PILLARS OF FLAME

PILLARS
OF
FLAME

Power, Priesthood, and Spiritual Maturity

Maggie Ross

1817

Harper & Row, Publishers, San Francisco

Cambridge, Hagerstown, New York, Philadelphia, Washington
London, Mexico City, São Paulo, Singapore, Sydney

This book is dedicated to

Sebastian and Helen
Simon and Rowan
two ordained
two not
all true priests

PILLARS OF FLAME: Power, Priesthood, and Spiritual Maturity. Copyright © 1988 by Maggie Ross. All rights reserved. Printed in the United States of America. No part of this book may be used or reproduced in any manner whatsoever without written permission except in the case of brief quotations embodied in critical articles and reviews. For information address Harper & Row, Publishers, Inc., 10 East 53rd Street, New York, N.Y. 10022. Published simultaneously in Canada by Fitzhenry & Whiteside Limited, Toronto.

Library of Congress Cataloging-in-Publication Data

Ross, Maggie, 1941-
    Pillars of flame.

    Bibliography: p.
    1. Pastoral theology.   2. Priesthood.   3. Spiritual life—Anglican authors.   4. Sacrifice.   I. Title.
BV4011.R67   1988   253'.2   87–46227
ISBN 0–06–254840–0

88 89 90 91 92 RRD 10 9 8 7 6 5 4 3 2 1

Contents

Readers' Guide: Readers interested in the theology and interrelationships of priesthood, ministry, and sacrifice may wish to begin with Part I. Readers interested in the commitment to transformation that is priesthood may wish to begin with Part II. Readers who are visually oriented may wish to begin with the chart of idea clusters in Appendix A.

Author's Note

This book is an attempt to communicate in today's terms what I understand to be the vision at the heart of the Gospel. It was the vision cherished by certain strands of early Semitic (Syrian) Christianity, and at one time it was also the focus around which institutional Christianity began to develop. Although it has continued as an underground stream, appearing here and there in Christian history, East and West, within the institution itself this vision almost immediately became distorted and today seems nearly to have vanished. Without it, Christianity, already moribund, will surely die.

I have tried to communicate this vision in theological and practical terms. I offer practical suggestions in Part II, Chapter 6, not as a definite plan to be voted on, but rather as a re-visioning to help us break out of the stereotyped ways we think about the institutions that have led us into a cul-de-sac instead of Christian freedom. But there is little point in changing the structures of the churches, as we do from time to time, if the changes are not based on the radical humility of God that is the heart of Christianity.

The creation of this book is a direct consequence of exploring the themes that make up *The Fountain and the Furnace* (Paulist Press, 1987). Since writing that book, I have attended Bishop Kallistos Ware's probing lectures on the history of christological and trinitarian doctrines, and I have found useful Geddes MacGregor's demonstration of the folly of trying to reconcile kenotic theory with the currently more familiar trinitarian model of God (*He Who Lets Us Be*, Seabury Press, 1975). One approach does not cancel out the other, and at points they can intersect; but to try to integrate them is a bit like trying to add apples and bananas. Another book in the more distant background is *The Form of a Servant*, by Donald G. Dawe (Westminster Press, 1963).

As I have observed the sometimes desperate discussions in theology today, it seems to me that there is a fluctuating middle ground between so-called academic theology, on the one hand, and practical pastoral training, on the other. The two have always informed each other, whether or not this exchange has been admitted; and discussion that sets up a dualism between them (as sometimes happens at conferences on theological education) is based on a questionable epistemology, one that admits only "reason," that is, discursive, logical, propositional (and therefore ultimately hierarchical and reductionistic) thinking.

This insight is an old one, but it does not seem to have become integrated across the spectrum of current thought. It is worth reiterating, however telegraphically. While propositional thinking is necessary to the development of ideas, even the hardest of hard sciences has rejected its primacy. It is, or should be, an epistemological servant, not master, especially in theology, where propositions often falsify more than expose truth. In *Computer Power and Human Reason*, Professor Joseph Weizenbaum of the Massachusetts Institute of Technology summarizes the problem:

A theory is, of course, itself a conceptual framework. And so it determines what is and what is not to count as fact. The theories— or, perhaps better said, the root metaphors—that have hypnotized the artificial intelligentsia, and large segments of the general public as well, have long ago determined that life is what is computable and only that. . . .

But, and this is the saving grace of which an insolent and arrogant scientism attempts to rob us, we come to know and understand not only by way of the mechanisms of the conscious. We are capable of listening with the third ear, of sensing living truth beyond any standards of provability. It is *that* kind of understanding, and the kind of intelligence that is derived from it, which I claim is beyond the ability of computers to simulate.[1]

While theologians have always invoked disclaimers that their propositions do not encompass the mystery of God, these disclaimers have a strange way of being ignored in doctrinal debates and inquisitions. In this book I am attempting to interrelate large areas of thought not only to expose the models of power that underlie the development of certain doctrines and the reason for the deathgrip some of them seem to have on us, but also, and more important, to show how that power cheapens, trivializes, and ultimately destroys the rich and fathomless mystery of kenotic life that is true Christianity. If nothing else, such cross-referencing keeps debate alive. We have so many studies of small and important areas and issues; we have very few that attempt to reveal fundamental problems that emerge only from a broad field of vision.

It seems appropriate to say a word about my affinity for the Syrian tradition exemplified by St. Ephrem (fourth century) and St. Isaac the Syrian (seventh century; also called Isaac of Nineveh). The controversies over the "how" of Incarnation (controversies that are being rehashed in some circles today) have always seemed to me misguided, because, for one, they insist on God's impassibility and, for another, the penal theory of the atonement seems to have the underlying (and mistaken) view that God has, at some point, left the world (which was created, in this view, gratuitously as an afterthought) or ceased to love it. Impassibility creates an artificial philosophical abyss, and the controversies themselves seem to be attempting to stick together artificial bits of ideas.

Although he never uses theopaschite language outright, Isaac seems to have *both* the sense of God's indwelling and working through our mortality, our creatureliness of the more "Nestorian" church to which he belongs, *and* the sense that it is the transcendent God who suffers, the divine compassion revealed to us in the Cross, that is the position of the Syrian Orthodox Church.

My attraction to the Syrians has come from within. As my theology has evolved, I have found very little in the Western tradition that seemed salvagable because it has been so picked apart in the stale atmosphere of academic and ecclesial word- and power-games. As a result, it is difficult to discuss a single idea in the Western tradition without getting into an enormous row, the roots of which are often in Greek philosophy.

Not so with the Syrians. The early tradition of Syrian Chris- tianity in Persia is not only relatively free from hellenization; it also is strongly Semitic. Christianity spread in the Persian Empire along with the Aramaic culture already present in the Mesopotamian region.

While we do not have a clear idea of the early dissemination of Christianity in the region and without elevating the Syrian tradition to the mythological status of "pure Christianity," this tradition is invaluable to us in the West as a resource of an ancient *Semitic* Christianity. It offers a passionate and unified vision of the love of God incarnate in Christ, indwelling the creation through the Spirit, unifying and transfiguring the universe, a vision toward which we in the West have been slowly and painfully struggling as we stagger away from the debris of exhausted philosophical categories, the shattered scholastic synthesis, the collapse of the illusion of objectivity, the corpses of holocausts, and the moral bankruptcy of nuclear commitments.

It was only when I began to work with the Syriac specialist Sebastian Brock (to whom I also owe thanks for the new translations of Isaac in this volume) that I realized that long before I ever heard of them, the foundation of St. Ephrem's and St. Isaac's vision, particularly their sense of balance be- tween intellect and experience, had somehow, by divine Mercy, begun to establish itself within me. And if in me, then perhaps this balanced vision is the same subliminal agent fomenting the restlessness those around me seem to share, an inarticulate restlessness that this book may, in part, articulate. I under- stand now that what has happened to me is part of an increas- ingly widespread movement in the West away from the *exaltation* of rational discursive thinking (*not* anti-rational "thinking," though that tendency is abroad, too) and thus from the perils of closed systems.

As Mark Taylor points out, it is possible that this illumination may "at least for a while, . . . delay and defer the terrifying arrival of the end. This is, admittedly, a fragile hope—a hope as fragile as our postmodern condition."[2] There is a kind of poetic justice in the resemblance between Ephrem's strand of Semitic Christianity that insists that it is blasphemy to posit God—God can be engaged but not posited—and our postmodern gropings toward what is unsayable.

However, we need to be careful how we apply theologically the deconstructionist program in both its narrower and its wider expressions. As a literary tool, wrongly used, it could destroy our understanding of the coinherence of divine and human acts. In its looser application, while it is necessary to break free of exhausted and isolative philosophical categories and to expose the anti-Christian structures in the churches, we have at the same time to be careful that we do not try to say the unsayable, the inarticulate exchange of love at the heart of Christianity, or else we will find ourselves where we began.

It could be argued—and it is true—that the insight that God can be engaged but not posited is not Ephrem's alone but also that of theologians in the West from Irenaeus through Augustine, to be found also in Luther, Tillich, Buber, and Heschel. But there are serious differences between the Syrian theologians whose exemplar is Ephrem and those in the West. The first and most important is that Ephrem's inheritance is relatively unscathed by Greek philosophy, and as a result his exposition is intensely Semitic in its love of paradox, use of characteristic images, and the poetry in which he writes much of his theology.

In addition, his style (and that of the later Isaac the Syrian) is clear and direct; the rhetorical decoration of the Greeks is absent. In this, the approach of the Syrians in the line of descent that includes Ephrem and Isaac is particularly appropriate for today. It could even be suggested that use of rhetoric in itself indicates self-reflection and the felt need for self-inflation, whereas the unadorned clarity of these Syrians' writing is perhaps evidence of the kenotic theology and self-forgetfulness of "awestruck wonder" before God that is its foundation.

Further, the Syrian tradition is uncompromising in its emphasis—not so much explicit as in the background—on *ihidayutha*, an untranslatable word that seems to embrace the inviolable vulnerability that is the love of God unifying all that is, in and with the Only-Begotten. Everything that is finds awestruck joy in the Love of God: the creation; human aspiration to have the watchful single-heartedness of Adam in paradise; linear time and sacred time with its promises fulfilled; integration of matter and spirit; the oneness in love of solitude and community; men and women; symbol and what is imaged—aspects of unity that add up to an ideal of passionate integrity, the only-begotten uniqueness of each creature, a notion that, even unfulfilled, most Western Christians would find staggering. It is holistic in the most profound sense and yet maintains clarity of distinctions; it avoids the perils of the sort of "unity" that masks as uniformity or that blurs creator and creature.

In short, the Syrian tradition offers us the possibility of once more living from aspiration instead of mere constraint, aspiration without which Christianity seems little more than a thin veneer of moral strictures coupled with a tepid and amorphous commitment to social concern. Aspiration gives energy and perspective to that which, under constraint, seems enervating and imprisoning; and without aspiration, constraint invariably evokes mockery, rebellion, and the opposite of its intended effects.

These and other features of the Syrian tradition, such as the image of the Holy Spirit as Mother and a new reading of its attitudes toward sexuality,[3] have special appeal for contemporary thought and offer a freshness that our stale theological climate badly needs. This is not a matter of laying blame but rather presents us with the opportunity to explore a Christianity equally ancient, yet alternative to Greek and Western traditions. Most important of all is the notion of *kenosis*, never very popular with the Greeks or in the West, possibly because of Western interest in self-reflection and self-mastery. *Kenosis* is of paramount importance because it seems to allow the absolute overcoming of theological and ontological dualisms, one of the main concerns of this book.

My fondness for Ephrem's inheritance and that of his spiritual descendant, Isaac of Nineveh, and my feeling that within the Syrian tradition is a major and largely untapped resource for theology today in no way imply a discarding of or lack of appreciation for the rich traditions of the West. I never would have found my way to Ephrem had I not first been nurtured by his remote spiritual heirs, and indeed the Western emphasis in trinitarian theology on the unity of God is perhaps a faint echo of the Syrian concept of *ihidayutha*. It is rather a matter of redressing balances and extrapolating from the insight of Christian sources relatively free from Greek influence. I have come to realize it is as much the Western *method* that is the culprit as anything else.

Dualistic tendencies haunt many religions, not excluding other strands of Syrian Christianity, but there are certain aspects of Greek philosophy that have a predilection for glorifying propositional thought, human mastery, healing of the wound of existence, and escape from creatureliness that are in irreconcilable conflict with Semitic love of engagement, parable, and paradox; and these aspects are, above all, in conflict with the Christian message of the glorious humility of our creatureliness exalted in the wounds of Christ on the Cross. Nonetheless, in Greek and Western Christianity a synthesis of these irreconcilable ways of relating the human with the divine was attempted, and the uneasy and illusory union that resulted is the source of many of the problems that plague Western Christianity today. The purity of the commitment to Christ's humility demanded by the Judeo-Christian heritage is so complete that it can come to us *only* as a gift of God's grace when we are willing to enter that humility. This primacy of grace does not deny intellectual endeavor; rather it is the completion and exaltation of what is highest and best in all human ways of knowing and engaging God.

There is a myth abroad today that says theology is reserved for the intellectual elite and that anyone else who wants to think about God's relationship with the creation but who does not have an advanced degree must have matters gently spelled out in the most elementary terms. I suspect this myth springs from the deliberate stunting of spiritual maturity that I describe in this book.

Theology that explores engagement with God (as opposed to nonnegotiable dogmas written in stone) speaks much more to the preconceptual and unconscious (and therefore what is unacknowledged and unconverted in us) than to the discursive, rational mind, a fact that may terrorize academics but that also means most people are far more capable of doing serious theology than they have been led to believe. Part I of this book has been offered in outline form to high school students, undergraduates, graduates, faculty, ordinary parish members, clergy, and scientists from Los Alamos Laboratories, and their insights, questions, and challenges not only have been invaluable but also confirm that nonspecialists can and will do incisive and challenging theology if offered the opportunity.

Last, it is only fair to say a word about my experience of the ordination question and my status in "the system." I am an Anglican solitary, solemnly professed, responsible to the Bishop of New York. In 1964, Bishop James Pike of California suggested he should ordain me deacon. I declined. After the ordination of women as presbyters (which I support) became legal in The Episcopal Church (ECUSA), other bishops, clergy, and nonordained people from time to time suggested that my ordination would be "a good idea"; some even took a more direct approach, saying, "Why don't you?" After three episcopal approaches, I did some serious questioning if perhaps this were an obedience I was being asked to undertake. But always I hesitated, not quite knowing why, and in the end I have refused. Initially, the only way I could articulate this refusal, this sense of "wrongness" for me, was that I felt no interior call to be ordained, and, more significantly, an even deeper conviction that to accept ordination would somehow compromise the priestly character of my solitary vocation and negate my striving for the willingness to fulfill it.

My perceptions of both the solitary vocation and the questions surrounding the ordination of both sexes have clarified over the years, and while the suggestion that I submit to ordination is repeated from time to time, my refusal becomes more certain. Some of the reasons are found in this book.

Only once have I reconsidered my decision, and that was during the first alarms about AIDS in England, when clergy often could not be found to comfort the dying, bury the dead, and support the bereaved because they were too frightened, or because, as in at least one infamous instance, the vicar defended his refusal to bury by saying, "I only deal in certainties." Although I knew that to request ordination would compromise my vocation, not to mention everything I have come to believe about the way the church ought to organize its ministry, at the time the situation was so appalling and the need seemed so urgent, that I wrote, raising the question, to my bishop and one or two trusted friends. Fortunately, I was persuaded that the ministry crisis would pass (it has), but the process of reevaluating the question on a personal level helped me to come to greater clarity on some of the matters discussed in this book.

My vocation is to Christ's priesthood in my being, not to function as part of the ordained secular power structure that currently organizes the church and (disclaimers to the contrary) regards itself as the church. My discernment suggests that while there are a few clergy (women and men alike) of singular priestly holiness, there are many more who may be ordained but evidence in their behavior that the meaning of *priest* is unknown to them. Their dedication is rather to power and expediency.

Dr. John Barton of Oxford University has provided help, encouragement, and criticism from this book's inception, but he is in no way responsible for the views it expresses. I am grateful to the Rev. Simon Holden, C. R., for permission to use the material in Appendix B; and for his wisdom, support, and affirmation. I also wish to thank Ms. Carolyn Kuykendall, whose unique philosophical gifts enabled the linkages between sections, and who created a personal context in which phrases and images that have long eluded me could emerge. I am also grateful to Bishop Kallistos Ware, Professor Rowan Williams, Dr. Gerald Bonner, Professor Mark Taylor, Ms. Sandol Stoddard, Canon Roswell Moore, Canon William Johnson, the Rev. Charles Hensel, and Ms. Sally Mitchell for their detailed critiques and encouragement, and to the Oxford University women's seminar organized by Dr. Janet Soskice, Dr. Paul Joyce, and Mr. Robert Morgan, where some of the key insights of this book coalesced. On discovering that I wished to use several extracts from *Riddley Walker* as epigraphs for this book, Russell Hoban telephoned to say that the usual fees would be waived. This is typical of his generosity, and his friendship and encouragement have been humbling and a great blessing. Dr. Sebastian and Helen Brock continue to offer scholarship, friendship, and prayer, without which this task would never have been completed.

Most of all, I would like to acknowledge the context that enabled the writing of this book: the atmosphere of freedom and warmth, of quiet, self-effacing support, and the daily round of prayer offered by the dean and canons of Christ Church, Oxford, in whom one can glimpse the priestly humility that is at the heart of the exercise of true Christian power and true greatness.

Abecedary: An Essential Primer of Theological Quanta

Have this mind among yourselves, which you have in Christ Jesus, who, though he was in the form of God, did not count equality with God a thing to be grasped, but emptied himself, taking the form of a servant, being born in the likeness of men. And being found in human form he humbled himself and became obedient unto death, even death on a cross. *Therefore* God has highly exalted him and bestowed on him the name which is above every name.

Phil. 2:5–10 (RSV, italics mine)

The heart of Christianity is the self-emptying, kenotic humility of God expressed in Jesus the Christ. It is from this authority, this ground, this experience that all discussions about the meaning of priesthood and ministry—and, indeed, all other discussions that are to be termed "Christian"—must proceed. What do we mean by the humility of God, the self-emptying of God, the *kenosis* of God?

At the heart of God's humility is this: God willingly is wounded.

God is willingly wounded in the mystery of divine *kenosis*, which we are shown in the Word spoken for us who is both First and Last. "God is most God on the Cross and most man in the resurrection," wrote Karl Barth. It is in the cry of dereliction that God is most deeply revealed, for dereliction is God's experience of God. Even God has to let go of God's ultimate idea of God in the divine *kenosis*, and *kenosis* is the wisdom of God.

It is as if God's speech is a wound in God, in which the creation comes to be and is cradled. God's willing woundedness is without hope of healing, as we commonly understand that word—for healing is the sign of finitude. In resurrection, Christ's wounds are open. The wound into which Thomas is invited to thrust his hand is not covered over or closed or scarred, but open and deep and glorified. The resurrection is the sign and celebration of the transfiguration being wrought by God's willingness to be wounded in the crucifixion of the Word.

The humility of Christ: we seem to have forgotten that for any worship, thought, or activity to be called "Christian" it must be rooted in the humility of Christ. In attempting to discern what is salvagable both in scriptural and ecclesial tradition, in sorting out what is cultural bias and what is essential, in attempting to recover life-enhancing religious symbols that have been put to corrupt use, we seem to forget, amid hurled accusations of prejudiced selectivity, that we *do* in fact have the criterion we need, and that is the humility of Christ. In Christian typology the Tree of the Cross, which is the humility of Christ, recapitulates and transfigures the tree of the Garden, which is the lust for control.

The Myth of Healing and Wholeness

If we are to mirror God, to be in God's image, to be like God, to invite God to indwell us so that we live Christ's life in today's world and in every day's world, we have to be willing to enter our individual wounds and through them the wounds of the community. We have to be willing to enter the wound of history, particularly the wound of Judeo-Christian history. We have to be willing to enter the wound of God. We have to be willing to enter these wounds, not hide them by casuistry, not seal them up, not scar them over. They must remain wounds in order that Christ's resurrection may enter and indwell us and our wounds be united and glorified with his. This is the way of transfiguration, which is an ongoing process, both within the arrow of time and outside of time's illusion.

Thus we reject as hope (as God has rejected it) what appears as healing within mortality, because too often the

appearance of healing becomes the denial of our creatureliness. We reject this mortal hope for the divine hope of transfiguration, which is our life with God. This rejection of healing
as hope does not, of course, in any way deny our longing to
relieve pain or our search for ways of healing our physical and
psycho-spiritual hurts in this life until we engage our death.
But we need to understand healing for what it really is; it is
not a vanishing act, but rather learning to live with, in, and
through pain, to adjust to our wounding, which cannot ultimately be denied, and to be willing to risk opening to change
that will lead to transfiguration.

We need always to keep in mind that healing is something
of an illusion, a surrogate for the immortality we desire. Our
physical wounds never entirely heal, though they may seem
to, and we may for a time forget them. Wounds and disease
always leave behind recognizable signs: a scar, a characteristic
way of walking, a minute change in the immune system or
retina that the skilled eye can read, above all what is written
on the human face. As skills and technology advance, height-
ening the illusion of our control over our destiny and our
mortality, it is ever more important that we cultivate and nurture our skills of discernment, and, most of all, growth in
wisdom in order to know how to apply this new knowledge.

The importance of our wounds lies in how we choose to
relate to them, how we choose to enter and to integrate them
into our lives, for ultimately this integration becomes part of
the choice for or against the process of transfiguration. And
with our interior wounds especially, while there may be "closure" in the sense of the ending of a particular phase of
coming to terms with painful reality, we must never yield to
the temptation to engage, in the name of "healing," a new and
often more destructive denial and repression such as T. S. Eliot
describes: "People change and smile, but agony abides." This
new denial is the hope that is betrayed by mortality.

Rather these are the wounds that need gently to be more
and more deeply entered as we sit in the dark and wait on

God to show them to us. In the dark these wounds embrace us, and we them; in the dark they show us our selves, wounded forever beyond any human alteration, and in this embrace we are brought to the focus of God's glory and God's glory to us, the dense glory of mercy. These become the transfigured wounds through which we offer healing to others; these are the wounds through which we come to the density of holiness.

The cry of dereliction from the Cross can be likened to our experience of sitting wounded in the dark; it is what Isaac the Syrian calls prayer that can no longer be called prayer, although he emphasizes the positive aspects because he doesn't want to frighten people. It is also, to name a contemporary issue, the experience of being woman, of being woman who in this society has been raped intellectually, psychologically, and spiritually, not to mention physically, who is told that her perception, her experience, her life must somehow be authenticated outside herself according to models, the idols that have been set before her by men and other women alike. These outsiders threaten her when her experience disagrees with theirs; they insist she must change her perception of her own experience (lie to herself). She is brainwashed into believing she is not entitled to living-space without justification as a commodity, much less thought-space or her own perception of life-enhancing uses of language or its creation.

And yet she endures in the dark, within the cry of dereliction, knowing that to be true to her self, to her integrity/ chastity, to the unique creatureliness that is peculiarly her; for her fluid existence to be become the density of the holiness of the image of God, she must sit there, damaged and wounded, without hope that her integrity is or can be otherwise. That is to say, without the comfort or security of the illusion of fixing herself up or allowing herself to be fixed up as a surrogate of herself, according to an idolatrous pattern, hers or anyone else's.

She sits there in her I AM (she can be no other) within the Wound that is I WILL BE FOR YOU (mutual *kenosis*—I WILL

BE FOR YOU is incarnational). The confluence of wounds flows from Christ indwelling in us creatures and the Person who speaks the wound.

This experience of dereliction that is the statement I AM is supremely, and most profoundly of all, the experience of the *anawim*, "the poor," whoever and wherever they are, and for whatever reason they are despised and rejected, desolate, and condemned. In fact, we might say that condemnation itself creates the condition in the other of *anawim*, no matter what the other's economic condition.

I am not limiting *anawim* to people or restricting "consciousness" to human beings, and therefore the burden of choice is on the whole creation. We can create *anawim* or we can enter our wounds to engage them and the transfiguring grace of re-creation. As with healing, this is of course *not* an argument against trying to better the situation of the materially and socially poor, but it does perhaps tell us, in part, why Christianity is supremely the religion of "the poor," and why inherent in it is the wisdom that the cost of the relief of suffering, ours or anyone else's, is *always* sacrifice.

We need to be aware that many of our efforts on behalf of the *anawim* are undertaken in the hope of avoiding sacrifice and fail as a result. Equally, the experience of entering our wounds can often make us open to the grace that sets rich and poor alike free from the determining patterns of the existing social order and bestows on us the courage to take the personal risks that its change requires.

Jesus heals at terrible cost to himself, yet he knows the significance of his message is not centered in either these signs or the power that they obscurely reveal. Jesus raises others from the dead. But even this act is temporary and the restored life finite. Mortality is not abolished, and resuscitation is not resurrection. Surrogates will not do.

Then some of the scribes and Pharisees said to him, "Teacher, we wish to see a sign from you." But he answered them, "An evil and adulterous generation seeks for a sign; but no sign shall be given to it except for the sign of the prophet Jonah. For as Jonah was three days and three nights in the belly of the whale, so will the Son of man be three days and three nights in the heart of the earth. The men of Nineveh will arise at the judgment with this generation and condemn it; for they repented at the preaching of Jonah, and behold, something greater than Jonah is here." (Mt 12:38–41, RSV)

Why adulterous? Because the people who seek these signs seek healing that can be seen and grasped and exploited, healing that provides a false sense of security, healing that seems to make the illness vanish and leave us "as before" (the fantasy of a static existence). They seek a sign that will provide them with a comfortable surrogate for life with God. It is significant that one of the heads of the beast in the Apocalypse (13:3) has "a mortal wound, but its mortal wound was healed, and the whole earth followed the beast with wonder."

Those who seek signs show by their asking that they have no real faith or understanding of how shattering it is to receive such a sign. Those who have received signs speak to the reality and permanence of God's wounding that accompanies a sign. They tell us of profound and unspeakable transformation that is more thoroughly penetrating, and often more painful, than the original illness from which they have been healed within mortality.

The issue of surrogates is an important one. In Matthew's gospel (11:23–24), Jesus says, "For if the mighty works done in you had been done in Sodom, it would have remained until this day. But I tell you that it shall be more tolerable on the day of judgment for the land of Sodom than for you." The reference to Sodom has more significance than is usually accorded it. The Sodom story (Gn 19:1–29) occurs in the midst of Abraham's journey, the patriarch's lessons in learning fidelity—not to security, not to what he can see, but to God alone known only in the darkness of faith.

Immediately preceding the story of Sodom (Gn 16–17), God denies Abram, who has relinquished hope of children from

Sarai, the surrogacy of Hagar and the tangible assurance of God's promise that Ishmael would have provided. Without denying the injustice of her oppression, it should be noted that Hagar in her destitution is more available to the promises of God than her former master.

Even so, she too must give up the security of surrogacy that her son's status within Abraham's family would have afforded. She has her own journey and heritage in the promises of God; she cannot receive them vicariously. Abram, if he is to realize his identity with God and God's promise of future genera-tions, must also give up hope and security against all common sense. God insists on promising what seems impossible, and Abraham's and Sarah's unfolding assent of faith bestows on them their full identity.

The entire Abraham story is one incident after another in which Abram/Abraham and Sarai/Sarah and other participants in the saga are repeatedly taught that to grasp at a tangible and presenting aspect of God's loving mercy is not to grasp God, indeed, that to try to do so is idolatrous and leads to death. In chapter 22 Abraham is asked for what seems the ultimate act of folly and hopelessness and therefore the ulti-mate act of faith: the sacrifice of Isaac. God wants to drive home the point that Abraham must not grasp even the fulfill-ment of God's promise in the person of his miraculously con-ceived son. In Christian typology the resonances of this moment are inexhaustible.

God constantly requires from Abraham the faith that relin-quishes surrogates in order to live without any security or assurance but that offered by the God he knows in darkness. His poverty thus focuses him continually toward God and away from himself, for if the promises are to be fulfilled, his efforts to create the illusion of fulfillment must be abandoned. When Abraham's self-emptying meets God's self-emptying, all can be accomplished. Only from this mutual *kenosis,* this engagement, can true fecundity arise; as with Abraham, so with us.

The meaning of the story of Sodom thus comes clear. It is not a story about the punishment of so-called homosexual behavior ("homosexual," "heterosexual," and "bisexual" are ambiguous and inaccurate labels and do not reflect the created order). The Sodomites are sexually indiscriminate (Gn 19:8). Lot offers his daughters, knowing that they will do just as well as the "two men" who are the presenting and tangible aspect of the mercy of God. The men of Sodom wish to grasp and know these surrogates to give themselves the illusion of grasping God.

Thus to interpret the story on a supposedly literal level is to miss its point. While it is certainly a story of violation of hospitality (particularly to God) as it has sometimes been interpreted, it is much more a story of spiritual promiscuity/adultery/idolatry told through a sexual metaphor. The story of Sodom is a mordant satire on the idolatry of that great shopping mall at the end of the Dead Sea, a consumer culture that can inculturate religion only as commodity by attempting to grasp an aspect of God. This consumer parable is told in a sexual metaphor with all the resonances of the multiple meanings of the verb "to know" ranging from wisdom to sexual intercourse, and all the paradoxes that we have seen throughout the Abraham saga of knowing that produces sterile surrogates that must be cast aside for fecund unknowing.

Unlike Abraham, the Sodomites do not repent of their sin, which is to desire, to grasp, to control, to feel secure with, to *know* God on their own terms, for their immediate gratification. They cannot be bothered with the unimaginable promises of faith.

This desire for secure, concrete, and finite knowledge of an aspect of God is an arrogant and idolatrous replacement for faith; and faith itself is the only security in the seeming insecurity of the vast love of God. This is one of the principal themes, if not *the* principal theme of the whole Bible from the beginning of Genesis to the end of the Apocalypse.

Gen 19

Repentance thus rejects "hope" offered by the "healing" or illusory surrogacy of human ideas of immortality, the blandishments of finitude. Repentance rejects them for eternal promises of transfiguration offered to us by God when we acknowledge and enter our wounds, the wound of our incompleteness and the wound of our unknowing, even as God in the divine humility is willing to be wounded and incomplete and unknowing. The great hymn of this, God's *kenosis*, in Philippians (2:5–11) describes God's unwillingness to be the arrogant God that humans often mistakenly think they require and even more often seek to reflect.

The Word is unwilling to betray, to arrogate, to grasp its own divine *kenosis*, to become a self-reflective surrogate, a distorted caricature of true and wounded divinity. If God's love were other than kenotic, there would be no Christ, God would have no wounds, and we would have no grounds for faith in transfiguring love.

It is only when we are willing to live in our wounds without hope of healing that we begin to live in faith—and thus in real hope—for it is only then that we give up the last vestige of the comforting illusion of control and exploitation and the denial of our creatureliness. Only when we wait, wounded, in the dark I AM, can we receive the sign of Jonah, God's merciful love for us as we are. Only then can Christ fully dwell in us; only then can our wounds become his glorified wounds; only then do *chronos* and *kairos* (linear and sacred time) come into fugal relationship; only then by the radiance of Christ's wounds in ours can the creation enter transfiguration.

The revelation of the wounded God has been a scandal throughout Judeo-Christian history, and perhaps today more than at any other time. It may help us to remember that in the English language the word "wound" and the word "blessing" have the same root. Our wounds are ultimately our greatest source of blessing because they become one with the wounds of our humble God.

wound &
blessing

The Myth of Baptismal Magic

In many churches today we baptize uncomprehending babies as if this ritual bestowed a vaguely social and even more vaguely religious magic stamp on them. While it has been argued that baptism is part of the churches' "service" to the world and that it would be hard to restore it to a place of dignity, the churches are not meant to be a service industry, and the death-and-life symbolism of baptism is too fundamental to be a service in the sense of a commodity. The baptism of each of us should have signification for the rest of creation; merely performing the rite does not accomplish the goal. The more we treat religious rites as technology, the more we give secular answers to the religious question.

Similarly, we allow adults to make their baptismal vows as casually as if this commitment were a fraternity handshake. Revised catechetical programs unwittingly perpetuate this trivialization by group activities and ceremonies that more resemble religious summer camps than initiation into mysteries of rebirth or death and transfiguration. In consequence, many so-called Christians regard their church as just another social club, just another card on which to score, to make a mark, to achieve, to wheel and deal in status and power politics. We reduce our baptismal commitment to living on a perpetual high of religious emotion or at least making our selves feel good once a week. With this attitude, the divine Humility has become just another rung on the ladder to be exploited, and the divine Ungraspingness is perceived as a Controller to be controlled.

By contrast, baptism rather requires from us a commitment that will bring us face to face with death in all its subtle forms and through death not once but many times. Baptismal vows commit us to the virginity of the single-hearted, to be on fire with the love of God encountered most potently in harrowed hell, to radiate the light of the consuming fires of love that transform even the fires of hell into the fiery dance of the life of God. Those who are willing to become such pillars of flame are the people to whom we should be looking for a way out of the current religious swamp, but they are often the most hidden, and despised by those who hold political leadership in the churches.

Christian morbidity is expressing itself in odd ways. Some of the motivation for this book arises from a deep concern for the many people for whom the community of the baptized provides so little support that they feel they are incomplete Christians without ordination or traditional monastic vows. While there is no question that God bestows ministerial vocations irrespective of gender, at the same time it is alarming to see both men and women inappropriately seeking ordination, not because they have vocations to leadership, but because they hold the dangerous conceit that ordination will authenticate their Christianity, will make them somehow "more complete" or "closer to God."

At the same time, an even greater number of people seem to give up their religious exploration because they find the baptized community the least helpful environment in which to live a deep and transformational life in the mystery of the kenotic God. They are discouraged by pastoral leadership that is afraid to insist on the primacy of never-ending interior conversion for the sake of the community.

Even when the importance of interior solitude in common life is emphasized, its nurture is too often stunted by inept spiritual direction and its related politics, direction that seems to deteriorate in direct proportion to its popularity. The word "direction" itself is of questionable value; its nuances communicate the wrong notion of power to the director and the wrong notion of process to the directee. Committed seekers are also confused by the the churches' substitution of incompetent and control-oriented political selection processes for kenotic discernment when it chooses spiritual leaders, and they are depressed by the resulting banality of these leaders' attempts to enable private and public worship.

The Myth of Two-Level Obedience

Moreover, some of us still perpetuate the illusion that there are two levels of obedience in Christianity, that only those who wear collars or religious habits (even invisible ones) have privileged access to the higher wisdom of God. While church leaders protest such assumptions, their unspoken signals often contradict their words. The people who drop out of Christianity are uneasy with the glib intimacy of those in visible ministry, whose source of authority purports to be the humility of divine Wisdom, but more often seems to have its origins in the most worldly sort of power politics.

In spite of the proclaimed Gospel, and in spite of renaming mundane housekeeping functions "ministry" (minister of raising money, minister of washing floors, minister of reading the Word but not, God forbid, preaching it), the subliminal and sometimes not so subliminal message even well-intentioned authority figures in the churches continue to give is this: the wisdom (certainly not the authority) of the humble (that is, those not holding institutional power) is not to be heard. The nonordained are allowed to have tiny hegemonies labeled "ministry"—ministry that is often manipulative power jealously guarded and ferociously defended, a model frequently learned from their pastors.

With such sops do many leaders attempt to placate and exploit the nonordained. The nonordained are manipulated, patronized, ignored, and pushed out of sight. Worst of all, there is no one to enable their greater spiritual maturity, especially since they are often more spiritually mature than their leaders. And their leaders take care that they do not become aware of this fact or else find ways to render them impotent if they do.

In spite of statements to the contrary, the "official" churches

still are composed of the ordained. In spite of verbal encouragement, those outside visible authority structures perceive
that their ordained leaders continue to be suspicious of nonordained ministry. These leaders are not only unwilling to
delegate closely held prerogatives, but also often seem panic-
stricken that their importance—which too often is self-importance—might be diminished. What have such attitudes to do
with enabling humanity to grow into the humility of God?

On the other side of this base coin are those of us among
the nonordained who support the neo-gnostic idea of two-level
obedience. We often use it to excuse ourselves not only from
ministry, but also from the costliness of the baptismal vows
that commit us to kenotic living, to becoming part of Christ's
sacrifice. Even more destructive, we use this false modesty as
a base from which to project romanticism and mystique onto
church professionals while belittling one another's gifts. We
like to fantasize that such vocations are "supernatural" because we would like to think that those who receive them are
able to deny the glory of creatureliness by the imagined mastery that leads to becoming "pure" spirit. This exaltation of
repression and hatred of the creation perpetuates the churches'
long history of diluting the implications of Incarnation, a process that possibly begins as early as the gospels.

In the very early churches, ministry was not a career; it was
not sought after, and the personal conviction that one might
have a vocation to be one of the organization's officials carried
little weight. In fact, the people who best understood the
practical implications of interrelatedness in kenotic love and
the dangers of power politics shunned ordination. They had
to be hunted down by their bishops, who were forced to
kidnap them to ordain them. To this day in some of the Orthodox churches, the one who is to be ordained is taken from
the congregation by two deacons, who grasp his elbows and
symbolically drag him before the bishop. Today the people
who are most likely to abandon the churches remain those
who cannot endure the suffocating and self-reflective politics
that characterize the institutions.

It is not only our trivialization of baptism that encourages false compartmentalization in Christianity and denies the eucharistic character of all of life. Religious people mistake mystique for mystery, self-image for self-respect, individualism for authenticity, dialectic for dialogue, gradiosity for grandeur, self-reflection for experience of God, gee-whiz for wonder, narrow-mindedness for the narrow way, lust (the desire to control) for sexuality, "the world" for creation, magic for miracle, pornography for eroticism, and religion for faith. Often this stunting of mature insight seems deliberate, an ongoing policy by the clergy to promote immaturity in those not members of the closed club of the ordained.

The congregation's pastoral and mystical gifts are belittled, discouraged, refused authorization, and ignored by frightened clergy who have a difficult time recognizing, much less fostering, such movements of God. As a consequence, these repressed gifts sometimes take bizarre forms. In addition, training programs teach clergy to mask rigidity and reductionism under the names "flexibility" and "fulfillment." Even the language of healing can be exploited for purposes of manipulation and perpetuating illusion, to enable the ordained to retain control.

Examples of this sort of con game are ubiquitous, not only in the obvious—television evangelism and rigged "healing" services—but also in everyday life. It is common practice in the restaurant business to teach servers the vocabulary and body language of intimacy for the sole purpose of extracting the greatest possible amount of money from the diners with the least possible time and effort. The server uses key words and gestures to elicit trust from the customers and then proceeds to manipulate them into eating what the restaurant wants them to (the subliminal message is what the diners "ought" to want)—not what they really want. The language of intimacy and trust is thus put to the purpose of dehumanization and exploitation.

Seminaries and theological colleges often seem to discourage the development of students' gifts beyond certain set, stereotyped, functional political goals. They render ordinands incapable of enabling gifts in other people even if they could overcome their instinct for dominance and elitism and their fear of God's indiscriminate bestowal of holiness and pastoral gifts. Spiritual maturity is a way of willingness for transformation, a way of kenotic *being* that is the heart of Christianity. People do not become spiritually mature by a spoken rite, by learning fund-raising formulas, management techniques, and theological arguments. God is living and active; so must religion be.

The seminaries and theological colleges often say (some do not say but imply by their actions) that fostering spiritual maturity is not their job. If enabling spiritual maturity in their students so that the students may in turn enable it in others is not the goal of clergy training and education, then we must ask, what *is* the goal? If ever we needed spiritual maturity, it is now. This shriveling of spiritual maturity is hastened by the churches' sanctioning of expediency, an attitude that seems more and more to dominate them. They justify and mask expediency with sacral lies, lies that become more destructive as the churches increasingly adopt the techniques of business and the marketplace. Perhaps we need to be reminded that Jesus' crucifixion was the expedient solution in his day.

There are some otherwise dedicated religious leaders who put on the sacral mask because they feel guilty about exercising the minimal amount of necessary functional power needed to keep their congregations from anarchy. But more frequently it seems as if religious professionals are primarily interested in increasing their power-base. This focus on control means that not only does the well-being of the institution take priority over the well-being of its members and the message of the Gospel; it means also that those who adopt this stance avoid the suffering necessary to their own growth into God, and as a result they do not have the capacity for suffering-with necessary to discerning and enabling others' growth into God.

These leaders take advantage of their poor, that is, those who are at their mercy emotionally, psychologically, and spiritually, not only economically. But this systematic exploitation is nothing new in the history of the churches; its contemporary appearance is simply a concentration of the besetting sin of the age, which affects us all. We are all vulnerable in a culture where greed perpetuates the illusion of ever-more narrowly focused control, where unenlightened self-interest promotes the grandiose delusion of omnipotence to be achieved by means of technology that fails. This dissipated vision can lead only to tyranny. We mistake confusion for paradox.

Having said this, however, we need to acknowledge that there is a necessary use of secular organizing power (as distinct from self-aggrandizing, worldly power) in the churches and give thanks for those who are gifted with administrative ability and willingness to take it on. But equally we need to stop confusing this functional power with Christ's priesthood, which rejects the claims of exclusionary dualism and control that any institution fosters.

In the *Didache,* one of the earliest documents of the Christian churches and one that may predate even the gospels, we see a very different concern for the second-class status of the individuals whom the community allows to offer its gathered prayer. Unfortunately the remedy was adopted too soon to have the effect not only of bestowing equality on them, but also creating a situation in which the conditions were reversed, and the ordained now had the opportunity to insist on an often idolatrous status, leaving the community without any say at all. We have been struggling ever since to reestablish the eucharistic knowledge that *the whole creation* is the Body of Christ in which Christ's priesthood indwells and that the ordained are its liturgical and administrative servants *when appropriate.*

Today we are beginning to recognize that there are community situations in which *any* ordained leadership is inappropriate, no matter how institutionally "valid." There are some passages of life in which liturgical leadership can come *only* from within the local circle of suffering and transfiguration, and this nonordained leadership is the *only* valid liturgical ministry for that group. These are occasions when the imposition of an ordained outsider is gross presumption.

The need for liturgical leadership from within, and the communities themselves, may be temporary or permanent. Committed communities of men and women, geographically isolated communities, retreat groups, support groups of handicapped people, communities of persecution such as safe houses for battered women—all these have the potential of being communities where only one of the members can legitimately preside at the Eucharist, give absolution, or bury the dead. Even if an ordained person is a member of such a community, this person is sometimes the least appropriate liturgical leader.

The appropriateness of nonordained leadership needs humbly to be acknowledged and recognized by everyone in the churches, both members of hierarchies and the nonordained alike. The churches need to take steps to enable these groups' responsible internal ministry without burdening them with ordination and the irrelevant and inappropriate politics that seem invariably to attach to ordination. It is not the ordained who authenticate the community's self-offering; it is rather those who make community, who gather to express the coinhering self-offering of their solitudes with Christ's sacrifice who authenticate leadership.

The suggestions—and they are only suggestions—I make in this book for the need to separate and redistribute kenotic and secular, that is, organizing, power may have to remain "in expectation," but I have tried to be realistic about what could be possible with only a *little* vision and only a *little* generosity. I am trying to suggest ways not of establishing further control, but of abandoning unnecessary and inappropriate control. Spiritual maturity in the churches cannot develop while they are hostage to fragmented and fragmenting power-games.

Non-Ordained

Thus, because I do not see the word "priest" passing out of theological and religious vocabularies, I have retained it with the proviso that this word must be kept free from any associations of secular, functional, administrative, or manipulative power and free from the mystique of any "priestly" cult. In this book, the word "priest" or "priesthood" is used to refer *only* to the mirroring of God's kenotic, self-forgetful love, which is irreconcilable, in human terms, with self-reflective, functional power, although one might dare to hope that when such power must unavoidably be exercised in the interest of minimal organization, it would be exercised with Christ's humility in mind and always from the equipoise of response within that humility.

Instead of the word "priest" for the middle position of threefold ordained ministry, I have used the New Testament word "presbyter." Under present conditions, and by these definitions, it is possible to be ordained and not be a priest at all; and precisely because of the depth of their priestly vocations, many people shun the idea of ordination. Conversely, it is also true that there are people who seek ordination precisely because they want to exercise control, control that will support the mask that covers their denial and their refusal to live out their measure of necessary creaturely suffering and *therefore* the glory of kenotic priesthood to which they are committed by baptism. This is not a glorification of suffering for its own sake, which no one should condone under any circumstances; it is rather a commitment to the willingness and self-restraint that lead to maturity and wisdom and invariably require suffering.

My reasons for insisting on this distinction between the way of being that is priesthood and the office of presbyter will, I hope, become abundantly clear. If this fundamental perception could be acknowledged across a broad spectrum, many of the problems that appear to be inherent in questions of ordination and ecumenism might seem less thorny, if not simply nonquestions.

However, it will also become clear that official ecumenism should stop at intercommunion and recognition of one another's clergy. Organic unity in polity among the larger churches especially is unwise because of what seems to be an ineluctable human tendency toward uniformity, reductionism, and tyranny. We need to recall the lessons of Babel. This is a hard saying, especially for one who has been involved in ecumenism since the beginning of Vatican II and whose vocation has been nurtured and sponsored across denominational lines.

Two obvious examples of issues falsely pleaded in the name of unity are the questions of clerical celibacy and the ordination of women. Large numbers of people perceive that it is wrong to require clergy to remain celibate simply because of a relatively recent tradition that has a highly questionable historical and incarnational base. And in the face of deeper knowledge about the way humans relate to God and one another, it becomes absurd. It is equally wrong not to ordain women simply because they are women, especially when we now recognize that in our doctrinal history we have persisted in fundamental errors of christology and anthropology. Not only are there not separate baptisms for men and women, there is only one kenotic model of priesthood and ministry, and that is the humility of Christ, a humility that indwells the creation irrespective of gender.

In addition, we face unprecedented social conditions that require the ministry of both married clergy and ordained women. If the churches are committed to the humility of Christ, then they are committed to Christ's equipoise of ready response or *apatheia* (my development of *apatheia* follows R. Williams; see Part I, Chapter 3 following). Dwelling in the ever-changing stillness that is the equipoise of ready response of being in God, and of God's indwelling can be likened to a gyroscope in a guidance system. Except that this equipoise of conversion I am attempting to describe operates without artificial horizons. If we are to begin to find this balance of moving repose, we must give up all geometrical coordinates in human terms, such as up, down, inside, outside, progress, failure, achievement, and respond only to the coordinates of grace. For the indwelling God suffuses all, and willingness requires us to give up all geometry, all human measures that lead us to self-reflection and the illusion that God is somehow "above" our creatureliness, instead of within it, around it, sustaining and transcending it.

By giving up the security of projected direction, we learn to ignore attempts by the institutions to impose idolatrous, static, and controlling fantasies about God and Christianity that are distortions of what must be a *living* tradition if it is to be Christian, a tradition that itself is in equipoise of response. If the churches attempt to come together on the basis of denial of these realities, how, then, do we serve unity in truth if this unity is based on perceived untruth? Not at all. And the problem will not go away.

The Myth of Uniformity

There is immense tension in the paradox of Incarnation (throughout this book I use the term "Incarnation" to mean the entire salvific event, both "eternal" and irrupting "in time"), a tension that is part of the essence of Christianity and therefore also responsible for the inevitable conflicts within Christianity. To attempt finally to explain this paradox, covering as it does the vast expanse of all that is creaturely and all that is divine, is a questionable undertaking to begin with. Attempts to establish guidelines for thinking about Incarnation have frustrated theologians from the beginning. Partly because of repeated attempts over the centuries to resolve this tension one way or another, to grasp and control the mystery of Incarnation, and in support of these efforts, to establish a mistaken idea that uniformity is the same as reconciliation or even morality, organized Christianity in Europe, the United States, and Canada finally seems moribund.

When the necessary tension within Incarnation is rendered ineffectual, we see institutional Christian life diminish. We see, for example, churches' insistence that they are exclusive ghettos of the baptized. They are disengaged from each other and the rest of creation except on their own terms. Similarly, there is resistance to new ways of looking at God, even when antiquated ideas of divinity become destructive. Much theology today still begins slavishly with the idea of a remote puppet-master creator, who is aloof except by condescension or appeasement or subtle forms of religious blackmail. It is hardly surprising, then, in this age of desperate struggle to save the life of the planet, that many people refuse to serve such a god or institutions that mirror it.

Christian theology must begin with creation as *expression* of the kenotic God's in-historicization. If we were to apply this more incarnational approach, vast areas of interpretation might undergo the radical changes that could bring hope to humanity in despair. Creation discloses the wounded God. The humility of Christ generates the creative potential and possibility inherent in our powerlessness. In this book, we can only begin to point to these implications.

In addition, much Christian theology has not yet put to use the tools newly available to us to implement this task, such as the analogical possibilities offered by contemporary science especially as regards space-time. Because of this failure of imagination, much of contemporary Christian theology (and therefore Christian life) seems as inert and two-dimensional as the cosmology of the Flat Earth Society.

We need to move in our theologizing from linear thinking to spatial thinking. Until recently, modern academic theologians have given little time to theology written in any but strictly logical and linear form. This way of doing theology was outmoded several hundred years ago as our perceptions of our world and universe changed. That theology attempts to persist in linear thinking to the exclusion of other ways of thinking (an illusion) is one of the fundamental reasons for its increasing irrelevance and thus the irrelevance of religion in general. To think spatially does not mean that we give up liner thinking but rather that such thinking is limited to appropriate use.

Spatial theology can best be expressed through poetry written as poetry (such as St. Ephrem's) or as prose poetry. Our most enduring religious (and some might say theological) texts tend to be poetic in expression. Yet, especially in the United States, poetry has not been taken seriously by the general population, and especially not by many theological academicians, for some time. They are perhaps quite appropriately reacting against the revolting sentimentality of much poetic religious expression. Yet in an age when scientists are naming newly discovered particles "blue" or "strange" we see the relationship between spatial thinking and poetry already at work. These scientists are still using linear thinking in drawing up their computer programs, but they have long since given up attempting to conceptualize their discoveries in this way.

What is most unsettling about making this shift is that no methodology or criteria have been established for the legitimacy of theology-as-poetry. This is a task we urgently need to undertake, no matter how controversial or threatening to those trained in a more inflexible tradition. Given the nature of the openness necessitated by spatial thinking and poetic expression, it is possible that only general and very flexible criteria could be suggested. And perhaps even more unsettling, the method required for doing such theology requires that an amount of time be set aside for the theologian to quite literally sit in the dark in silence where all words and thoughts are left behind, time equal to at least half of that we spend poring over texts.

To cite two brief examples in space-time, we could give multi-dimensionality to our theologizing if we could find ways of thinking spatially that are analogous to Poincaré's insoluble conjecture or by imagining ourselves floating weightless in space, so that theology would lose its flat coordinates of horizontal and vertical. It is important to have a spatial sense underlying our theology because the confluence of God and creation, life lived under the condition of no up or down, is in fact the condition of our lives in which our theology is supposed to assist us.

In a recent *New Yorker* article a description of an astronomer's vision nicely illustrates the linear-spatial shift:

In his mind's eye, Gene holds a peculiar vision of the solar system, and it is not any solar system that I had ever heard of. In schoolbooks, the solar system is pictured as a series of flat concentric circles centered on the sun, each circle representing the orbit of a planet. In Gene's mind, the solar system is a spheroid: a dynamic, evolving cloud of debris, filigreed with bands and shells of shrapnel, full of bits and pieces of material likely to be pumped into long ellipses and tangles, and wobbling orbits, which carry the drifting projectiles all over the place—minor planets that every once in a while take a hook into a major planet, causing a major explosion.[1]

Time, as we all know—but haven't yet fully integrated into our thinking—is linked with space, a matter of where we are located in relation to others in terms of velocity. New explorations of time theory have turned up some fascinating possibilities. J. R. Lucas in *The Nature of Time* points out that there is no inconsistency between the idea of time that is past or future, depending on your point of view, and the notion that agents can decide their own future. He goes on to say that both in Newton's and the new physics we should in theory have memories from that future, but no one can figure out why we don't.[2] I would like to suggest that one reason we don't is that we are making so much noise in our logical traps that we never shut up long enough to listen to our memories. In silence is not only possibility but the primordial moment.

To come to terms with time theory is important because we already need practical tools for integrating new discoveries into theology. Astronomers are rapidly improving their equipment, looking backward through time to the universe before the stars began to spill light into the dark. This is not to suggest that scientists are going to come up with a formula to penetrate the divine mystery, but rather to suggest that having even a nodding familiarity with current time theory can help us *by analogy* to break out of our squirrel-cage of first-century cosmology into awe before the humble majesty of God. If religion is to be viable, it must be able to relate to the creation as God made it instead of how we might like it to be. Even more, theology and religion need to understand history, and therefore incarnation, in terms of contemporary perceptions of the space-time continuum.

Linear thinking makes us follow our noses along tightly logical lines, consuming or rejecting what immediately appears in front of us according to the limited criteria that it *is* in front of us, and that it makes us feel good or not. Linear theology leads us to such absurdities as so-called natural law that has nothing to do with the way God in fact made the universe. This so-called natural law has, among other tragedies, led to condemnation of a whole segment of the population. The homophobic seem unable to perceive that in addition to condemning people of same-sex orientation, they are also condemning *God* for making the world according to the divine wisdom instead of according to their pinched human prejudices.

Religion also is cultural, and its problems mirror those of the surrounding culture. One of the greatest perils the culture and the churches face today is a growing unwillingness, a fear even, to live within the continuum, in the tension of paradox. We seem to have a compulsion to oversimplify complex problems in order to take action on them, when often the exercise of self-restraint would allow enough time to pass so that appropriate action—or refraining from action—could be discerned.

Conversely, we in the churches seem unable to resolve false paradoxes, and these are among the issues of power explored in this book. Those who most wish to chain us to uniformity polarize issues, create the false paradox, the dialectic that is a *dead* end (see Appendix A). Or, in the political arena outside of institutional religion, we seem to have a reluctance to see through the illusion of "security" based on technology that is highly vulnerable to variables as simple as storms that devastate the power grid. Ordinary life today is rendered helpless without electricity. We seem to have got exactly backward what is acceptable as paradox and what is not, and it rarely seems to occur to us that true paradox can be the needle's eye through which we may move toward freedom (see Appendix A).

Our inability to discern and tolerate appropriate paradox is expressed partly by our growing fear of ideas offered for informed dialogue and debate and the effort to inform ourselves for such dialogue and debate. This tendency is dangerous if only because we can arrive at clear discernment by no other means than dialogue and exchange, whether this dialogue is silent within our selves or articulated with others. Some of our fear of debate and our mental sloth may have a social root. We seem to have mistaken the demands of equality for lack of discrimination, that is, discernment of variation and the implications of choices.

We seem to want formulas and technology for living, but few formulas can be applied universally (especially to creatures who are by nature unique), and while every view arises from a point of view, some points of view are at the bottom of canyons and some are on the tops of mountains. This leaves us with the dilemma that while every point of view may contribute to discernment, in a particular situation or context every idea is *not* of equal value with every other idea. Without dialogue and debate we lose our ability to establish criteria to discern among them.

Similarly, while we badly need to continue to develop equality of opportunity, people have different gifts in different measure and combination requiring specialized nurture. To work, a republic or a democracy requires discernment, commitment, and energy; otherwise equality becomes banal conformity, and apathy gives birth to tyranny.

The Myth of Immortality

The most important product of our culture's deification of technology is the illusion of immortality. This illusion thrives on the denial of the existence of difference and defuses every spark of debate. To perpetuate itself, this illusion requires not that technology be user-friendly, but that users be technology-friendly. We are required to reduce complex problems we barely perceive to the simplistic, logical framework computers can understand. This leads to simplistic and logical (and therefore often destructive) solutions.

Because technology gives us the impression that every problem has a solution, we have a desperate compulsion to *do* something about every difficulty, real or imagined. We are thus developing an ever-narrowing spiral that reinforces our illusion of control. This lust for control, for secure, closed systems, feeds our fear of boat-rocking, our fear that our illusion of safety and a static world will be destroyed. It is so much more comfortable to linger in a reduced fragment of an idea, to outwardly impose a temporary and provisional resolution as if it were permanent and encompassing. We continue in this way to try to tidy up the messy complexities of creatureliness and delude our selves with false clarity, lest the status quo be threatened and we discover to our horror that we are not, in fact, in control.

These cultural and religious fears inevitably extend to interpersonal relationships. Again and again we encounter people who seem to think that to be friends or spiritually related we must have identical ideas, tastes, and opinions, to the exclusion of complementarity in the name of "love." Such an attitude precludes mutual illumination and criticism. The true friend, the one who truly loves, is the one who calls to our attention the chasm in front of us when we, blinded by illusion, are about to fall into it.

These attitudes of denial amount to fear of life, life that

of importance of Diversity

constantly tests the edges of experience, as Barry Lopez's *Arctic Dreams* reminds us life must if it is to continue and without which there is no life at all.[3] Illiteracy in the United States and elsewhere is more than the inability to read and write. Even among those who have these skills there seems to be a kind of notional illiteracy, an illiteracy that is *chosen* on the frightening grounds that information and ideas that do not appear immediately and tangibly to affect a person's life are irrelevant to that person's life. People don't want to know.

This shortsightedness and accompanying isolation arise from individualism carried to an unimaginable, but very concrete extreme. The cycle seems to be, "I don't want to make the effort to incorporate any more knowledge than I must to survive; I exclude anything that doesn't seem immediately and tangibly to affect me. The ideas I am forced to deal with I want in predigested and simplistic form. Having thus established my prejudices and let others do my thinking for me, I do not want to admit that there are implications I have missed, much less that there is much I do not know." This attitude is not new, but on its reversal now depend both free government and the fate of the earth.

As a result of this petulant desire for homogeneous thought and opinion, and as a consequence of our increasing dependence on technology to tell us what and how to think, we have become addicted to heedless action. We desire to "solve" all problems according to the dim lights of our prejudices, to fix up, that is, exploit, first our own immediate territory (no matter what the cost to ours or other environments) and subsequently to fix up everyone else's according to our increasingly narrow vision, no matter how different others might be or how inadequately we understand their circumstances.

Underneath this frenetic drive to action, what we are trying to fix up is death. That, of course, is impossible, so instead we try to project a sense of security and an illusory self-image that exists within that security onto everyone and everything around us. Thus committed, we spend all our energy trying to sustain fantasy as reality, to preserve the artificial environment

that supports it. We defend our delusions and their destructive, uninformed action with increasing ferocity when we feel
the mirage dissolving and our resources becoming exhausted.
In the end we are sacrificing life for environmental and spiritual death, a death that is cursed, a death more profound and
final than mortality. In reality, mortality, embraced as part of
our choice for life, is the final thank-offering of our earthly
sacrifice in Christ. Our addiction to the myth of omnipotence
means we abandon the mysteries of life and death that bond
our solitudes into community.

In spite of the many environmental disasters that we have
caused, we still have not understood that we create more and
greater problems when we rush to impose our private percep-
tual resolutions on the outside world. Without humility before
its immense and incomprehensible variables, without critical
discernment, without much, in fact, beyond the desire for
short-term gratification, status, and control, particularly the
control that fosters the illusion that material or theological
technology can dispel our mortality, we insist that there is an
ultimate cure for physical death and a shortcut to ecstasy if
only we develop the correct sequence.

This heedless quest for gratification is pursued on more
levels than mere consumerism. It stems also from a kind of
ideational drunkenness, a sense of controlling power that leads
to insanity such as physicist Jeremy Bernstein experienced at
the atomic bomb test site in Nevada:

Someone counted over a loudspeaker backward from ten to zero.
There was a flash of light, and after a few seconds we all turned
around. My first thought—and this seems to have been common to
many people who saw these tests—was "My God, that's beautiful!"
An orange-red-rose cloud was rising out of the desert, and it *was*
beautiful. Then, as it cooled, it turned darker and darker—a
purplish-black, menacing color. When I look back on that moment,
I think of the lines Robert Oppenheimer remembered from the
Bhagavad Gita, after the first bomb explosion: "I am become Death/
The destroyer of worlds."

Then we were taken to a small, low building, which was covered in concrete and set away from the rest. . . . What I saw caused me to start backward. The concrete hut was filled with atomic bombs and parts of atomic bombs—enough, no doubt, to destroy a continent. The heart of an atomic bomb is a perfect sphere of plutonium or uranium. I was given one of these spheres—about the size and weight of a bowling ball—to hold in both hands. Don't drop it. It had a bright, silvery sheen and gave off warmth—radioactivity. . . . In the bomb storehouse . . . there was a woman, who sat there knitting, while a man—perhaps her husband or a boyfriend—filed on the high explosive wrapped around the metal sphere that is the heart of the bomb. . . . As I write this now, I see her there, dressed in a sweater and a skirt, knitting silently while this man files on a bomb. . . . It somehow became the meaning to me of the whole visit. . . .

As I reread what I have just been writing, I am afraid that it may give the impression that I was made wise—instantaneously wise—by seeing the bombs; I mean wise about nuclear bombs. I was not made wise. I was made foolish. . . . I had seen bombs explode, and I had held one in my hands. *The effect of this was to give me some feeling of power to which I was not entitled.* I wanted the aboveground testing to go on. I thought it was all very important and necessary. . . . [He then tried to see Adlai Stevenson to persuade him to withdraw his platform plank against nuclear testing.] I knew so little about weapons technology that I don't see what I could have told . . . about their importance, or, above all, about why we needed to test in the atmosphere. In retrospect, such tests seem so crazy to me that I can't imagine what I said [italics mine].[4]

Here is a haunting echo of the myth of the Garden: the lust for presumptuous control leads to death, spiritual death first and foremost, then death of the created order. Bernstein's experience shows how the mere attempt to possess this kind of power, epitomized in nuclear weapons, is *inherently* corrupting and leads to insanity, not only in individuals but even more in whole societies. Possession of this sort of power even potentially corrupts quietly and absolutely in the dark, out of our sight and consciousness, under the guise, the rationalizing lie, that it is "good," that it "protects" us.

When we presume to act out the illusion of absolute power, whether in physics, or theology, or any other area of life and thought, we are by definition unable to engage God, to reciprocate the divine eucharistic relatedness. It is precisely this kind of oppressive and violent power that Jesus the Christ renounced and to which the divine humility is the antidote. "Blessed are you poor" refers *not* to those who are materially destitute, but to those who are able to relinquish the need to establish and maintain their identity by controlling others.

At the same time, death proper to our creatureliness is not to be pushed out of consciousness or regarded solely as an enemy. Death is the one sure background against which, without in any way devaluing the goodness of life and creation, our lives are illumined and from which they derive their meaning. Paradoxically, if we consciously choose the inevitable, if we choose the fact of our death as part of our createdness (though not, under ordinary circumstances, its time or season), we have chosen life; we have engaged the future with the eternal *living* sacrifice of Christ indwelling. This sacrifice does not require the objectifying of life by ritual slaughter, which the Christ-event has ended; rather this sacrifice *enhances and transfigures life.* And when the time comes to prepare to engage death itself, our having lived within the sacrifice of Christ enables us to discern the choices that will complete that sacrifice as we, or the person for whom we are caring, would wish.

But devotees of technology desire to take this choice away from us, especially as we approach our dying. They seem to want to ignore the distinction between lives that run their natural course and artificial prolongation of dying. In an article in the February 28, 1987, issue of *America,* Dr. Robert J. White writes of three desperately ill patients, all of whom, from his Olympian height, he elects to "save" no matter what the cost in suffering to the patient and even in one case against the patient's explicit wish. Dr. White is trying to issue a warning that "we may be rapidly approaching the time when it will be

JN The truth will
12 set you free

decided that physicians and hospitals can no longer care for such patients regardless of the wants and desires of their loved ones."[5] However, not only does his arrogance deny patients control over what they are made to suffer, his desire to throw technology at problems indiscriminately is shocking.

While in one place he rightly points to those who more or less recover and for whom such treatment may be justified, he admits that the patient who wishes to die has no other future than as "a head on a pillow." If, after time, counseling, and prayerful deliberation the patient wishes to die, who is the doctor to overrule that patient in the name of technology, in the name of "life" at any cost? Who is the physician to dare to appropriate the only significant human choice left to this patient? It is true that we must take every step to ensure that the lives and rights of those who are physically and mentally disabled are preserved; it is equally true that we must protect the right to choose the amount of suffering we will endure and, when the possibility of choosing appears, the kind of death to which we will submit.

If there is a right to life, there is also a right to death. To take away the right to engaged my own death is the same kind of thinking that makes possible human-induced mass annihilation, whether by nuclear war or Nazi gas chambers. The denial of death increases the possibility of the extinction of the planet because it feeds the illusion of immortality. It leads to and in turn is fed by the delusion that we can control the effects of a technology already wildly out of control, and that we therefore have a right to control others' lives and deaths simply because that technology exists. Being made ciphers, we are denied the deepest mystery of our humanity.

It is this kind of "thinking" that lies behind the ill-considered "heroic" medical interventions that physicians force on patients even at the end of long life and attenuated, debilitating illness. Let us look at a real-life example (details have been altered for anonymity's sake). A woman in her eighties has lymphoma, which recurs after five years' remission. There are tumors on the liver, kidney, and colon; there has been fluid in her lungs for some months, cause unknown. The doctor has never told her that lymphoma is incurable. He has not told her that scarring from apparently unrelated recurring intestinal inflammation will eventually lead to blockage and may kill her before the lymphoma does. He has not told her she is too weak to have surgery to prevent this obstruction. In recent years she has repeatedly expressed her wish to be kept off "machines" at the end of her life and that no extreme measures be taken when it comes time for her to die.

Because she does not know the facts, she becomes alarmed when her condition deteriorates, as does her family. Instead of telling her the truth, the doctor "does something," that is, he embarks on a course of in-patient chemotherapy, which not only renders her already fragile constitution more susceptible to infection, but also causes extreme nausea and makes all her hair fall out, causing her acute embarrassment. Within weeks she has a virulent infection.

Suddenly the intestinal obstruction occurs. The woman is taken by ambulance to the hospital. She is in great pain and rapidly going into severe shock. The doctor does not inform the bewildered and frightened family that she is dying. He offers them no choices. He does not ask them what her wishes are. He does not give them the chance to authorize him to give her morphine and let nature take its course. Instead, he puts her on a ventilator, stabilizes her as best he can, and calls in the surgeons for a heroic and "life-saving" operation, which he justifies as "the only way to stop the pain." The patient's postoperative agony is acute; she fails rapidly; she dies within eighteen hours of being taken to the surgical suite.

For the unprepared family, her death is devastating. Later, when the husband asks questions here and there, he is left with a shattering sense of failure, failure to have made the decisions that would have implemented his spouse's wishes, failure associated with the knowledge that she died in acute pain "on the machines." He is haunted by the phrase, "If only

I had . . . " He is left with the question, "Why . . . why if she was too weak to prevent the blockage in the first place was surgery attempted when she was already dying?" Much of his suffering is unnecessary, as was hers.

Doctors who engage in such interventions may seem well intentioned when they boast about keeping patients "alive" by throwing technology at them, but the medical industry—and medicine today is a commodity—is much too complex to admit simplistic and egotistical motivation. Such treatment often prolongs the death of patients who, after due consideration and prayer, no longer wish to be kept alive, or who have never been consulted about their wishes in the first place, or who have been blackmailed by the hope of a "cure" so that research can continue, or who are simply pawns used to increase the profits of the medical industry in the name of "research."

This battle to prolong dying at all costs is fought in pursuit of an idea of "life" that is an artificial construct in physicians' minds. It is a battle invariably lost. It is fought by doctors who are afraid of death, who no longer diagnose by engagement with humanity. Instead, they anesthetize themselves with technology that enables them to reduce humanity to biomechanical objects. Medicine today is drunk on the power of technology exercised at the price of our freedom from pain and our relationship with God in the mystery of death.

This intervention amounts to human sacrifice exacted by the medical profession, a kind of sacrificial slaughter demanded by the great god technology in order that we may finally be allowed to die when technology ultimately fails in the face of death. It can be compared only to the Aztec sacrifices in which the officiant tore the still-beating hearts from living victims to offer to the bloodthirsty tyrant-god, the sun, to prevent its going out and their world coming to an end. The medical rationale is identical: the sacrifice of lives to the tyrant-god, technology, is offered to justify its high cost; for if the sun of technology dims, the doctors' little world of prestige and high finance and the medical growth industry will be threatened.

The Hippocratic maxim "First of all, do no hurt" applies even more today than it has in the past twenty-five hundred years, for as we acquire increasingly invasive technology that inflicts great suffering even as it may prolong life or death, we have in our hands more subtle ways of doing hurt. We need always to weigh for ourselves and others for whom we may be responsible the amount of suffering treatment may cause against realistic prospects not only for length and but also, and more important, for quality of life.

The analogy to Aztec sacrifice may seem extreme, but a professor of medical ethics at one of the world's leading university medical schools agrees that it is appropriate. He adds that the most important issue in medical ethics today is the question of patient autonomy. He says, further, that physicians are even more concerned about giving up a little of their presumptuous control over the lives and deaths of their patients than they are about the potential decrease in the medical growth industry such patient autonomy would imply.

It could be argued that patient expectations often drive doctors to extreme measures, but the medical industry does little to bring patient expectations in line with reality. It could also be argued that helping patients to come to terms with death is time-consuming and costly, but there are already hospital staffs who have developed these skills and testify to the fact that helping families prepare for the possibility of death makes all other aspects of care go a lot more smoothly.

The spiritual and physical pain exacted by medical tyranny is insupportable. It is not technology in itself that is evil, but rather its indiscriminate and ill-considered application. Always reluctant to mirror the God whose power is expressed through the wisdom of self-restraint, we now appear to have rejected self-restraint as either impossible or undesirable. There seems to be a direct relationship between the rise of technology and the decline of wisdom.

We have mastery on our minds, mastery that says we know better when in fact we know comparatively nothing and can never know to the limits of our wishful thinking. The desire to know to the uttermost limit of human capacity is *not* the sin of the Garden. The sin of the Garden is rather the presumption that we can know *beyond* human capacity, that we can know as God knows, that we can have God's wisdom and perspective in applying our knowledge by taking away others' choices for death or life.

Perhaps the Garden story will end up being prophecy: we will be turned out of the Garden, Planet Earth, which we will have made hostile to life, because in our state of denial we cannot restrain our shortsighted tinkering and insatiable greed. Medicine is an obvious target for criticism, but it is only one culprit among technologies run amok. We could apply the same criticism equally to a theology that has taken refuge in closed philosophical constructs or religion that has degenerated into magic.

Myths of Power

In her parables *The Farthest Shore* and *The Wizard of Earthsea*, Ursula Le Guin powerfully portrays the relationship between heedless action and the fear of death. She understands the resonances of action and how important it is *not* to act without a constant listening for new possibility outside our limited knowledge and experience, without reverence for each person's freedom of choice to live or to die. Her exposition of "equilibrium" and "balance" is not the closed system of the pantheist, nor should it be understood in terms of uniformity and stasis. It is rather the open system of the Gospel's radical questioning, the faith that provides the security that enables us to live in insecurity.

Within our lives is paradox, seeming opposites in relationship within a continuum, and if we seek freedom, we must have the willingness first to live within the tension of paradox:

"Why should you not desire immortality? [Ged the Archmage is talking to Arren, the boy who will be king in *The Farthest Shore*] How should you not? Every soul desires it, and its health is in the strength of its desire.—But be careful; you are one who might achieve your desire."

"And then?"

"And then this: a false king ruling, the arts of man forgotten, the singer tongueless, the eye blind. This!—this blight and plague on the lands, this sore we seek to heal. There are two, Arren, two that make one: the world and the shadow, the light and the dark. The two poles of the Balance. Life rises out of death, death rises out of life; in being opposite they yearn to each other, they give birth to each other and are forever reborn. And with them all is reborn, the flower of the apple tree, the light of the stars. In life is death. In death is rebirth. What then is life without death? Life unchanging, ever lasting, eternal?—What is it but death, death without rebirth?"[6]

Or, in more ostensibly Christian terms, to violate another's freedom for the sake of illusory immortality means that the oppressor ultimately faces the prison of a closed system without salvation, death without hope of resurrection, for resurrection can come only from the humility that is Christ's. Yes, there is risk; yes, there is pain; yes, the insecurity can fill us with something like despair. But life without aspiration, life without testing the edges, life that does not risk itself, life with the choices taken away—is it deserving of the name? I think not.

In his introduction to Goethe's *Truth and Fantasy,* Humphrey Trevelyan writes:

It seems that two qualities are necessary if a great artist is to remain creative to the end of a long life; he must on the one hand retain an abnormally keen awareness of life, he must never grow complacent, never be content with life, must always demand the impossible and when he cannot have it, must despair. The burden of the mystery must be with him day and night. He must be shaken by the naked truths that will not be comforted. This divine discontent, this disequilibrium, this state of inner tension is the source of artistic energy. Many lesser poets have it only in their youth; some even of the greatest lose it in middle life. Wordsworth lost the courage to despair and with it his poetic power.[7]

Le Guin is talking about this same precarious disequilibrum, this balance that continually seeks its equipoise of conversion, of ready response. When Ged frees Arren from a slave-ship, he tells the slaver, "I do not punish . . . but in the cause of justice, Egre, I take this much upon myself: I bid your voice be dumb until the day you find a word worth speaking."

And explaining to Arren, he continues:

"I left none bound on that ship."

"But Egre's men had weapons. If you had bound *them*—"

"Aye, if I had bound them? There were but six. The oarsmen were chained slaves, like you. Egre and his men may be dead by now, or chained by the others to be sold as slaves; but I left them free to fight or bargain. I am no slave-taker."

"But you knew them to be evil men—"

"Was I to join them therefore? To let their acts rule my own? I will not make their choices for them, nor let them make mine for me!

" . . . Do you see, Arren, how an act is not, as young men think, like a rock that one picks up and throws, and it hits or misses, and that's the end of it. . . . When it is thrown, the circuits of the stars respond, and where it strikes or falls the universe is changed."[8]

Ged is willing to live in the tension of not knowing, of the self-restraint that keeps him from himself becoming a slaver by attempting to predetermine the outcome of other people's action. Yet he is not without discernment; he is not without morality. His integrity is impeccable, yet he has the humility to know that even he, the archmage, cannot comprehend all variables, cannot see the pattern entire, and he will not enslave others to guarantee his own security.

"Lebannen, this is. And thou art. There is no safety, and there is no end. The word must be heard in silence; there must be darkness to see the stars. The dance is always danced above the hollow place, above the terrible abyss. . . .

"You will die. You will not will live forever. Nor will any man nor any thing. Nothing is immortal. But only to us is it given to know that we must die. And that is a great gift: the gift of selfhood. For we have only what we know we must lose, what we are willing to lose. . . . That selfhood which is our torment, and our treasure, and our humanity, does not endure. It changes; it is gone, a wave on the sea. Would you have the sea grow still and the tides cease to save one wave, to save yourself? Would you give up the craft of your hands, and the passion of your heart, and the light of sunrise and sunset, to buy safety for yourself—safety forever?"[9]

Perhaps some of contemporary reluctance for debate comes from our misinterpretation of the biblical injunction not to judge. We seem to feel we must never look at another's action and have an opinion about what we see or how it affects us. In bending over backward in order not to "judge," we have in fact allowed those who seek controlling power to make precisely that kind of judgment, to say this or that is from God or is under God's judgment. People who desire to control move swiftly into the vacuum left by our abrogation of discernment. Their fearmongering reinforces our reluctance to "judge" because they imply not only that we are morally incompetent, but also that the nonspecialist has no ability to think about such matters. They whisper that it is dangerous to trust our own admittedly incomplete discernment, that only self-certifying "experts" have this right. In the end, their brainwashing makes us feel we have no right to any legitimate opinion at all.

It is claiming to judge from God's point of view that we are to avoid, not informed critical opinion, not observation of the interconnectedness of diversity according to the vision and integrity given us, not criticism of those we see destroying life by the tyranny of their control. We must bend over backward to understand other points of view without relinquishing our own; we must offer our discernment as possibility or option to be measured against the discernment of others, to contribute to synthesis of new insight. We are to avoid imposing it

on others or coercing them, but we are not to deny the faculty itself.

When we refuse appropriately to voice our discernment from fear that disturbing others will cause us to lose our status and power, we lose the kind of judgment that is essential to life, and we condemn ourselves to slavery. Neither Ged nor Arren hesitates to say that Egre is evil, nor does he go without the effects of justice. But Ged knows when to stop; he knows that all power systems, if they are not themselves to turn evil, must be short-circuited, that power can be exercised and has authority only under conditions of utmost self-restraint and humility.

In our day we have confused morality with popular opinion, both the pressure of mass opinion and seeking others' approval at the price of our integrity. As Christians we are bound to discern and to transform the pressure of prevailing prejudice by declaring a different morality irrespective of threats to our own status and without coercing those to whom we speak. This is both the poverty and freedom of the blessed. Further, we are to live out our declaration, often without apology or explanation, and the resonances of this living-out are still the most powerful, effective, and perhaps the only true way to illumine others: it is Christ's priesthood and therefore our priesthood. The price of this living-out may be our lives, but without this risk, life for us and others around us is living death.

To live out this vision requires humility, the humility to say we do not know, the humility to revise our morality when new information about the way God makes the world conflicts with our prejudices, the humility that leavens with painful awareness any action that is part of our experimenting at the edges and insists that our movement into the unknown be undertaken with all deliberation.

"But then," the boy said, frowning at the stars, "is the balance to be kept by doing nothing? Surely a man must act, even not knowing all the consequences of his act, if anything is to be done at all?''

"Never fear. It is much easier for me to act than to refrain from acting. We will continue to do good and to do evil. . . . But if there were a king over us all again and he sought counsel of a mage, as in the days of old, and I were that mage, I would say to him: My Lord, do nothing because it is righteous or praiseworthy or noble to do so; do nothing because it seems good to do so; do only that which you must do and which you cannot do in any other way."[10]

And this brings us to the central insight of Christian obedience and freedom—which are the same thing. The freedom of obedience is not the freedom of choice found in a supermarket, but, as the Master Summoner says to Ged in *The Wizard of Earthsea* after his abuse of power through hubris has unleashed a darkness in the world, "You thought, as a boy, that a mage is one who can do anything. So I thought, once. So did we all. And the truth is that *as a man's real power grows and his knowledge widens, ever the way he can follow grows narrower: until at last he chooses nothing, but does only and wholly what he* must *do*" [italics mine].[11]

To act heedlessly and shortsightedly, instead of doing only what we must in fear and trembling, is the fundamental difference between the creation of the illusory, controlling, power-hungry, self-reflective, ultimately evil *gebbeth*, the living death of our own dark pseudo-selves, and the reality of being so found in God, so becoming, so fully realizing the person God created us and knows us to be, that self-reflection is no longer necessary or even possible.

We do only what we must because we have been found by God in the creation and have found our true being in God through our createdness. To act otherwise would be to opt once again for slavery to appetite and the illusion of immortality and to set ourselves over and against our creatureliness. Morality that emerges from the pursuit of self-image (and it is questionable if the pursuit of self-image, as opposed to self-respect, is in any way moral) is exercised by imposed constraint alone.

The morality that emerges from the true freedom of God is self-restraint that naturally irrupts from aspiration, the mirror of God's *kenosis*. And aspiration toward God's freedom does not fear debate conducted with humility before the facts as we best can know them. Whether we give priority to constraint or to aspiration speaks volumes about our fundamental attitude toward ourselves and the community of creation.

The created order—not just humans—tends both to appear and to be imprisoned by our expectations. Joe Clark, the successful principal of tough Eastside High in Patterson, New Jersey, understand the difference, as reported by Frank Rossi in the *Sunday Times Magazine*: "He believes that young people will do what they are expected to do. If you expect them to be addicts and rapists, that's what they will be. From the beginning, he made it clear that his expectations went quite beyond that."[12]

It is important to think as clearly as possible about issues, but it is equally important to acknowledge that whatever clarity we come to can be no better than a staging area for going forward into the unknown. At least, then, we move with care, even if at the same time we are more acutely aware of our confusion. To be aware and tentative is to be in reality, even if sometimes we need to move with boldness. Boldness requires acute vigilance to consequences and willingness to remedy or withdraw if consequences should prove us mistaken. Faith is the security to risk going forward in insecurity; it seeks the equipoise of ready response and hope that arises from our reciprocity in the love of God that is Eucharist.

To be aware and tentative would be less destructive, for example, than racing to spread Western discoveries and control throughout the world as part of a planetary ego trip, discoveries and control that, no matter how beneficial they may seem in the West, may do incalculable harm in a different climate, a different culture, a different genetic heritage. A dialogical method that challenges our wholesale efforts at control sets up a proposition to be considered, attacked, analyzed, and modified and is not to be feared.

That such a process *is* often feared today is a sign of the need for this book on power, because malignant, self-aggrandizing power can destroy under masks of helpfulness and conciliation. While my primary focus is on power and maturity within the churches, it is obvious that these fundamental issues touch every aspect of our lives.

But the churches have a particularly important role to play, for truth is not served if differences are concealed under a miasma of pseudo-charity, and the churches today often seem to be engaged in the trivial pursuit of so-called unity at the expense of the diversity of truth, while the world around them seeks meaning in despair.

Dialogue is at the heart of Incarnation; the mystical coinherence of human and divine, the humility of God, is the mystery of our salvation. To live in that tension is not Christ's alone. It is the vocation of each of God's creatures. This does not mean living an escapist romantic fantasy. The Incarnation is ultimately the most practical action of all time. True mystical life, God's in ours, is *always* practical, though it is neither facile, nor simplistic, nor finished, nor static. It is especially our brokenness that is cherished by the divine Humility. Priesthood is opening to and living out that Humility within our brokenness, Christ's outpouring and indwelling that engages, transfigures, and re-creates.

Feast of St. John the Baptist, 1987

I. PRIESTHOOD AND THE CHRISTIAN

"There is a certain bleakness in finding hope where one expected certainty."

URSULA LE GUIN, *THE FARTHEST SHORE*

"You are not thinking; you are merely being logical."

NIELS BOHR TO ALBERT EINSTEN

"I think the whole of theology will come to be seen in a different light. . . . "

EDWARD SCHILLEBEECKX, *GOD IS NEW EACH MOMENT*

1. Priesthood and Ministry: Ordination Does Not Bestow Priesthood

"You have great power inborn in you, and you used that power wrongly, to work a spell over which you had no control, not knowing how that spell affects the balance of light and dark, life and death, good and evil. And you were moved to do this by pride and by hate. Is it any wonder the result was ruin?"

URSULA LE GUIN, *A WIZARD OF EARTHSEA*

"If I brung him down for any thing it ben becaws he thot you cud move the out side of things frontways and leave the in side to look after its self. Which I think its the in side has got to do the moving its got to move every thing and its got to move us as wel. If I say diffrent time after this itwl be fearbelly talking I know I aint brave."

RUSSELL HOBAN, *RIDDLEY WALKER*

"Sayin' a sheep has five legs don't make it so."

ATTRIBUTED TO ABRAHAM LINCOLN

God is related to the creation in kenotic (self-emptying), eucharistic, indwelling *engagement*, the love shown to us in the priestly humility of Christ. The hierarchical orders that exist in many Christian churches are true neither to the disclosure of Christ's humility nor to New Testament Christianity. As we shall see, any hierarchy entails a dualistic class structure that invariably fosters immaturity.

Hierarchies define themselves by precisely the sort of dominance condemned in the New Testament. Thus, to call these orders "priesthood" is both anomalous and self-contradictory. Further, claims that Jesus established this system have been systematically disproved by biblical scholars.[1]

Even before these critical tools were available to us, for many centuries Christians have felt that a manipulative power structure that also purports to represent the confluence of divine and human sacrificial love is blasphemous. Those in control quite naturally silenced the voices of these critics, and Christianity has become progressively more sterile because of its self-contradiction.

Some theologians appeal to tradition to justify perpetuating this contradiction, and their appeal, particularly to the subapostolic and patristic ages, is fatally flawed. It is flawed not only because New Testament evidence will not support the churches' claims that their system of orders was established by Jesus, but, more important, it is flawed precisely because the tradition is dedicated to preserving its own inordinate control even at the price of its reason for existence, which is communicating the revelation of forgiveness, service, possibility, and freedom in the humility of Christ.

Indeed, this flaw is so fundamental as to call into question much of the theological tradition that is known as "Christian." Such an assertion neither dismisses the tradition nor opts for anarchy, but rather points to the fact that organizational, that is, secular, functional power tends to make creatures into objects to perpetuate itself. Organizational power has a strong tendency to deteriorate into self-aggrandizing, or worldly, power and creates closed systems. That the churches create closed systems is one of the deepest wounds of Christian history, a wound we must enter if Christianity is to survive.

There is no salvation in a closed system. If institutional Christianity is to find salvation, the power systems that operate at every level need to have built-in, fail-safe devices, means to short-circuit power before it becomes self-perpetuating. Power systems need tripping mechanisms like those in pressure-sensitive transducers on household alarms. However, unlike most alarm systems, which are designed to prevent intrusion into a guarded space, these would maintain the integrity of the churches' vulnerability and compassionate response that is Christ's.

The question of priesthood and ministry is under discussion everywhere. It is a central issue in ecumenical dialogue, the debate about the ordination of women, the crisis brought about by shortage of clergy in the Roman Catholic Church and the Church of England, and the extraordinary growth in clerical numbers in The Episcopal Church in the United States. In addition, nonordained people are increasing their ministerial roles in every church, especially where Christianity is persecuted. These and other movements within the churches seem to have led to wider and perhaps freer questioning about the nature of priesthood and ministry than has occurred since the first three centuries of the Christian era.

We cannot seek answers to these questions in the context of an unexamined tradition. Rather we need to decode that tradition's inherent self-contradiction, the self-contradiction of controlling power that gave rise to the separation of the institutions from the humility of Christ in the first place. These questions cannot move toward illumination until we reclaim the practicality of the divine Humility. But first we must review the dilemma and the loss of vision.

A Brief Survey of the Present Confusion

The self-contradiction and incoherence of our theology of priesthood and ministry is as old as Christianity, because there are always those who wish to twist the humility of Christ into a religion of power. In every generation there are people who wish to take the Cross, turn it upside down, and sharpen one end into a sword.[2] This self-contradiction has disorienting and catastrophic results. It means that for centuries we have been giving secular answers to religious questions. When we fall back on these secular answers, a fissure develops in our ontology: we fall away from our being-in-God, for a religious question is engagement and a secular answer is mere technique.

We in the churches have reduced our search for religious answers to technology, to a series of controlling propositions that together make a closed system in which we become trapped. Our insistence on technique means that we perceive and try to manipulate religious questions, God, the creation, and ourselves as if we were isolated fragments, objects, instead of creatures engaged with one another in the kenotic Love of God. When we treat something as an object we remove its capacity for engagement; we encapsulate and kill it.

There is nothing in the fabric of creation and the interrelatedness of the creation that is *inherently* worldly, not our work, or our play, or our committed love-making, or anything else. It is we who create the secular when we make any part of the creation fall away from its engagement with the rest of what is moving in and out of existence by making it object, by isolating it as a fragment and exploiting it, by thus taking its life to support our delusions of power. The worldly character of a person or process results from the choice to fall away from being.

We become reductionistic when we confuse the internal tension of faith that moves within the continuum of Incarnation with the tension that desires to maintain by control the false synthesis that ostensibly integrates two contradictory models of power. These models are the Zeus-god of objectifying, controlling power, who demands our life (*pace*, classicists, it is indeed a popular caricature), and I WILL BE of kenotic, eucharistic engagement, who enhances our life (see Appendix A).

When we attempt a false synthesis, we create static and artifical resolutions. Instead of regarding these resolutions as temporary stopping places where we can catch our breath before we seek a still wider perspective, we seize them, delighted with our own cleverness, and turn them outward to impose them as "answers" on our own, and worse, on others' lives. Or, equally facile and equally destructive, we repeat the same insight over and over, without any engagement or self-critical realization, "all is question, there is no answer, and happily we run along." We are lazy and self-reflective (as opposed to creatively self-critical), and our tidy resolutions feel comfortable.

Any seeking that is properly called Christian must be free and open and grounded in the self-emptying humility of Christ, which means that it must be willing to be in unknowing and seeming insecurity as it finds its equipoise of response in the love of God. By this standard, much of today's power-oriented religious propaganda that calls itself "Christian" is mislabeled, if not frankly deceitful. Television evangelists give one version of this message, the Vatican another; an organization that might call itself "Christians for Nuclear Weapons" would be an absolute contradiction in terms.

By absolutizing our reductionistic resolutions and techniques, our religious questing becomes synthetic and we become trapped and isolated in our closed system. We fall ever farther away from being, seduced by the fragmenting, individualistic self-image we are intent on creating and projecting. Or, to use another image, our devotion to self-image removes us from the confluence with Love, who gives us being, and our life drains away through the ontological fissure. We widen the fissure in our being when we use selection instead of discernment to choose the people we hope will enable us to close it, to restore our engagement, to find religious answers.

When we use these worldly sensibilities and controlling techniques to search for religious leaders, we tend to select people who are expert in worldly (self-aggrandizing) political techniques and who will only aggravate our falling away from our engagement with God. We are puzzled and disillusioned when they cannot enable our religious maturity, refusing to see that we have fallen into our own trap. Because we deny the impossibility of our false synthesis of the controlling Zeus-god and I WILL BE, our search for religious enablers and religious answers becomes indistinguishable from the illusory problem-solving power-struggles of the politics of self-aggrandizement.

In the churches where people are flocking to ordained ministry in numbers far in excess of jobs available, the people responsible for ordination are asking two questions: "Should we ordain them?" and "Why are they offering themselves?" Can all these people truly be called to the organizational hierarchy, or are they haunted by something more fundamental for which the churches have no response, or perhaps once had but do no longer? The people offering themselves for ordination give a variety of answers as to why they feel called to be part of the hierarchy of their church. All their answers boil down to one: a call from God, which is a mystery.

Those who counsel and examine these people often have an uncomfortable and frustrating task. The idea of "interior call" is a relatively recent one. In earlier centuries, churches would have regarded such certainty of a call to ordination with deepest suspicion because it would have been a sign of desire for worldly, that is, self-aggrandizing power. The church depicted in Acts and the church of the Egyptian desert described in the saying of the desert Fathers *(Apopthegmata)* are two examples of churches in which "interior call" was not a consideration for ordination. Certainly a balance needs to be struck between interior call and the churches' desire to ordain people chosen by the community, but the scales seem to have tipped too far over toward an often poorly discerned interior urge.

While it is true that many of these people do in fact seem to have a call from God—each of us, without exception, has a vocation—it is also evident that for many of them, ordained ministry is the last place they should try to live out this call. How can the churches respond to them? (For a discussion of this problem, see Part II, Chapters 5 and 6.)

The selection committees seem hard put to describe what they are looking for when they screen candidates. On a committee of ten there may be eleven (or more) opinions as to the differing natures of priesthood and ministry. Candidates accepted by one screening group are sometimes turned down by another.

Sometimes the committees make these decisions with painstaking self-searching and inner distress at the delicacy required for a discernment that will affect the whole of a person's life and hopes. On the other hand, sometimes their decisions are tinged with political agendas—power, favoritism, vendetta—that have little to do with discernment. As one bishop has lamented, "It is distressing to realize that my ordinands end up regarding me as an adversary." As a clergy member of a Commission on Ministry observed, "It seems to me that all the people who seem to have potential for the spiritual nurture of others get turned down, and all the politicians get approved."

The selection problem, from a parish point of view, is a nightmare. Let us look at a hypothetical clergy selection process based on several actual parish experiences (and two diocesan searches for bishops) in The Episcopal Church in the United States. (Some form of selection torture seems ubiquitous, present in every church.) This hypothetical example is not intended to show how the process *ought* to work but how it seems to work in fact.

A parish is asked to make a profile of itself that describes its group personality, and the members are asked to agree on what kind of pastor they seek. The parish makes this assessment statistically, and a politically selected committee writes the final version of the profile. Invariably there are some people in the parish who are dissatisfied with the profile and feel that their particular needs are being ignored.

This profile is sent to a central computer, which in return sends a list of candidates to the parish, which, combined with other candidates suggested by the bishop and those nominated through word-of-mouth, can present the selection committee with over three hundred names to choose from. Note that this committee is called a selection committee and not a discerning community. The selection committee then begins an agonizing weeding-out process. It can hardly meet each of the candidates, much less make any kind of deep discernment even if its members could agree on what ministry or priesthood is.

Since the descriptions on the computer printout or letters of nomination are based on material written by the candidates themselves, the process from the parish point of view resembles choosing a new friend from the columns that advertise the needs of the lonely at the back of the *New York Review of Books*. From the candidates' point of view, it becomes an exercise in self-marketing. Right from the start, the process loses those most suitable for the spiritual nurturing of others because they are the people who are least likely to be able or inclined to sell themselves.

In addition, any committee process is by nature more political than contemplative, and politics virtually eliminates the possibility that the Holy Spirit will have any say at all. The Holy Spirit, after all, is self-effacing. While some will argue that that "group process is the playground of the Holy Spirit when entered into openly and freely, without predetermining its outcome," such groups are rare. Members become members by behind-the-scenes maneuvering because they have a political stake in what is going on. The process is thus not entered "openly and freely," and to assume that in even a few groups all members enter the proceedings "without predetermining its outcome" is naive. It could be argued that I am committing the same error of expectation outlined at the end of the Abecedary, to which I must respond that expectation about individual development is one thing and expectation about group process quite something else. History has given us too many examples of the workings of group process for us to remain naive about the human lust for power. And for group process to work, the members of the group must have a motivation other than greed and self-promotion.

Power-struggles within the committee are often responsible for weeding out names; these struggles only obscure what little information is at hand. But somehow the committee gets through the list and makes recommendations. Sometimes the candidates are invited to preach and be viewed; in any event, the wardens make their selection. They call a new pastor and work out a contract.

A former clergy deployment officer adds:

Parishes lie about their needs and their spiritual condition. So do clergy.

Parishes often call someone they intend to control like some neophyte priest or the present curate.

Parishes often call someone they don't really want because they can hire him/her cheap.

The rectory, its size and condition, is often the factor that determines whether the cleric is issued the call. I know more than one church that has always called bachelors because it will not buy a bigger rectory or consider a housing allowance.

Vestries call desperate priests needing jobs to desperate parishes that fear no priest will have them.

Parishes often call clergy from several states away when many capable people are available locally. In many cases this seems to be related to the degree of unresolved problems in the parish. The worse the known problems, the farther the distance of the called and supposedly ignorant cleric.

A Roman Catholic concurs:

It seems that even though the example you draw out is for churches who select, the same fundamental problem of criteria and implementation exists for churches who appoint. And appointment carries the additional stigma of having the "good old boys" perpetuate themselves and their ideas by who they appoint where. The Roman Catholic church is scandalous on this count. Not only do priests get appointed to "good parishes" by who they know and how political they are, but grave injustices, not to mention crimes, are hidden and perpetuated by reassigning problem priests to different parishes without ever dealing with the problems. Both the archdioceses of New Orleans and Minneapolis/St. Paul have been or are being sued because for years they reappointed priests to parish after parish, priests who should have been prosecuted for molesting young boys.

Sometimes the selection process results in a reasonably harmonious relationship between parish and pastor; most of the congregation is happy with the new minister. Sometimes the selection committee or the appointing hierarchy realize they have made a disastrous mistake. Once in a while a senior warden has the courage to say so, refuses to sign or recalls the contract, and calls for another finalist. More often, the parish feels it is stuck and hopes for better luck next time. There is often a sense of futility: surely among all those names was hidden the right pastor for the parish! But, for the most part, tenures are short, and with luck the parish will have another opportunity in five years' time.

Why are tenures short? Is a short tenure as desirable as some church administrators would suggest? One answer frequently given to these questions is that a pastor comes with a particular task to do, and at the end of five years that task is usually accomplished, changed, or failed. Another explanation is that the energy and motivation of the pastor shifts about this time; creativity is tempered, and either the relationship settles down for the long haul, or everyone gets restless for a change. A third suggestion is that frequent change keeps a pastor from getting too powerful. Rarely is it suggested that tenures should be different lengths in different situations; for example, in highly mobile or rural communities, a pastor with a long tenure can be a hub around whom the highly fluid or geographically remote group can find some common life.

But tenure problems aside, the foregoing description reflects a commonly held view of ministry, one that is political, if not politely cynical. Today's attitudes toward ministry include the mistaken assumption by the congregation that the pastor and ordained, paid assistants are not only able to meet the needs of everyone in the parish, but also that it is their job alone. Some denominations have attempted to counter the nonordained's abrogation of shared responsibility for their own maturity and the problem of increasingly politicized religion by stating that the role of the pastor is frankly administrative.

Yet whatever the official church position, the congregation usually has unspoken expectations, hardly realistic, that the administrating minister will also be able to care for their spiritual needs. In their turn, candidates for the job consciously or unconsciously incorporate into their profiles tacit signals indicating that they are ready and qualified to be discerners capable of enabling spiritual maturity whether or not they have the gift and the experience. These signals are given in addition, of course, to those indicating that they are good administrators.

When the selection committees read these profiles, common sense seems to disappear. No one seems to remember that the coexistence of these qualities in equal amounts in one person is, with very rare exceptions, unlikely. The selection committee, reflecting the desires of the congregation, makes choices based on wishful thinking, reflecting a choice against creaturely engagement, a choice for nonbeing. By choosing illusion, we fail to be.

The ministers, too, are subject to wishful thinking; at the end of five years they feel burned out. They have spent all their energies supporting the illusion of their omnipotence, of their own nonbeing; they have tried to meet and perhaps have even been encouraged to meet the congregation's unspoken and unrealistic expectations that they be administrator, finance expert, fund-raiser, labor-mediator, liturgist, counselor, and spiritual midwife. Both sides, by supporting illusion, have denied the possibility of relationship in the glory of creatureliness, transfigured by the flow of God's loving mercy.

The congregation is disillusioned because the pastor has been unable to meet their demands in regard both to running the parish and making them feel holier or closer to God. That congregations hold these consumer—sometimes quite literally devouring—ideas about what any one human can or should be expected to do and what it means to grow into God, can also be laid at the feet of churches' teaching and polity. Ironically it is in the moment of disillusion that the congregation has the greatest opportunity to reclaim its being. But few recognize this opportunity; after pinning the blame on a convenient scapegoat, most try to get on to the next grandiose vision as soon as possible in order to forget their unfortunate failures.

The ennui, disillusionment, and loss of focus that today beset ECUSA are also rampant in most other churches, Catholic or Protestant, regardless of whether their pastors are appointed from the top of the hierarchical pyramid or called from the bottom by the congregation. The illusion of human omnipotence is a story as old as the churches themselves.

But what about the omnipotence of God, if omnipotence is denied to humans? Why, some ask, can't God solve all these problems for us? In the popular mind, the word "omnipotence" seems too often to imply an intervening Zeus-like puppet-master. This god is the negation of the humility of Christ. Such a god's controlling intervention renders the creature object and takes its life.

A humble, kenotic, Christian God will not intervene, but co-creates only as we allow or invite. Such a God infuses, supports, and enhances our life, without making us object. While God will use any cracks and ambivalences we leave (we are always mixed in motive and desire) and while God is committed and able to suffer with us no matter how we try to shut out divine engagement, political processes are rarely conducted in this atmosphere of eucharistic reciprocity.

The humble, kenotic God does not intervene when the noise of politics shuts out the resonances of being. Politics is a matter of choice, and to choose politics means we have to take the consequences of falling away from being. But if we would return to creaturely engagement, the forgivenness and power of co-creation are eternally and immediately available to us in the open and generative context where our aspiration, our kenotic mirroring of God, enabled by Christ's indwelling, meets God's self-outpouring love. We can call this meeting by any number of names that do not have nuances of a divine puppet-master or a controller we need to control. Some of the names we can use are: a confluence of love, loving coinherence, the divine Ungraspingness, mutual *kenosis*, eucharistic reciprocity, interpenetration, interconnectedness.

Although God is active in secular (morally neutral and minimally organizing) processes to the extent that we are willing to open ourselves, it is blasphemy to call worldly institutional politics "God's work"; an institution and those with careers within the institution are by nature self-serving. In addition, ministry was never meant to be a career. It would be more honest and effective to say, "We need leaders to exercise the necessary, morally neutral organizing function in the churches, and this is inevitably a political process in which, as far as possible, we hope to open ourselves to God."

[handwritten margin note: They were created good]

There is an important distinction here between secular, that is, functional organizing, power kept to a minimum, which may be morally neutral, and worldly, or self-aggrandizing, power, which is evil. For functional power to be morally neutral it must proceed from kenotic, open and deeply listening engagement, the eucharistic coinherence with God that enhances the creature and the creature's reverence for the mystery of others. Too often functional power objectifies, and functional power seems to have an ineluctable tendency to become worldly power, which is evil.

Priesthood-Being Distinct from Ministry-Function

The words "priest" or "priesthood" have not been used in the forgoing description of selection processes in the churches, because the contemporary method of selecting ministers is secular, not religious, and has nothing *per se* to do with priesthood. Priesthood is the eucharistic being of the creature in confluence with the eucharistic God. The relationship is one of equipoise, the always-seeking-balance of ready response or *apatheia*.

When two or three are gathered together in God's name there is *politics*, and politics is concerned with *power*, and the exercise of executive—as opposed to kenotic—power is *not* the primary message of Christianity, no matter who is wielding it: popes, bishops, presbyters, deacons, selection committees, or the people of God.

Presiding at the celebration of the Eucharist is *not* the executive privilege many ecclesial power-brokers would insist upon extorting from their flocks. Nor is blessing or invocation a magical summoning by an administrator, who by virtue of his office presumes control over the Spirit of Christ and on whose magic the life of the congregation depends. Readers may express shock at the force of these statements, but they reflect the experience, the cycle of despair that constitutes life in the churches for many nonordained, kenotic Christians whose being is focused with awestruck wonder on God, and not on themselves or their status in the community. (Mt 18:5–10)

The ecclesial system largely in place by the end of the third century abrogated true Christian priesthood. It reestablished the very model of controlling, objectifying, and life-denying sacrificial cult of the Temple rejected by the new dispensation. This shift came about because of the bishops' desire to justify and consolidate controlling power over the churches in their own persons (see Chapter 2). This move was in direct contradiction to the radical message clearly spelled out in the letters commonly attributed to Paul, and the Letter to the Hebrews. We have lived for centuries under the suffocating effects of this betrayal of Christ's humility, and as a result we fail to recognize true priesthood even where it does exist. We fail to look for it in the right places. It is rarely to be found in the clerical club.

Most arguments about the ordination of women seem to be based on this inappropriate third-century model, with little or no reflection as to the model's lack of religious ground, of its secular, if not anti-Christian, nature. Once we realize that the model is antithetical to the Christian priesthood disclosed in the humility of Christ and once we see that being has been confused with function, arguments put forth by *both* sides of this debate are exposed as arrogant, trivializing, and irrelevant. No one, man or woman, has a *right* to ordination, and ordination does *not* bestow the humility of Christ, which is priesthood.

To cite just one example: the argument about physical representation, that is, whether a man or a woman can represent Christ at the altar because Jesus was a man, completely misses the point both of Christ and of Eucharist. This argument usually speaks about physical representation in the context of the Last Supper. Eucharist is not Jesus' action before the crucifixion alone; it is a foretaste of the completion of the salvific event in time, erupting through and out of time and within, transfiguring all time. In the Eucharist we experience the Silence of God from which the Word who is both First and Last is spoken in the present, is spoken in the world and time.

The most important element in the breaking of Bread and the drinking of Wine at the Last Supper is the understanding that "This is my Body and this is my Blood" refers to the coinherence of Jesus' life with the disciples' lives. Eucharist goes far beyond recapitulation of the Last Supper as an event in time because Jesus' life has disappeared into the disciples' lives and into our lives by the grace of the Paraclete. The Eucharist is the reenactment of *the entire salvific event* from the first to the last moment of creation. Eucharist is, with Christ indwelling, the self-offering of the *people* continually being transformed into Body and Blood and meeting in sacramental confluence Christ's self-offering in Body and Blood. It is in this shared life, in this eucharistic coinherence that the humble, kenotic Love of God transforms our fragmentation and unifies us in and by Christ's eternal offering. Blessed and broken with Christ, we are sent forth in unity to live this eucharistic sacrifice in the world.

The Last Supper event is but one movement of Eucharist. Christ is risen and has disappeared into the people, *particularly* into those who are despised, outcast, homeless, degraded, disgusting, and useless, who receive the Paraclete, with or without the confirmation of the institution. To isolate the moment of the Last Supper, to point to the humanity of

Ευ Χαριςτ

Jesus in isolation, as if this one evening and single gender signified the entire salvific event, is to engage in the worst sort of literalist trivializing distortion and to drain the life from both the humanity of Jesus and the Eucharist itself.

The "humanity of Christ" is not mental imaging but rather the understanding that the Christ *seeks* to indwell in our humanity. The churches' ancient insistence on the humanity of Christ is not only so that we avoid the pitfalls of seeking a nonincarnate god at the expense and denigration of our createdness, but also that we recognize that it is *our* humanity that has the name of the Father written on its heart (cf., the *Didache*) because Christ indwells us. It is *within our humanity* that we begin to understand the eucharistic engagement of all things in the Love of God. The contemporary emphasis in some churches on the humanity of Christ as "seeing Jesus" either external to us—"my buddy Jesus"—or "when we die" is another example of the effort to make the humanity of Christ into a lifeless, controllable pet object. What the Eucharist shows us is that *we* are Jesus and that we look on the face of the Father.

The action of the Last Supper points beyond itself, as did every action in Jesus' life. In the Eucharist we receive, become, partake of God's outpouring kenotic divinity, which is our being and our life even though we are still distinct from God, created by God. We do not partake of Jesus' incidental physical characteristics. If celebrants are to be transparent liturgical icons of Jesus' offering in the true sense of icon, that is, windows who help us look *through* into the eternal *kenosis* of God, which is reflected back into time in the sacramental action, then these people, men or women, must be self-effacing as Christ is self-effacing. We need this transparency so that our lives can become more deeply commingled, can gather the communion of our solitudes in Bread and Wine. Love of God and neighbor is a single movement of Love, grammatically indistinguishable, and thus difficult to speak of.

In a proper eucharistic celebration, the effect of words and voice and gesture and garments, ritual appropriately splendid or simple, points kenotically beyond the people speaking, moving, and wearing them. Thus the gender of the representatives at the altar is irrelevant because the people must be enabled to focus not on the celebrants but *through* them to the humble and hidden presence of the *invisible* Christ indwelling, surrounding, coinhering, into whose Body and Blood we are continually and ever more deeply being transformed and commingled by the self-effacing Paraclete whom Christ has sent.

Self-effacement, self-forgetfulness, and humility are hardly the distinguishing features of the predominantly male clerical elite. Those who use the gender argument—and it is often in terms of a nontransparent image—are engaging in an exercise of self-reflective self-serving self-importance, if not self-idolatry that is hubris. Their principal concern seems to be that all eyes be focused *on* them and not *through* them, as if they had some exclusive claim on God's *kenosis*, not to mention the questionably elitist god this self-reflection implies. It also seems to follow from this argument, usually by carefully unspoken implication, that men are somehow more "perfect" than women in some absolute sense. The arrogance of "perfection" (in its static Latin sense, certainly not in the Greek sense of maturation) necessarily obviates the wounded Christ and the glory of our woundedness that is transformed in the Eucharist. These observations are not anti-male bias; they are pro-*kenosis*. Women are quite as capable of assuming the self-reflective, elitist role as men.

It is *Christ* who gathers the people of God and indwells them in priestly being, into Body and Blood; it is *Christ* who meets them in Bread and Wine to be fused, renewed, broken, and sent out. It is *Christ* whose indwelling bestows and enables our priesthood that is the mirroring of divine love that goes to the heart of pain to find and generate new life, hope, and love in each of our human solitudes and *therefore* in the common life. *Individual* kenosis *enables eucharistic community.* Kenotic life in common—the Kingdom—cannot be accomplished without the commitment of each member to this aspiration that mirrors God's *kenosis* and transforms us into God's image.

It is *Christ* who bestows—scandalously and indiscriminately, for those who like their religion neat and tidy—pastoral gifts of making Eucharist, healing, shriving, comforting, and counseling, irrespective of the political patterns (including ordination) of the institution. The scandal of Christianity today seems to have become a scandal to the very institution that wears its name. As Choan-Seng Song has observed in *The Compassionate God*, today's elitist-ordered Eucharist is no longer offered to feed the outcast, to free sinners and the poor with forgiveness, compassion, and new life.

Now the eucharist appears to be a *skandalon* not to church authorities but to sinners outside the eucharistic community. The eucharist has become *descandalised* insofar as the church is concerned, but *rescandalised* in relation to those who have no access to it.[3]

Or, as Andrew Reding writes in his review in *America* of *Faith of a People* by Pablo Galdámez,

Galdámez recognizes that a whole community of men and women had—in the deepest moral sense—progressed through the stages by which laity become priests.

They had begun as porters (doorkeepers) as they formed C.E.B.'s [base communities]. Next they became exorcists, as they cast out the demons of alcoholism, of machismo, of selfishness that further fragmented these poorest of the poor. As they came to appreciate the miracles that occur when people come together in *agape*, they became lectors, capable of interpreting the Bible in the light of the Holy Spirit's immanence in their lives: "Gradually we discovered that the dichotomy between personal conversion and social transformation was a false one. After all, behind every personal conversion is, at least in seed, a social commitment. At the same time, of course, no social commitment is possible without a corresponding conversion of heart. The correct solution to this false dilemma, then, was a personal, interior commitment of the social task."

They were now ready to become acolytes (followers) and deacons (servants): "In a flash, we saw that the 'acolytes' of our communities were going to have to go out to the highways of our land and be Good Samaritans to the stricken—those the system had struck down and left for dead. . . . The reason there were poor, so many poor, in El Salvador was that there were rich, a few rich, who monopolized everything." This was very dangerous knowledge, and it was not long before the death squads began descending on the neighborhoods of the poor, whereupon the communities assumed their blood-ordination into the priesthood.[4]

Here is the source of confusion: ordination is *not* a "special call to priesthood." All are called to deepest priesthood. We are called to be, to the glory of our creaturely engagement in the Love of God that is the humility of Christ. Ordination does *not* bestow magic power and privileged access to God. This idea is a perversion of eucharistic leadership, the excuse for the bishops' political power-play that solidified in the third century, that sets organizational leadership over and against the community in a dualism instead of being an indistinguishable part of it (see Chapter 2).

Priesthood *is* a commitment to a way of being; it is not ministry, which is merely practical and functional, and has been ever since New Testament times no matter what trappings it has worn. The action that is ministry *should* be an expression of self-giving, self-forgetful, kenotic priesthood, of the self-immolation and consequent resurrection of the humble Christ. If ministry does not arise from and communicate Christ's life-enhancing sacrifice, if its motives are primarily self-seeking, ministry makes object of those it purports to serve, destroying their engagement, draining away the very life it says it wishes to enhance. It becomes demonic.

Priesthood is a way of living through the paradox of God's self-emptying transcendence-immanence and is inherently integrating, integrating both fragmentation within the individual and among the individuals that make up the community (see Appendix A and *The Fountain and the Furnace,* especially Chapters 6 and 8). Ministry is a pastoral function, a sociological necessity, a means of oganizational efficiency. Priesthood is the

Ordination

willingness to sustain in ourselves the tension of the paradox of self-emptying love. It is unfortunate that the current discussion of ministry, wrongly labeled "priesthood," continues to externalize this self-contradiction, attempting a false synthesis of the two models of power. It reduces *both* priesthood, a commitment to mirror Christ's humility, *and* ministry, the organizing function in the churches, to the level of worldly concern for career, status, and power.

That ordained ministers over the centuries increasingly have seen their task in light of worldly power and professional careers is a fact that compromises, consciously or subliminally, everything that they do. Theirs are secular questions, cultural and economic questions, worldly questions that reveal unknowing acceptance and transfer of obedience to the controlling model of power that is directly in conflict with the kenotic priestly offering. The force of the Matthean teaching of Jesus, "You cannot serve God and money," is one of the few biblical teachings we can take absolutely literally. To pay someone to be self-emptying is a contradiction in terms.

Sometimes the churches have excused their worldly power by claiming a foretaste of Christ's coming in triumphant power at the end of time. But those who use this excuse forget that they are talking about a triumph that evidences itself only through total self-giving and that the triumphant coming of Christ at the *parousia* will not be in the jewel-encrusted patriarchal robes of an Eastern potentate accompanied by clouds of sycophant-acolytes, but rather in the humility of God once seen in Jerusalem, riding the wildness of an ass' colt tamed by Love, surrounded by the cries of the *anawim*.

There seems to be the occasional exception to this rule that the two models—the *kenosis* of priesthood and the organizational power of ministry—cannot dwell in the same person, but *exception* must be emphasized along with its gratuitousness. To be able to have these abilities coexist with integrity in one person is not a skill that can be taught. These rare clergy (stipendiary) by their own lived-out understanding of the nature of kenotic Christianity manage to convey not only function but also *symbol* of the spiritual authority of the gathered people of God. Such ministers are able to be kenotic symbols in spite of being stipendiary, because they recognize implicitly that their authority comes from the body of Christians, each of whom, according to capacity, lives out the commitment of baptismal vows, the priestly mirroring of God's kenotic movement of love. Such people therefore constitute a living, diverse, *still-unfolding* tradition, a tradition whose authentic spiritual authority rests on the humility of God in Christ.

We also can see the development of this symbolism today in the lives of the few nonstipendiary clergy who have profoundly understood their ordination to be more than the mere acquisition of a certain kind of status. Their visible self-emptying has potential legitimacy and importance for discernment and for liturgical purposes far beyond their present, somewhat amorphous role (see Part II, Chapter 6). In churches of the future, education for priesthood must be mandatory for all, and education for nonstipendiary ministry must not be lumped with that for career, administration-oriented ministry. The two must be kept increasingly separate in identity and complementary in service, if institutional Christianity is to survive. We must render distinct these two models of power; for the most part they cannot beneficially coexist in the same human being from the point of view either of the congregation or the clergy themselves.

These observations in no way contradict the tradition of *ex opere operato*, the notion that expresses, according to the *Oxford Dictionary of the Christian Church*, "the essentially *objective* [N.B., italics mine] mode of operation of the sacraments, and (their) independence of the subjective attitudes of either the minister or the recipient." All very well and good, and many of us sigh with relief, because we know we desperately need grace when often we are in anything but the "proper" frame of mind. But this is not the way this notion has been used. Instead, since medieval times, it has been used to cover up the appalling morals of clergy. In consequence, their attitude becomes something like, "As long as the sacraments work, why do I have to do anything about cleaning up my own act? I'm just a functionary," all the while, of course, claiming the privileges of being in a special ontological category, claiming that the ordination authorizing them to function has also somehow made them a special kind of human being, a little closer to God than the common (nonordained) run of humanity.

But there is an even more fundamental problem. While it is comforting to know that God's grace can be within us no matter what, *ex opere operato* and similar attitudes are rendered irrelevant by their closed and mechanical metaphysics. The implication is that God is not free, that God acts only within closed systems—"more Masses, more merits." The attitude that confines sacramental grace to the eucharistic rite is deeply misleading. Sacraments by their nature tend to open systems up. In addition, *ex opere* fails to take into consideration the profound impact of psychological signals vital to the transformational context of liturgy. That the early churches realized the importance of these signals is self-evident in some of the liturgical documents and mystagogy that have come down to us. The purpose of the eucharistic liturgy is primarily the transformation of the *people*, of which Christ's Presence in the Bread and Wine is sacramental sign. United physically with the Bread and Wine, the people are made aware that *they* are the sacrificial offering and gift being consecrated by the liturgical action, and that the epiclesis is a prayer for the Holy Ghost to transform their lives into confluence with the kenotic Christ who now sacramentally indwells them in the ordinariness of food and time and their daily round.

Thus the unspoken signals sent out by both the celebrant and the liturgical context *do* matter; they often have a deeper influence in enabling (or, sadly, more often not) engagement than anything else in the life of the worshiper. The liturgical context should be appropriate to the situation: sometimes it will be splendid and mysterious; sometimes it will be incorporated into a communal meal and be equally mysterious.

Eukarist

Appropriate context enables the self-offering of the people of God as Christ's Body and Blood meeting God in the Bread and Wine taken into and renewed by Christ's eternal sacrifice. It is not the kind of pneuma-alchemy we see developing in such writings as the sermons attributed to Cyril of Jerusalem, which are in marked contrast to earlier statements (such as those of Irenaeus).

As this alchemy develops, the sacrificial life of Eucharist becomes progressively externalized, technologized, analyzed, fragmented, and dead and finally devolves into the notion of transubstantiation, in which the transformation "wrought" by the celebrant is focused solely on the bread and wine. A presbyter making Magic Cookies is perhaps not its intent. In theory it emphasizes the transfiguration of createdness, but it ends by turning the sacrament into a cipher.

Transubstantiation is defined by the *Oxford Dictionary of the Christian Church* as "the conversion of the whole substance of the bread and wine into the whole substance of the Body and Blood of Christ, only the accidents (i.e., the appearances of the bread and wine) remaining." The emphasis in the dictionary and in catechesis has been on the elements themselves, not on the Body and Blood as the expression of the transformation of the *people* by their self-offering commingling with the once-for-all sacrifice of Christ both in and out of time. It is this meeting, mingling, transformation, this confluence of love, that is celebrated under the sacrament of Bread and Wine.

Ex opere and transubstantiation end up being what amounts to an attempt to render a mystery into a technique for control—control both of God and people alike. Over the centuries the alchemy becomes patent magic, whose potency is increasingly dependent on the people's submission to hierarchical power (false validity), which renders them object, noncreatures, and trivializes the mystery of the Eucharist into a blasphemous parody that one wag has described as worship of the Magic Cookie. Tom Lehrer has summed up Magic Cookie theology with devastating accuracy in his savagely funny song "Vatican Rag":

Get in line in that processional,
Step into that small confessional.
There the guy who's got religion'll
Tell you if your sin's original.
If it is try playin' it safer,
Drink the wine and chew the wafer,
Two, four, six, eight,
Time to transubstantiate!

The words may seem blasphemous, but it is rather the pre-sumptuous, dead-end theology that is blasphemy, a parody of the living mystery of Eucharist. Some people might argue that the sort of thinking that has fueled the transubstantiation issue and Magic Cookie theology is dead. It is not dead. As recently as 1982 the Sacred Congregation of the Faith objected to the fact that the ARCIC agreed statement did not use the term.

Michael Sheridan reports from Rome in the October 31, 1987, issue of *The Independent* (London) that Cardinal Ugo Poletti has barred the music of Bach, Mozart, Beethoven, and other great composers from Rome's churches because it is not "religious music" and not "suitable for performance 'in the presence of the Most Blessed Sacrament.' " (We cannot help but speculate what kind of music His Eminence might con-sider suitable. Gounod?) The cardinal is not alone; the diocese of Bologna instituted a similar ban some months earlier.

But blame for this sort of thinking is not confined to the Vatican. Anglicans and Protestants are just as guilty of false polarization as the Council of Trent. In their Reformation fervor and in reaction against Magic Cookie theology, many Protes-tants mechanized and trivialized the sacrament by going too far in the opposite direction. The Anglican middle ground of "Real Presence" is no better when it is used to justify both extreme points of view as well as no view at all and when the essential implications of the sacramental nature of sacrificial living and transfiguration are hardly mentioned. Perhaps the churches are afraid of speaking of *kenosis*, of the necessity for self-forgetfulness and sacrifice and, horrors, *pain*. After all, isn't religion supposed to make us comfortable? And who wants to hear about sacrifice in our narcissistic culture? We come to church to have God fix us up so we feel good.

If the churches want to know what is wrong, it is precisely *this* that is wrong: they refuse the implications of the Cross, that "Christ became sin for us," and the living, kenotic response God's action requires. Instead, the churches, especially those with a conservative thrust, continue with the sort of teaching that drove Lehrer to write "Vatican Rag" more than twenty-five years ago, and doubtless today's "warm fuzzy" school of theology at the opposite end of the spectrum could inspire him to equal heights.

The people are prevented by magic from engaging God. Instead of enabling the transformed and transfigured community, magic reduces them to fragmented, isolated, worthless objects who receive a dead sign of a dead god, or the opposite, the "feel good fix" of a warm fuzzy god they can cuddle like a teddy bear or who, they hope, will cuddle them. The life, the communication, the communion, the confluence of love, the humble and aweful majesty that is the commingling of the living sacrifice of our individual lives made one each with the other, in and with the living sacrifice of Christ, is gone.

The theology founded on this depraved metaphysics is a form of psychological blackmail that exacts credulity in exchange for the illusion of the efficacy of ministerial magic. It operates on a subliminal linking of power and death, as Lehrer's song so clearly shows. Those concerned with the self-perpetuation of power are blind to the destructive spiritual conflict inherent in trying to combine in one person the self-aggrandizement arising from the failure to be and the creaturely glory bestowed by the humility of Christ.

It is essential that the model of power communicated in the celebrant's unspoken signals both express and enable the transformation of the people in sacramental action, that is, that the celebrant convey a model of God's divine vulnerability, the kenotic power that will encourage all present to abandon self-aggrandizement or worldly power so that the humility of Christ may be joyously reproduced in their solitudes and therefore in their community thus engaging their true being. It is essential that these signals convey unconditional acceptance, love, and forgiveness that deny nothing and transfigure all. The importance of psychological signals in liturgy and ministry is not a startling new insight; it is implicit in ancient liturgies and mystagogy.

Ordination *in itself* does not bestow the least spiritual authority, personal holiness, specialized knowledge of ways into God, or privileged access to God. Neither does ordination bestow prerogatives of coercive power. Conversion is not submission to a persuasive demand for conformity; it is an awakening that frees from bondage to fear of death in all its forms. Ordination does not bestow a "spiritual" power that controls the Holy Spirit received magically through the hands of one similarly ordained, citing a mandate from a tyrannical puppet-master god who deigns to give his ear to an elite and chosen few who wield power over forgiveness and resurrection, that is, over death and life.

The authentic symbol of authority in either stipendiary or nonstipendiary ordination does not originate in the self-certifying and questionable legitimacy of an institution. Rather it flows from the authority of the individually lived-out priesthood of each of the people of the humble God, the priestly people whom Christ gathers and in whom Christ indwells.

Thus secular and sacramental leadership, that is, organizing and celebrating-discerning ministry, *both* receive their authentication not from a presumptuous institution imposing leadership from above, but rather from the humility of Christ's indwelling handed on from generation to generation in the living priesthood of the people of God. *This* is apostolic succession, not the solemn pronouncing of a proper formula with a proper intention while smug bishops lay hands on the newest member of the club so that the magic chain will not be broken. Any consideration of apostolic succession must begin with baptismal commitment and the handing on of Christ's kenotic *life* bestowed on the priestly people by the scandalous, indiscriminate, and *living* Spirit, not a prepackaged dead body (even a "risen" one) or mechanical doll. Thus, commitment to *kenosis* is an absolute prerequisite for ordination.

Ordained people who attempt to grasp God's indwelling power and use it to dominate betray their role and the mind of Christ. God's kenotic power can rightly be used only by those who mirror the divine self-emptying, which in us means primarily the emptying out of the urge for domination and illusory self-image. A person, male or female, who understands ordination as a model of controlling power, who represents a puppet-master god and does magic on its behalf, is set over and against the community as its "mediator," creating an illusory gulf between God and creation, for the humility of Christ has already bridged every abyss.

To change the image, such a person stands between the people and God, blocking their mutually kenotic gaze. In addition, the sacrifice made by a controlling person places a dead thing between the people and God: it is a recapitulation of the *taking* of life, of Temple slaughter. If what is offered is controlled, its creaturely engagement is denied and taken away and it is made object; by being made object its life is encapsulated and destroyed. It is killed, whether or not its throat is cut. God meets us in a *living* sacrifice, a sacrifice that neither denies our creatureliness nor destroys life, but reveals to us the glory of our creatureliness and *enhances* life, uniting with life even as it is offered in eucharistic reciprocity, broken and sent forth. Sacrament is ultimately about mortality and the salvation that comes to us through our mortality.

Seen in this light, eucharistic devotion is not idolatry of the Magic Cookie. Rather, it is an opportunity for focused still-prayer, the means by which we deepen our engagement with God and each other. Eucharist is the way we and the community come to be in the Word who is both First and Last, spoken in the Sacrament from the silence of God, in reverence for

Christ's indwelling, in reverence for each other in the transfigured glory of our engaged creatureliness. If only we could allow our selves to believe what kind of God we are serving, the Love in whose circumincession we dwell, then some of the discarded eucharistic devotions of the past (but certainly not all of them) could be powerfully renewed, as could the sacrament of reconciliation, not only for the more "catholic" churches but across the ecumenical spectrum.

By contrast, when the controlling servant of the puppetmaster god makes an offering it is not Eucharist; rather it increases the community's fragmentation because as object it is fragmented and isolated, and such a rite sets up competition. It is no longer thanksgiving, the adoration that arises from and elicits self-forgetfulness, but the self-protective narcissism that hungers for an immortality that denies the glory of our mortality and is the reflexive response to one who clings to the mystique of human power over life and death in God. The controller is hardly a model of the servant Christ or Christ's self-effacing priesthood. Thus, the wrongly labeled "priesthood," that is, church orders, over which many churches are wrangling today, not only are *not* Christian priesthood, they are not even Christian ministry. In fact, there is nothing Christian about them at all.

Christian priesthood is a way of incarnating God's ungraspingness shown us in Christ, but church orders attempt blasphemously to grasp and direct this divine outpouring by means of hierarchical status, self-aggrandizement, and money. Worst of all, it is not a long step from the churches' attempt to "justify" the Temple model of priesthood to the kind of mentality that leads to nuclear war, because both negate creaturely engagement with God through mortality and devalue life. When we start thinking about people or the creation, and especially relationship with God in terms of numbers, we have already taken life.

As we shall see, the ministerial offices of the New Testament seem to be borrowed from pre-Christian models. Episcopal ceremonial, for example, has its heritage from the law court of imperial Rome. How can imperial ritual communicate the God whose majesty suffers and dies on a cross, and whose message is, explicitly in one place in the Gospel, to avoid the courts? The ministerial offices of the New Testament are a response to the necessity for social organization in the churches created by the leadership vacuum in the wake of the death of the first followers of Jesus. There is nothing *inherent* in the nature of these offices that is sacramental (as opposed to what is bestowed by a congregation), and thus there is every reason why such administrative offices should be kept separate from sacramental service.

2. Priesthood and Sacrifice: Ways of Life, Ways of Death

We ben roading like all ways with the black leader josseling nexy but 1/2 way acrost the barrens he pusht his nose in to my han. He never done nothing like that befor I cudnt beleav it. Him what lookit like Death on 4 legs with his yeller eyes what dint even care if he livet or dyd and he wantit me to pet him. Thats when I cryd for the dead.

After a wyl I cud feal on my face a littl stilness where the wind wer cut off I cud hear the sylents of the stannings of the Power Ring. Feal the goast of old Power circeling hy over me. Only this time I fealt a Power in me what circelt with it. Membering when that thot come to me: THE ONLYES POWER IS NO POWER. Wel now I sust that wernt qwite it. It aint that its *no* Power. Its the not sturgling for Power thats where the Power is. Its in jus letting your self be where it is. Its tuning in to the worl its leaving your self behynt and letting your self be where it says in *Eusa 5:*

> . . . in tu the hart uv the stoan hart uv the dans. Evere thing blippin & bleapin & movin in the shiftin uv thay Nos. Sum tyms bytin sum tyms bit.

Looking up in to the black where the goast of Power circelt blyn and oansome like a Drop John roun the los hump of Cambry I larft I yelt, "SPIRIT OF GOD ROAD WITH ME!"

RUSSELL HOBAN, *RIDDLEY WALKER*

We have described priesthood as a commitment to a way of being and ministry as a function proceeding from this commitment as *one* of its fruits. Neither priesthood nor ministry under this definition necessarily has anything to do with ordination, nor does ordination make a person any more a priest or a minister in terms of the heart's reciprocity with God or bearing God to others except, perhaps, in the eyes of a highly fallible and self-serving institution.

Christian priestly power is the self-emptying, self-restrained, concentrated power of love (love is by definition ungrasping) commingled with the self-emptying, self-restrained, concentrated outpouring Love that is its source and model and sustains the life and coinherence of the divine with the creation. Priestly power is not "self"-seeking, that is, it does not seek to create an illusory self-image to project on to the world as a form of domination. Christian priestly power is exercised only for purposes of salvation, that is, for springing from traps, from the "slavery that is the fear of death" (Heb 2:15); fear that is the wages of sin, that is our falling away from our responsiveness to the Gaze of God, in whose contemplation we come to be and away from which we have no existence (Mt 18); fear that is both caused by and arises from living for self fragmented from and set against the community, a self-debasing fear that drives us ever farther into isolationist self-inflation and away from being.

The revival of the Old Testament idea of "priestly" cult that came into church order in the third century is a sterile hybrid of the transcendent half of the Jewish paradox of God both transcendent and immanent and the central forces in Greek philosophy that have their source in non-Christian worship of power. This worship of power includes worship of techniques of self-transcendence, of the attempt to acquire divinity through self-mastery, not through transfiguration by grace.

The tradition that gathers around this worship of power exalts a very narrow way of thinking that claims to contain and control by ideas, the same kind of presumption of control condemned in the myth of the Fall, that is, knowledge and control of that which is *beyond the capacity* of creatures. This presumption is most readily seen in the traditional mystique that attaches to ordination. This mystique insists that ordination effects an ontological change in "kind" as well as a change of degree in elevation in the human hierarchy. It presumes that God has given limited creatures mastery over the unlimited divine wisdom and prerogatives of being.

In the myth of the Fall, it is not exalted human thinking that is sinful; we are to use all our created gifts to the full. It is rather the presumption that the capacity to change human

true Ordination

sin

ontology is available and limited to, and can be grasped by, humans, handed on from one to another; or that the vision of God can be acquired by techniques of self-mastery, or that God's wisdom and perspective are given along with creaturely gifts. It is the churches' insistence on sustaining this mystique, this presumption, that is the source of the ontological fissure that leads them to respond to religious questions with secular techniques. While the Protestant churches claim to have rejected the idea that ordination bestows a change in "kind," wherever we see domination at work in any form in a church we are seeing precisely this mystique and this presumption.

It is ironic that the Greek philosophers who were most obsessed with rendering themselves impassible to reactions, feelings, and ideas succumbed, by this very obsession, to the passions they sought to control. Theirs is an attempt to reshape a created person into an abstract idea (the true meaning of lust); they succumb to an aesthetic fallacy. The theologians who follow them succumb to both an aesthetic and an ontological fallacy.

Worldly power, that is, self-aggrandizing control or mastery, is an expression of lust, and lust is a counterfeit of sexuality. Sexuality pervades all of life and gives life to everything we do; lust compartmentalizes, objectifies, and kills. It is not sexuality that is at the heart of the story of the Garden but rather this antisexual lust, a lust that breeds insatiable envy, fear, and blame. Adam and Eve's envy of God's *kenosis*, God's hidden wisdom (which they mistakenly perceive as control they wish to exercise, without regard as to whether this control was actually God's action in the world or possible for creatures) caused them to eat the forbidden fruit. The result is that Adam not only has not gained what he misperceived as divine control—he has lost even some of the self-restraint that issues naturally from aspiration and the gaze on God and has to cover himself. In the same way, those who presumed to control religion and access to God in first-century Jerusalem crucified Jesus: he was "out of control." *The presumption to control destroys our communion with those who most love us and keeps from us from what we most desire.*

Paul Bradshaw suggests that the *Didache* shows us envy at work in those merely elected to eucharistic leadership (elected to supplement the numbers of the gifted). Their destructive envy is aimed at the "prophets" (those few who had the gift of extemporaneous eucharistic prayer). It is this envy that led to consolidation of power by the second-raters to the exclusion of the gifted, and it is this envy that creates the mechanistic metaphysics to support their claim. In *Liturgical Presidency in the Early Church*, Bradshaw discusses the shift from charism to office and the ensuing impertinence that claims that office bestows charism:

It may well be that the unusual step of providing a written prayer-text was taken by the author in order to help prevent them [elected leaders] from appearing quite as liturgically incompetent, in comparison with those leaders possessing the charism of *propheteia*, as they might otherwise have done if they had been required to extemporize prayer. . . . It is not really surprising that such formally appointed community-leaders were not generally content with a second-class status and began to claim endowment, through their appointment to office, with the same *charismata* which their predecessors had possessed, and with the right to exercise the same liturgical functions within the congregation, not merely the presidency of the assembly and the improvisation of the eucharistic prayer, but also a major responsibility for the teaching of the community. Indeed, their adoption of this latter function was almost inevitable.[1]

In today's churches, at least at the official level, envy continues to reserve the eucharistic prayer as the exclusive right of members of the clerical club. This may be a harsh and unpalatable reality, but it is time we faced it before the worship of self-seeking power destroys not only Christianity, which is the worship of self-emptying love (and therefore self-restrained power), but also the whole earth. Exploring these truths with naked honesty, even ruthlessness, will release us into Christ's freedom and a new hope for the future.

Being, Function, and the Resonances of Being

Priestly power is self-effacing and points away from itself. Its bearers are often indistinguishable from the surrounding "secular" community. Priestly power is hidden power that releases into our awareness the life of the indwelling God, who sustains the creation with the divine self-emptying. This *kenosis* is the hidden power that hopes, transfigures, celebrates; it is the power of resurrection that is preceded by and has its source in the dense glory of the Cross. It is the power of true healing that radiates from the open wounds of Christ into and through ours. It is active, but for the most part out of sight, out of sight even—or rather especially—of the person exercising it. It is active primarily through our being and much less through direct action or function. To put this another way, priestly power, Christ's salvific power, is the resonance, the radiance of our gaze on God, our willingness to be transformed (Mt 18). And as we are transformed, the radiance of our growing density of glory offers freedom and transfiguration to the creation.

Functional power, that is, necessary secular organizational power, is a consciously active and directed exercise of power. If we are to be honest, this kind of power in human terms is always also worldly. It cannot be exercised without in some way being "self"-seeking (seeking glorification of illusory "self"-image as opposed to seeking the self found in God). The Archmage's speech in the epigraph at the beginning of the last chapter expresses this truth succinctly.

"You have great power inborn in you, and you used that power wrongly, to work a spell over which you had no control, not knowing how that spell affects the balance of light and dark, life and death, good and evil. And you were moved to do this by pride and by hate. Is it any wonder the result was ruin?"[2]

Lest Christianity come to a similar end, functional power in the churches should be exercised with the greatest reluctance, and then only from the kenotic engagement of being-in-God. We should act only by offering options that may set people free, options that, if they are accepted, may heal the fissure in our being, that is, enable us to enter our wounds and free-fall in the abyss of true being that is the wound in God. What churches must *not* do in the exercise of this power is to make demands that cause us to fall even farther from our being, that force us to find our spiritual authenticity by submitting to the controlling stereotypes that promote uniformity and evidence our lust to make creatures into ideas (Mt 23:4).

We exercise functional power in a kenotic way all too rarely. It is not merely a matter of desiring that motives be unmixed; this is impossible. We cannot be or act entirely without self-interest. But we can exercise a constant vigilance over which aspect is predominating and be aware of the increasing sub-tlety with which self-interest takes on camouflage that imitates self-emptying, liberating power. And we can and must estab-lish ways to safeguard against self-interest that pushes aside the transforming humility that is the resonance of being-in-God.

Humility has to do not with "self"-conscious "self"-abase-ment (which is really vanity), or, more important, with the kind of self-negation that leaves terrorized women or men at the mercy of psychologically and physically abusive superiors, spouses, or children, or that leaves children burdened with what should be their parents' guilt for their parents' assaults. Humility is not the "self-giving" that is a form of isolating and imprisoning self-encapsulation (experienced particularly by women with children), nor is it accepting being cast in the role of a victim or a nonperson.

Rather, humility is inviolable vulnerability; it coinheres with chastity (as distinct from celibacy); it is the focus of the whole being. It has an unself-conscious dedication to seeing through the camouflage of creatures and processes. While humility accepts what is, it also discerns and exposes what lies beneath the surface, not stopping at the level of appearance, of what is pretended. Humility penetrates disguises not for purpose of dominance or malice but simply to reflect the life of God that sustains each creature in order to rejoice in its creaturely glory. More is changed in the world by resonances of this clear-eyed being, by its vision and exposure of shams, than by any amount of coercion or manipulation. Let us be clear about humility; it is not a romantic fantasy of self-abuse palely loitering, but rather a discerning, steady commitment to truth for the sake of the transfiguration of the community, and it carries the knowledge that the price for doing so may be life itself, a price exacted by those who are dedicated to inertia, to maintaining appearances and the status quo.

In sum, if we want to know what priesthood is, we have to look at God in Christ. What does God do? What God does is God's priesthood reaching across the abyss of illusion we create by presumption to control. As God's image we seek to mirror God's outpouring. God creates with self-abnegation outpoured, continues and sustains this creation *by going to the heart of pain that dwells within the Creator's self-restraint and is inherent in creation's freedom, and from this total self-denudation God generates new life, hope, and joy.* We come to know this priesthood in the humility of Jesus the Christ.

It is this priesthood of humility to which the vows of our baptism are supposed to commit us: *we are to be willing to go to the heart of the pain that is our creaturely freedom mirroring God's self-abnegation outpoured and, there, meeting God's own self-emptying love that engages and fills us, indwells us, to co-create, through eucharistic confluence, new life, hope, and joy.* This sacrifice is our identity and our salvation. Through this freely-chosen, confluent sacrifice we are sprung from the trap of dispersing our energies to support the illusion that we are and should be in control, when in fact we are trapped by the prison of our limited perspective in the fissure created by our desire to control and by our noisy protestation against our fear of death.

Baptism

Division of Powers in the Churches

What kind of eucharistic community could evolve from the priesthood of humility? In a eucharistic community there should *ideally* need to be no other commitment beyond baptism, only a recognition of charisms, of gifts—such as discernment, healing, counseling, forgiving, preaching, teaching, celebrating the Eucharist—within the community of the people of God by the people of God. The prodigal bestowal of these gifts within the churches is part of the mystery of God's life within them, and they are unrelated to ordination to administrative hierarchy. They are gifts of God, not the QED result of "office bestowing charism."

Confession, for example, has been the hegemony of the ordained only since the fourteenth century. In a eucharistic community, when one person seeks another to confess, it is because the penitent experiences the forgivenness, the life-enhancing resonances of the confessor's being-in-God. To enter into these resonances is to receive forgivenness and to recover the forgivenness of being-in-God. Because the penitent has fallen away from being, the penitent's discernment, that is, attraction to the confessor's resonances of being, authenticates the authority of the confessor. This authentication is not bestowed by the penitent in isolation but also is a bestowal of the authority of the "church," of the eucharistic community, because the penitent, by seeking assurance of forgiveness, seeks re-engagement with the community and, by confessing, confesses on behalf of the community.

This is theology proper to the words "by authority committed unto me," not magic power derived from a Zeus-god. Ordination by the institution does not a confessor make; ordination by the penitent's seeking the confessor's absolution does.

But given the reality of human propensities, we need organization, and we need to subject these charisms to scrutiny and education because we can be deceived by illusion; we need to recognize these charisms and cherish them. Thus these gifts need to come under some kind of minimal jurisdiction and discernment. But because of their kenotic nature they should most emphatically *not* be exercised by those wielding functional, that is administrative, power, and those wielding that kind of power should *not* be involved in the discernment of these gifts, because even with the best will in the world their discernment is compromised by their position of control and their salaries.

To check the insidious growth of self-aggrandizing power in the churches, perhaps there need to be, in addition to nonordained discerners, local nonstipendiary presbyters and bishops whose sole function is discernment and without whose concurrence decisions involving people and their gifts cannot be made. This would give the nonstipendiaries power, to be sure, but it would put this power in the hands of those who, if they have themselves been properly discerned, are more kenotically oriented to begin with. And not being paid administrators, their discernment might be less compromised. One danger might be rivalry between the two groups, the paid and unpaid, the discerners and the administrators, but no system is going to be perfect. In any event, we need to remove discerning power from the administrators; they must be servants, not tyrants. We have to be realistic about the nature of the human beast in power-struggles within organizations, recognize these struggles for what they are, and put sensible checks on them.

For a eucharistic community to act in the world we need an organization delicately balanced between administration and discernment. A balanced administration can help us with the practical compassion of eucharistic ungraspingness, to give to the *anawim*, in whom we see God, in such a way that our charity is neither a waste of our resources nor an exercise of dominance over those whom we seek to assist. Such balanced discernment can help us with engagement, because in spite of the seeming shrinking of the world by communication, we are increasingly separated from one another rather than in communion with one another. In a technological age, we no longer need to have either face-to-face human communication or human relationships to gather information for survival.

Administrative power held in check by discernment can enable both our communion and our anonymity, our ability to engage one another and to give to others in a kenotic way, preserving their freedom within communion and preventing the establishing of power-and-dependence relationships. These are the sort of relationships exploited by secular governments and the churches past and present. (How, for example, did the symbol of the Cross, the sign of the glory of utter *kenosis*, become so twisted as to become the sign of conquest?)

Administrators would then be committed to *listen* to the discerners and to obey; the discerners, listeners by nature, would be committed to discern and teach. These commitments would be effective whether or not the discerners and administrators were ordained (see Part II, Chapters 5 and 6).

We need administrators who are dedicated to organizational tasks and who even make their living at it. We need organization to deal with the world, to render to Caesar—for the caesars, like the poor, are always with us and will thrust themselves into any available power vacuum. Those with administrative gifts can free the rest of the people of God to live in a Christian, kenotic way, though it is devoutly to be hoped that, as far as possible, the administrators too will strive to live in this way and that their exercise of secular power in the churches will have constant reference to the humility of Christ and be disciplined by it, disciplined by aspiration and not merely by imposed and hollow constraint.

We need symbolic figures such as bishops around whom the community gathers as focal signs of the living, still-unfolding tradition from which we spring. But they should be signs of God's self-emptying love, which is generated even as it spent, *not* signs of self-aggrandizing power, which is spent faster than it is generated and devours what surrounds it to maintain itself—and certainly not aggrandizing power sacralized with a veneer of piety, mystique, or quasi-divinity.

In addition, we need to make sure that the role of more visible secular power that invariably threatens the engagement of ungraspingness does not obscure what is or should be our primary movement for the sake of the community of creation, our willingness to be transformed by Christ's indwelling, the resonance of Incarnation, the hidden, self-effacing power of *kenosis*, which does more to leaven and redeem what is evil than any well-intentioned action that is not deeply rooted in stillness. Action that does not derive from stillness is mere technique and diminishes the life of those acted upon.

The two movements are mutually exclusive. This is not to say that those who are in charge of administration are by definition second-class citizens or that their job is diabolical. But too often administrators have confused the role given them as the exercise of the power of God. While there are many career clergy who are also holy in themselves, there are equally as many who have assumed because they have been "set aside" that this "holiness" of apartness automatically confers personal "holiness" and a "right" to exercise secular, self-seeking power in God's name.

Those who exercise power in this way do indeed become diabolical. The traditional devil is the truly false puppet-master. The worship of self-aggrandizing, worldly power wielded in any name is idolatry and cult, not the stuff of Christianity.

In short, while there are notable exceptions, it is more often true that those who have a gift for administration are the least qualified (no matter how well-educated) to teach by work or their own being the kind of self-emptying love that is at the heart of Christianity. This is not to imply that they do not grow in holiness: their struggle is different, difficult, and not self-evident to the observer. And the reverse is true: those who are most qualified to teach this kind of love are usually on the fringes, shun politics, and go unnoticed. They should be able to minister without the burden of ordination.

For administrators to grow in holiness may also be dangerous. The story of the Rich Man and Lazarus (Lk 16:19–31) is a cautionary meditation for administrators. In the hell the Rich Man has created for himself, at the nadir of the abyss of illusion, he continues to manifest his self-aggrandizing worldliness. It is not enough that he still regards Lazarus as an object to be "sent" to protect his earthly interests, he presumes to give Abraham instruction on technique.

At the same time, it was precisely for their kenotic presence that people oriented by self-forgetful aspiration were sometimes kidnapped and ordained by bishops in ages past, because the holiness of their lives taught more than any book or sermon could. Ordained as reluctant presbyter-bishops, they were often poor administrators—if they escaped being exiled or murdered. But they became shining icons, and their lives show the importance of distinguishing between being and function in ministry. We need such people in nonstipendiary ordained ministry as much today as then, not only to be discerners and to keep examples of kenotic holiness before us in the liturgy, but also to relieve them of the conflicting function of administration.

Scriptural Tensions

If this distinction between being and function is so critical to the life of the eucharistic community, how then did the exclusionary hierarchical model come to predominate? To answer this question we have to begin by looking at the scriptural source from which it was borrowed.

The fundamental tension between paradox and dualism exists within Scripture itself as well as between Greek and Judeo-Christian notions of divine power. The kenotic power of I WILL BE (see Appendix A) and the engaged relationship that life in I WILL BE requires are inherently paradoxical. Secular and worldly power require thinking that is inherently dualistic. Far from being of merely philosophical interest, the refusal by a person or institution to engage the tension of paradox

Lk 16.19-31

means that the choice for more comfortable dualism determines the nature of all the prayer and theology that will follow. This notion will be explored in more depth in Chapter 3.

Here we need only to remember that paradox is in reality a continuum, an integrated unity, whereas a dualistic view of the same material deliberately excludes essential elements that make up the whole. Paradox can be seen as "both-and" and dualism as "either/or"; the elements of paradox refract off each other; they are inclusive of each other. Because we are creatures and lack the divine perspective, what appears to be excluded even when we are willing to live in paradox is a reflection of the finitude of our creatureliness, an *unintended* exclusion of what has not yet come to our awareness or cannot come to our awareness. However, we remain open even to what we, in our finitude, cannot know. Paradox is a way to freedom. Dualism *chooses* to exclude, chooses illusory stasis, and becomes pernicious when in spite of this choice for small-mindedness it claims a vision of the whole.

The relationship between light and dark illustrates this distinction between paradox and dualism. There are ancient texts that express the unity of day and night, not only "darkness and light to thee are both alike" but also the fading of night into first light, first light into dawn, dawn into morning, and so forth through the full circle of light-and-dark that makes up a single day-and-night cycle. Equally, light and dark can be pitted against each other as in "the children of light and the children of darkness." The first analogy expresses the light-dark symbolism within a paradoxical continuum. The latter takes a dualistic view: one aspect must triumph over the other. One is "good" and the other is "evil"; one has "value" and the other is "devalued."

In both Hebrew and Christian Scriptures, there is a constant tension between paradoxical and dualistic views of God. The paradoxical view is expressed in the statement, "God is both utterly transcendent, and more immanent than the very cells that make up our bodies." In the tension of paradox, immanence and transcendence are inclusively related: the meaning of immanence receives its life and depth because it is in relationship of seeming polarity within the continuum with transcendence, and vice versa. Equally, God's *kenosis* is inclusive of the potential for the exercise of controlling power.

What is difficult to remember is that dualism falsely polarizes, whereas the extremes of paradox only *seem* to be opposite. The churches today often get caught in a false polarity between a position of dualism and stasis, which quickly becomes diabolical, and the way of paradox, which is set up as if it were the other "pole." This too is a trap; we rarely seem to be encouraged to go *through* the way of paradox into true Christian freedom (see Appendix A). Rather, religion too often seems to trap us between two illusory points known as "the devil" and "God." While the resonances of evil choices gather and insinuate themselves into available existence, of themselves they have no substance (for once a scholastic category is useful).

Evil does not constitute a "pole" of our existence; its seeming existence is part of the dualistic point of view that claims perfect knowledge and a static universe. Neither is God the other "pole," and it is this mistaken perception of outpouring divinity that we are most reluctant to let go. We want a point at which we can aim, a mental goal toward which to strive. Such a dualistic view precludes Christ's indwelling, or our aspiration. A dualistic view allows only for life by constraint and understands "God's will" as a spiritual railroad track onto which our lives must be forced if they are not to fall into perdition. This is linear thinking at work in theology. Spatial thinking allows us to engage the divine Love that is all-pervasive in every dimension and beyond all dimension, around us, within us, behind us, beyond us.

A dualistic, exclusionary expression about God might speak exclusively of God's "triumphing" over God's enemies by force, thus devaluing them into objects and forcing them out of relationship. One of the Midrash texts reminds us of the constant struggle against dualism. "Do not rejoice, Israel," says God after the Exodus, "for my people are drowned in the sea."

This tension runs through the Hebrew Scriptures. Even though the law is given as a covenant (a reciprocity, a bonding, an engagement, an integration that is relationship, between God and God's people), much of the concrete *development* of that law in practice, development against which Jesus was preaching, tends to be dualistic. Dualism—in this case, legalism—is in some ways more comfortable. It is more *graspable* to make commandments explicit and concrete in detail to support the human lust for mastery, to be able to know self-reflectively and empirically in this closed system that one has satisfied the requirements of holiness by deed. It is easier to be able to tick one ritual act after another off a list, than to attune one's whole being to live in an open system of creatureliness, of possibility and unknowing.

There is marvelous irony in realizing that our grasping for the illusion of immortality and security precludes the very possibility we desperately seek to take to ourselves. Life with God is a gift; we can prepare to receive it, but the moment we try to grasp it or technologize it we have lost it.

The command to "choose life" is covenant. Even though the command appears dualistic, a choice between seeming opposites, the "life" and "death" to which it refers are engaged in the paradox that is the shape of human finitude, of being in the world in time. But the command refers to more than physical life and death. Choosing life and focus in God may mean allowing good options to die, which is a form of death we fear greatly in our contemporary subjugation to the tyranny of ostensibly good options.

But the subtleties do not stop there. Even choosing moral death (the death that is a curse) can be a way of relationship and life if only through the tension that feels like separation caused by sin (though in fact what we are feeling is our rage because we are loved in spite of, through, and *because* of sin). Repentance makes even the sin that is death a vehicle for deeper relationship. We see the working-out of this paradox of relationship throughout Judeo-Christian history.

By contrast, relationship is reduced to dualism when repentance becomes a matter of accounting, and sacrifice of animals or money is presented in terms of cost-effectiveness, whether we are talking about the "pharisaical" style condensed in the gospels, or Christianity. The religious style that says that God's continuing relationship depends on Temple sacrifice, or buying forgiveness with money, or rituals, or doctrinal formulas renders relationship into a means for compartmentalized and externalized control of salvation that degenerates into magic. It reduces the love of God to blackmail, to materialism and technique, and makes the people into objects, draining them of their life even as the animal is drained of the blood poured on the altar (Heb. 9:13–14).

In these times, the price of relationship with God, of life, thus becomes submission to human mediation, the giving up of our authentication that is direct engagement with God. The illusion of life dictated by subjugation is a vicious cycle of death and power. The more we are subjugated through fear, the more we are denied our creaturely engagement, the more unsure we are, the more we seek tangible authenticity outside our selves by manipulating others or being manipulated by them, at the expense of our intangible engagement with God. And this idolatrous pseudo-authentication is given us through the death of falling farther away from being. When we fall from being, we lose the self-respect that is one of the fruits of our gaze on God and begin to construct the self-image that is the fearfulness of narcissism.

This tension between paradox and dualism, between direct relationship with God and mediated relationship with God, is focused by the prophetic tradition, on the one hand, and the development of political leadership, on the other. In Exodus 19, God proclaims "You shall be a nation of priests." But the people do not want either the engagement or the responsibility and demand leaders from God. God gives leaders only with great reluctance. In later days God is particularly opposed to their demands for a king on whom they may project their developing self-image.

After the Exile, priestly leadership and its accompanying ritualism gradually dominate the people so that Temple sacrifice becomes not an outward expression of God's transforming relationship with the community, enhancing their life, but rather an act that takes the place of that relationship, distinct from and dominating the community, rendering it object and draining its life along with that of the sacrificial beasts. Sacrifice becomes a dualistic act separating the believer from God and maintaining the position of a power elite, little different from the magic, divination, and appeasement of the nonbelievers who surround the Temple. It is highly significant that Jesus is not a member of the levitical tribe and therefore in Jewish terms a layman. It is only because he is a layman that he is able to be the eternal indwelling high priest. To put this the other way around, because Christ is the eternal high priest, the divine priesthood can be incarnated only in the humility of one who has no status in human politics and dies a death that is cursed.

By contrast, rather than releasing the people from traps of their own making (salvation from idolatry), rather than releasing them into the life of God and releasing the life of God in them, ritual sacrifice, once the expression of the people's covenant of salvation with God, has now replaced engagement and thus become death, a dead end, a closed system. "I hate your sacrifices," says God in prophetic literature.

God wants the sacrifice that enhances life, the free engagement of a loving heart, a direct and unmediated relationship of sacrificial ungraspingness. Far from being the sign of salvation from a trap, Temple worship has itself become the trap. It is not sacrifice that is wrong but rather the people's abrogation of direct relationship, commitment, and responsibility, for which it has become a substitute.

Sacrifice

In prophetic literature God begs and woos the people to return to their divine vision. God does not rape, dominate, overwhelm. God, who could control, refuses to control. Freedom of response is too important to God: God's power is exercised in God's self-restraint. True, there is a theme of monarchical power and might, judgment and destruction that runs through the Hebrew Scriptures, but this is expression of religion in the crudest of presumptive human terms and not the strand that finds fulfillment in Jesus the Christ.

One of the most profound themes in prophetic literature is the repeated emphasis on return to the equality and trust epitomized by the tribes' wanderings in the desert. This emphasis can be found not only in prophetic literature, but also in the law itself in the declaration of jubilee years. The purpose of the jubilee years, whether or not they were ever observed, is to reassert the total dependence of the people on God, to remind them that life comes not by mastery but by grace. The nomadic life, the desert, the wilderness are great levelers. The people who survive must have reverence for the fragile environment, must be intensely alert and aware. In these wild places, there is no privileged access to God or to life decreed by the status of one's birth. Survivors are those who listen with every fiber of their being. But the people shrink from dependence on the unseen God, from relinquishing control over what is visible, and from the risk of trust and responsibility. Instead, they seek the security of being controlled by human hierarchies. Even at Horeb they not only demand that Moses speak for them, they cannot even bear his face, which reflects the glory of his kenotic mutuality with God.

Later, the prophets point to this refusal of relationship and remind the people that if prophets seem to have special knowledge, it is the engaged knowing that all are intended to have (Joel). This particular theme is picked up by the Letter to the Hebrews: the Temple priesthood is finished. There is no privileged access to God. Chapters 11 and 12 are the great recitation of the faith of those from every walk of life who in ages past have lived the courage of faith, who have staked their lives on a promise, "having seen and greeted it from afar" (11:13), for we, like they, "have not come to what may be touched, a blazing fire" (12:18) exterior to us, but rather to the heavenly city, to be pillars of flame with the God who is "a consuming fire" (12:29).

At this point in Hebrews an interesting shift takes place. We move from the recital of awe, from "here we have no lasting city" (13:14) to the practical, "Obey your leaders and submit to them; for they are keeping watch over your souls, as men do who will have to give account"(13:17). This plea for obedience is given in the light of aspiration, and the leaders' accountability arises from the joy of aspiration. We have not yet arrived at leadership that demands obedience by coercion, with threats of exclusions and anathemas. There is a haunting echo here of the time of transition of *Didache*.

We seem to see the ancient cycle beginning again, the story of the problems of enabling human response to an elusive God. The churches long to communicate the vision to a new generation without reestablishing the rule of law, and yet without willingness to pay the price of the same commitment, the same vision and inviolable vulnerability of those who have gone before. The temptation to replace vision and integrity with technique emerges anew. The Temple priesthood may be finished, but it is clear that within the churches' struggle to communicate the new dispensation, the same issues continue.

Authentic leadership elicits courage, openness, and integrity, and caretaker leadership that does not inspire is always tempted to point to itself instead of to the elusive vision from which it derives. If it does so, it no longer nurtures a community in which the vision can renew itself. Religion seems always tempted to try to capture this vision and render it technique, instead of humbly waiting in hope. Waiting in hope is in itself part of the vision, and the temptation to try to technologize it is ever with us. At its best, religion creates an environment for the vision, but there is always the danger that religion will presume to take its place. *Religion can provide food for the journey; it is not itself the journey.* As with Abraham, so with us: there can be no surrogates.

As long as Christianity is a lived expression of the vision, the promise, the intrinsic kenotic engagement between the divine and the creation, it serves a useful purpose. When Christianity later attempts to take the place of this engagement, claiming to reproduce the vision in the institution set over against the community, then it is in self-contradiction. It is easy to point fingers at the pharisaical style, but are we willing to admit our solidarity in sin? Are we willing to admit all the ways in which we, individually and collectively, try to avoid the wounding that is necessary to have the vision embodied in our selves?

We still try to rationalize our clinging to surrogates, and they become more and more subtle. When we try to re-create the vision by prescription we will fail. When we try to assure our selves by set ritual that we have prayed, we will fail. When we constrict our lives and perspective by locking our selves into complacent religious practice that avoids the glory, suffering, and uncertainty of aspiration, we will fail.

To sustain the balance is perilous, but it is the risk we must take. We see the shining lights of religious founders and in their wake the humdrum of a subsequent generation, humdrum because people have tried to capture the vision instead of allowing the vision to capture them. They have attempted to systematize the founder's vision. To cite a specific example in religious practice, the inviolable vulnerability of aspiration that is virginity degenerates into the commodity that is genital intactness.

Attempts to convert vision into technology seem to occur everywhere. And in doctrinal struggles, technologizing by one side invariably stimulates the same reductionism in opponents. Equally, admiration of a human exemplar can degenerate into mystique. Mystique encourages us to try to squeeze our selves

Church

into the fantasy stereotype we have projected onto the dead object into which our humbugging has made the other, and thus we miss our own mystery of being.

A vision can be communicated and received only by the willingness to be the unique icon God would have each of us be, not by slavish imitation of someone else or a grandiose fantasy about our selves. Under the influence of true aspiration, religious discipline falls into place; the difficulty and suffering are forgotten in the light of the vision that is sought. But there is always a two-edged danger that the seeker will, on the one hand, take refuge in rigorism in order to externalize the suffering or, on the other, will grasp the freedom that aspiration bestows and, finding discipline irksome, rationalize it as irrelevant and take license. Mysticism and common sense are one in the mystery of the ordinary.

Equally with leadership, one who lives the vision may come to power, but having received it, must be willing to live under the obedience of the increasing self-restraint that is required in one who embodies the projections of others and leads them out of their immaturity. In our immaturity we do imitate, we do project, but a wise and inspired leader can elicit and enable our maturity, our letting go these childish things. Every community contains a spectrum of maturity among its members. But there is always the danger that leadership will fall into tyranny, on the one hand, exercising power for power's sake, or into trendiness or rabble-rousing, on the other, appealing to what is most base and unexamined in us. One of the deepest wounds of our coming to maturity can be the moment when we realize that the task to lead others has become ours, that it is now our turn to nurture the immature and to wait for the vision in the dark.

Institutions must learn to wait for the vision in humility and hope, not attempt, like Judas, to precipitate it. It appears that nature and institutions and our interior lives hate a vacuum; but deeper examination discloses that in all of these, focused stillness offers room to test edges and discover wider

Judas

perspective. Like the synapse in our nervous system, stillness is the space in which connections may be made. In ecumenical endeavor, as the Swanwick Declaration affirms, the deepest unity is in the "silence beyond words" in which we become no longer strangers but pilgrims. Ecumenism is founded on shared vision, not on the "how" of religious technology.

While tradition is important, each bit is a response to a particular context and questioning; it might be said that tradition is religion's technology. Like modern technology it has its uses, but it cannot be universally and indiscriminately applied, and like any technology, most of it soon outlives its usefulness. And when, by grace, the vision does come, it comes in poetic leaps for which, Joseph Brodsky reminds us, "You're grateful . . . but the gratitude costs you your previous identity."[3] The gratitude, thanksgiving that transforms, is Eucharist.

Who among us will have the courage that puts life on the line, who will use every faculty to live the vision to the end? Who will arise with the perspective of unity-in-diversity that helps us to restrain ourselves from grasping what is cheap and shortsighted? Who will fuel the fire of aspiration in us that becomes our virginity that cannot be exploited and is willing to die for the promise barely glimpsed? *These* are priests. There is no priesthood but the priesthood of Christ in which each Christian shares by Christ's indwelling (1 Cor 1–3). So must we all be.

Ransack and criticize the gospels as we might, the predominant message is the humility of Christ, one of self-emptying, of giving up ambition, pride, control: "Who is last shall be first"; "Who gives up life shall gain it"; "Do not despise these little ones, for their angels look on the face of my father which is in heaven." It is summed up in the great hymn of Philippians 2:5–9 adapted by Paul: "Let this mind be in you which was in Christ Jesus, who, being in the form of a servant . . . " In short, Jesus is fighting the dualism of his day: observance of law that imperils life with God; hatred of the creation God has called good; domination of and condemnation by one group over another so that there are superiors and inferiors and those who are utterly rejected.

Shifting Power in the Early Churches

The New Testament churches recognized that gifts of the Holy Spirit and consequent gifts of ministry were given as part of their members' being-in-Christ. *In addition*, and in a move not necessarily related to the bestowal of these gifts, leaders appointed morally upright functionaries to deal with other, practical matters relating to organization. There is disagreement over whether the models for these offices were taken from non-Jewish or Jewish tradition. At the moment, the former seems to predominate in scholarly opinion.

These offices did not have a static character, and their functions were fluid. The deacons and presbyter-bishops took care of organization, distribution of goods, the decent and orderly conduct of the gatherings of the community, and teaching. Those with charisms, with gifts of healing, prophecy, and the like, were recognized by a discerning community, but there is no confusion in the New Testament between office and charism.

In addition, there is no evidence whatsoever to tell us who presided at the eucharistic meal. Aside from the *Didache*, it is not until the second century that we have any real idea what form that eucharistic meal might have taken. If the *Didache* is an authentic document (and the scholarship establishing its pregospel date so far has not been refuted), it gives us a very different picture (as do the later writings of Justin, to name but one author) than one of the threefold hierarchy that was eventually to dominate.

And it is also an utterly different picture from what Ignatius of Antioch, if we take his letters to be authentic, seems to have been trying to impose on the churches. Recent scholarship by R. Joly, however, suggests that the elements in his letters that are exclusionary and encourage domination by the bishop are later Greek interpolations.[4] Whether or not Joly's scholarship is accepted, the argument from Ignatius does not provide authoritative ground for the dominance of the three-fold hierarchical ministry because its concept of authority is defective: it is not based on the kenotic humility of Christ.

More to the point, and contrary to what conservative scholars would assert, Ignatius unwittingly shows why there can be no eucharistic validity when the eucharistic community is dominated by monarchical bishops. What leaks through Ignatius' letters in the vehemence of their protest is an uneasy and inarticulate sense that if the bishop invalidates the in-Christ-ness of the people of God—the name of the Father written on their hearts—he also invalidates the possibility of his becoming Eucharist for them with his own life. This conjecture is even more plausible because in his time, community leaders were still part of the community and indistinguishable from it, not set over and against it as Ignatius desires to be. Such a stance twists the eucharistic community's shared experience of relationships of ungraspingness in the kenotic love of God into the fear of a puppet-master's petty tyranny.

There is a long, dark tunnel between the year 70 (after *Didache* and the gospels) and the few documents that have survived from around the turn of the century. These documents give a picture of continuing diversity in order and practice. There is another long tunnel between Ignatius and Irenaeus. In these tunnel periods we know virtually nothing of how developments in the churches came to be.

In sum, while we can make few positive statements about the first three centuries of development of the early churches, scholarly consensus (as opposed to ecumenical consensus, which tends to be less daring and perhaps less honest) suggests the following: the threefold, ordained hierarchical structures we know now were unknown in New Testament times. What offices existed in the churches were concerned with practical organizational matters and with teaching—though teaching was not primarily the concern of and certainly not confined to those appointed.

These "offices" were unstructured and highly fluid in terms of who did what. There were no claims to an ontological change of "kind" implying unique and permanent status. While there was an attempt to choose responsible people for these offices, there was no sense that the office was either a "reward" for particular holiness or that it bestowed holiness. The death of the apostles left a leadership vacuum in the churches, and the conflicts we see beginning in the New Testament become deadly as one or another interpretation of leadership abandons the humility of Christ and seeks to dominate.

When we arrive at the second-century period, there is still great diversity in pattern and theology in the documents. The theology of the Letter to the Hebrews still prevails. What happened in the second tunnel? We can only wonder how many documents were destroyed by those seeking to seat themselves firmly on thrones of power.

By the time of Irenaeus, the pattern of threefold ministry is established, and it is only in the third century that ideas of levitical priestly cult and dualistic language and imagery relating to Temple sacrifice begin to be used widely in reference to Christian hierarchy (Cyprian uses it consistently, to name but one author). The fact that authors felt it necessary to borrow this language and symbolism at all suggests the anomalous and deadening nature ministry was taking on and its need for self-justification.

That the churches at about the same time suddenly became respectable, united with and supported by the emperor, increased their need to justify the implied rejection of the model of humility of Christ by whatever means available. This meant ongoing devaluation and objectifying of the gathered community so that power might be concentrated in individual bishops. Thus by the fourth century the churches reestablished the same religious style against which Jesus revolted.

Jesus' affinity for the poor and outcast (which made him ritually unclean during most of his ministry) and his condemnation of those who condemn were the scandal that led to his death. His position undermined the ruling powers, the status quo. And the folly that is the glory of the Cross, the humility of Christ, simply puts his exposure of the illusory nature of these ruling and condemning powers into sharper focus. We can come to be only through God's humility; we have no existence apart from engagement with God, which means we must abandon our grasping after illusion. This is the scandal of Christianity that the emerging rulers of the early churches seem to have wished to forget and that, especially after Constantine's conversion, was turned upside down to become a means of dominance.

The inviolability, wildness, invisibility, prodigality, and indiscriminate bestowal of our in-Christ-ness by the Holy *Geist* (the German word has a sense of wildness, the Spirit blowing where it will) is a scandal to the churches because of the human tendency to want to have a tangible point of focus around which to build a closed mythology, the kind of idolatry exemplified in the story of the golden calf. The risen Christ is only too aware of this lust for idolatry, which is why the divine life disappears and leaves the life-giving but invisible Paraclete active within the creation. God was reluctant to give Israel rulers because the people would become dependent on their projected self-image rather than on God. We see this wisdom of God most clearly in God's insistence on self-effacement in the bestowal of the Holy Ghost. Yet we have made a golden calf out of both the Holy Ghost and ordained ministry.

In addition, there is now as there was in the ancient world a human tendency to prefer to believe the fabulous to explain the workings of the universe, in preference to acknowledging the wonder and mystery of invisible engagement, the ungraspable eucharistic confluence not only of humanity but of all creation in and by the indwelling Love of God. We also seem constantly to be tempted to attribute supernatural power to people who make specious claims to have God's exclusive mandate to control our coming to be. We fall prey to their attempts to grasp and maintain power. They become idols, illusions of divine manifestion.

Today as we stagger on the nuclear brink, we are experiencing yet another resurgence of interest in spiritualism, communication with the dead through mediums, and trust in the magical powers of crystals. Even a patently bizarre illusion can seem reasonable under threatening circumstances if it pretends to provide us with a visible savior that is able to grasp the threat and the fear and control them. In the modern world this desire to control fear means that we also have exalted scientific research to an untenable position, and the scientific community has not hesitated to create its own pseudo-religious mythology. Yet even in our mistaken pursuit of these chimeras, we are still seeking after the essence of our interrelatedness.

While we are unable to assign an essence to Christianity (or perhaps to any religion), there is within it a certain inarticulate engagement that, if we attempt to reduce it to speech, is rendered more false than true. Early in volume one of his monumental patristic study, *Christ in Christian Tradition*, Aloysius Grillmeier writes of the significance of the intuitive communication of early Christianity. He points to the church in Smyrna (quoting Hippolytus), which, when challenged by Noetus "did not resort to high theology; [and] contented themselves with the simple formula which they had heard."[5] This was not anti-intellectualism. The supra-conceptual experience and interior transformation behind the formulas had been communicated with such clarity that the elders could discern when someone held a different understanding and belief.

Why the churches corrupted the humility of Christ into dominating power and why this perversion was and continues to be maintained is a complex historical tale far beyond the scope of this book. But in addition to being a political narrative, it is also a story of the domination of certain kinds of thought processes.

3. Ways of Thinking About God: Can Athens and Jerusalem Ever Meet?

"Whatre you then are you the Asker of the Worl?"
   I said, "It seams like every body elses got ansers only I havent got nothing only askings."

RUSSELL HOBAN, *RIDDLEY WALKER*

"Can Athens and Jerusalem ever meet?" was the great question that preoccupied theologians during the patristic period. Behind this question there is infinitely more at stake than the clash of cultures or the political domination of Byzantium or Rome, which nonetheless played their own crucial roles in the development of Christian doctrine.

Behind this question lies an intuitive understanding that the Zeus-god and I AM or, better, I WILL BE [FOR YOU] WHAT I WILL BE [FOR YOU] contradict each other (see Appendix A). The central forces in Greek philosophy that arise from the worship of power exalt the kind of reasoning that controls and manipulates static ideas, reducing the search for "truth" to the power-struggles of human intellects, conflicts that finally dead-end. Dialogue with the divine becomes the dialectic of humanity dedicated to illusion. The transactional I WILL BE tells us of the constancy of God's ready response to indwell all times, seasons, conditions, suffering. I AM is the means to life; through God's willingness to take on I AM, the creation receives its being and existence.

The chart in Appendix A shows us the false sense of polarity we tend to create between the dead-end Zeus-god and the willingness to enter and be entered by I WILL BE. Most of us get stuck in this false dialectic, fleeing toward the dead end (with the emphasis on *dead*) of the left side when we are afraid and longing for the promises of the right-hand column, which we seem to regard as the other "pole" of this seeming polarity. But we are not to stop at the right side, which is a *way* and not an end. I WILL BE is a *way* of salvation; the equipoise of faith found in I WILL BE enables us to move *through* the right-hand column because the heart of the way is abandoning the "need" to have closure, giving up the illusory and destructive "need" for artificial polarity. We move into ever-widening Life; we are far beyond the Hegelian thesis/antithesis interplay.

The right-hand column, which represents escape from constricting dialectic, is not a "pole" or polarity but more like (the analogy is two-dimensional and hardly exact) a transponder that focuses and magnifies a signal before sending it on. In scriptural terms, this is the "narrow gate." Expressed in a plumbing analogy, this means that the point of greatest pressure in a constricted pipe is not the point at which water enters the constriction, but where the pipe begins to widen again. Emerging from the narrow way, we are caught in vastness and energy beyond knowing in any terms, and we must be willing to be thrust out into the Wound where creation is transfigured.

We are asked, with Christ indwelling, to give up the satisfaction that there "is" another pole. So while we are still caught by our projected self-images it may feel as though there is polarity, but we cannot posit (and we must give up trying to posit) the "other" pole. We can be willing only for engagement with the divine and self-forgetfulness beyond dimensionality that is the confluence of mutual *kenosis*.

While I WILL BE is named in the language of being, it violates all the existence/nonexistence "rules" implied by the grammar of being. The kenotic God is beyond categories of being and non-being, but takes on being, and bestows being upon us through this willing self-denudation that is Incarnation. I WILL BE is an incarnational Name. I WILL BE is transactional because through the Name the creation comes to be as *thou*. The old categories of being are static and absurd. But the *language* of being is still the most resonant language we have. It expands theology and liturgical expression, erupting through the finitude of creation's timespace. The beauty of such language carries a transformational power that springs from the density of glory that is I WILL BE. It is never exhausted, and cannot be matched by the most elegant argument.

Our task is to resist locking this language into static categories. Rather, we must be cognizant of its ability to commune us with what is unsaid, the Word who proceeds from Silence and brings us to Silence, who has spoken words— those who have gone before, those who are yet to live, and ourselves. By this language of being we are in communion with them, with each other, with all creation, all timespace, all dimensionality; we are earthed or densified or whatever language is appropriate for the fluidity that is "existence" in sacred time. There is a sense in which this language creates us and our world of lived experience. We must restore to theology equally a sense of earthedness, the resonances of divine Mercy, and the utter inarticulateness with which we must approach the aweful glory of the kenotic God.

The popular (not scholarly) concept named "Zeus" begins with a primitive, somewhat rueful, picaresque mythological character who sometimes dominates and sometimes is duped. Zeus ultimately becomes pure functional power, one who rules by a massive and impassible intellect, utterly self-contained and disengaged from creation yet manipulating it by thought alone—when he chooses to think about it. Creation is an object, and whether or not it has life or its life is enhanced does not seem terribly important. The worship of this kind of power and the exaltation of analytical reason that devolves from it, is *inherently* dualistic.

We need to be aware of the illusion of control and containment that dualistic reasoning gives us, especially in theology, especially in the examination of tradition. Like the Greeks, we have tended to endow linear thinking, discursive reason, with value that exalts it above all other aspects of our created being, even if its narrowing perspective means the destruction of life itself. Discursive reason in turn, even as it narrows our focus, enhances our wishful thinking leading us to imagine that even within the reality of the creation's unimaginable interconnectedness, we have a greater and more objective perspective and control than is possible to us. The idea that we might have absolute objectivity is absurd; we would not exist; we would have fallen away utterly from being.

Thus if we exalt this power of discursive reason above all other criteria of discernment in our relationship with God or believe it is possible to make accurate statements about God by manipulating ideas in a controlling way, we *cannot help* but project the image of Zeus the controller (which is a projection of human egotism) onto the humility that is I WILL BE.

When this exaltation of the power of human reason is mixed with Egypto-Roman ideas of pyramidal/hierarchical power for controlling the social order and then is transmuted into the Christian organism, *kenosis* as God's self-revelation and the essence of individual and community life in Christ becomes almost totally obscured. When we accept these controlling models of power, we *cannot help* but become prisoners of a kind of fundamentalism that seeks security in controlling and being controlled, blaming and being blamed, fundamentalism that says, for example, that human perception of the Word of God is perfect. This is the reasoning behind the idea of biblical inerrancy, and it is another example of the presumption that is the sin of the Garden.

Biblical inerrancy mistakes static human constructs about God for God's living and active Word and by implication points to the smug, immutable, self-contained popular caricature of the Zeus-god. Biblical inerrancy cannot help but lead to the positing of a puppet-master because a Zeus-god, controlling power, points to itself by its intervention. Those devoted to biblical inerrancy measure themselves to see how well they are

Biblical inerrancy

doing according to a static model or closed system and quote "inerrant" Scripture to "justify" their intervening action whether or not it accords exactly with that model or system. Because a Zeus-god can be posited, the questions of the existence and intervention of this god become real questions.

On the other hand, the idea that we can posit the kenotic God is a philosophical *trompe l'oeil*. It is a little like trying to levitate in St. Paul's Cathedral: we will hit our heads a lot sooner than we think. Experiment with trying to make controlling statements about a self-emptying God. It is much more difficult. It is almost impossible to make positing statements about something that is pointing away from itself. This God's self-emptying ungraspingness is ungraspable by definition. Even theological statements about the kenotic God tend to be about *how that God acts*, not *what that God is*. We cannot posit this God strictly speaking because this God is not a static point or concept like the Zeus-god. This God's contextual, interpenetrating, generative, transfiguring self-outpouring is eucharistic engagement with and within creation.

We can point only to God's movement of love, and this perception cannot be arrived at except by engagement. This God points away from God toward the experiential life of the creation. God always seeks kenotically to share in a union of eucharistic indwelling, confluence, and reciprocity. Since neither an encompassing and coinhering context nor ungraspingness can be contained, the question of positing the existence of this God is absurd: only engagement is real. Even though we are free to choose to live in a trap, in a closed system of our own devising that does not acknowledge anything outside itself, we cannot really disengage God; we can have only the illusion of disengagement.

Paradoxically, the impossibility of disengagement is not a trap but is the condition of our true freedom. The arrogance that insists on illusory disengagement does not accept either the interdependence of creation or the eucharistic engagement that is the source of its being.

Disengagement, isolation, is the illusion that causes the fissure in our being. Our attempt to live in the illusion of disengagement by manipulating self-image leads only to the closed system of perpetual failure. No matter how successful we may seem to be to ourselves and perhaps to others (judging by the fantasy criteria of the illusion), the more we try to control, the more we *are* failure, because we have fallen away from the equipoise of our responsive and engaged being.

The perception of the kenotic God rides the boundary between contemplation and notion, never reaching conceptual grasp precisely because of God's ungraspingness. Engagement with God means commitment to an open system, to vulnerability, to risk. It means that we are always looking not only toward God but also through God, because this God points away from the divine self and through us, and through this God's life creation is magnified so that we see God's glory within creatureliness with ever-greater clarity.

Through our self-forgetful aspiration that mirrors God's *kenosis* we no longer are able to categorize and to objectify other people or any of the rest of creation because we perceive the kenotic mystery that indwells all that is. We are dependent and interdependent on the security of God's self-outpouring, not on the illusory security of a closed and static structure. Our gaze, undistracted by concern to know if static boundaries are in place, is turned away from our selves; there is no time to wonder how we are doing because we are always being led through the deeper clarity and ever-widening perspective of life in God. In such engagement, Scripture, far from being confined to the static framework of inerrancy, takes on luminous and fathomless depth, and the resonances of symbol and metaphor transform through still-prayer, from which imageless contemplation proceeds. This imageless contemplation, by which we come to be, is a process glimpsed only occasionally by concept, and transformation occurs out of our sight as we gaze on God.

The counterfeit of the engaged approach is literalism or any other device that creates a closed system. *Christianity must leave its conceptual and verbal system open.* Its essence cannot be conveyed in language; it is inarticulate precisely because God is engaged with the creation by the love that is *kenosis* and not by the imposed domination of a closed system of articulated concepts. Christianity is articulate through the resonances of our being-in-God.

Religious questions engage; secular answers control. So also in our mirroring of God it is much more through the resonances of our *being* that we communicate the divine mystery than by our thoughts, words, and actions, though these are not to be discounted. Propositional high theology can be just as secular and distorting to Christianity as biblical inerrancy; conceptual theology can become a form of fundamentalism in its own right.

Thus *the method we choose to explore religious questions determines the way in which we relate to one another and divinity, and thus that divinity will determine the method by which we relate to God and one another.* When we try to posit God, we are trapped in a circular argument. We need to make all the dissonant noise required to sustain a closed system and distract our selves from the yawning abyss we have created, to convince our selves we have in fact grasped both being and salvation.

When we are willing to engage God, we are not trapped in a circular argument. Rather, in the equipoise of ready response we are opened to possibility and co-creation. All is Eucharist; and from the Silence of God, the Word of loving engagement, the Word that is First and Last is spoken.

We can think about a god with Zeus-nature in a structural way, and to posit such a god will entail a closed system of universe and thought. This universe discourages religious questions because religious questions will reveal the synthetic, secular nature of the system's controlling, life-draining answers. In such a system there may be security but there is no salvation.

But contrariwise, if we risk *engagement* with a kenotic God, we recover our being in the love of God that is eternally open and can never be a trap. Religious questioning is essential to this faith that is engagement, for in both the religious question and the religious answer are found ever-deeper engagement. This engagement gives us grace to live in the wondrous and ever-expanding freedom of self-forgetfulness that is our divine inheritance and our salvation.

Both approaches engage God to a certain extent. But in the first, the thinker predicates God, and in the second, the thinker must first acknowledge being predicated by God. In the first, God is made object and engagement is destroyed; in the second, God is subject, but there is no object, only thou-engagement. (It is perhaps because of this necessary open "engagement," the willingness to experience thou that is prerequisite to attempting any intellectual approach to the kenotic God, that structural positivists are unable to admit that meaningful statements about God can be made.)

In consequence, *how we relate to God determines the way we commit ourselves to our own and others' salvation in Christ.* One will reinforce the other. And the characteristics we ascribe to God may very well be determined by the factors that we find meaningful. If we find meaning in control and exercising controlling power over others, then we will doubtless be happier with projecting a Zeus-nature onto God so that we are able to think about that nature and act with others in a controlling way in order to sustain our grandiose fantasies.

However, if we find meaning in gazing on God in still-prayer, seeing through God's eyes (or being open to God's looking through ours), if we find meaning in becoming willing to mirror that God's self-forgetful love, we will be content with engagement, and we will engage others by the resonances of our being.

While we need very much to think as closely and rationally as possible about what we believe, we need also to admit to our selves that we cannot do it in a disengaged way, or else in

How we act is how we perceive God to act

our delusion we soon elevate the love of the control of our ideas about God over and above our engagement with the incomprehensibility (literally, uncontainability) of eucharistic reciprocity with God. Too many of the arguments surrounding the development of the unfinished doctrine of the Trinity, for example, are compromised because they reflect the arguers' intoxication with their own controlling ideas, not to mention the context of threat of political exile, anathemas, crusades, and murders. We always have to remember—even if its creators did not—that trinitarian theology developed as a series of responses to specific problems, and while its artificial propositions are useful guidelines for thinking about God under specific conditions, they are not descriptions of God, and they are not immutable and eternal or appropriate to every context and age.

The hardest of hard scientists, particle physicists, have been among the first to abandon the idea of absolute objectivity, not only because the dynamics of matter must be spatially engaged, but also because they understand that the interlocking of all creation is too subtle to be observed in fragments and that it is impossible to disengage either the fragments or themselves. They understand that there is a continuum within which lies essential paradox. Matter has a way of appearing as we wish to see it. If an experimenter is studying waves, energy seems to tend to appear as waves rather than particles. The observer is part of what is observed and in some way has a part in determining what is observed. While we must strive to be as objective as we can, we must not continue under the illusion that our objectivity is or ever can be absolute. Even computers cannot be objective, for they have the bias of their programmers in them, and they may interact with the surrounding world in ways we do not yet understand.

This is not to say that utter subjectivity is to be embraced. We need to distance ourselves as we attempt to look as clearly as possible at what is under examination, but we must always have the humility to realize that we are somehow engaged with what we are looking at and that our perspective and awareness of variables is severely limited. We are becoming aware of the perils of the illusion of objectivity in theology— a kind of scientism—and we must return to a way of doing theology that takes experience into consideration or begins in reflection on experience.

If we refuse, we are just engaging in another form of gnosticism, both in terms of arcane knowledge and in denial of creatureliness and the sanctity of creation. This is not to say that we might as well take our books and burn them, because eventually "pure" academic theology does trickle down the artificial pyramid to the grass-roots level. But the difference in our age from any other is that *we don't have time.*

Theology has an essential task to acknowledge the language that already goes so deep as to strike genetic chords in us; to receive its *kenosis,* silence, and stillness from which transfiguration resonates; to be infused with meaning that we in times of our preference for a Zeus-god have sought to bypass, obscure, or destroy. In our age we don't have time to wait for speculative theology to become fashionable, because if we don't make the kenotic God accessible, in one of those moments when we are vulnerable to the Zeus model, we *will* end by annihilating the planet.

In a world that understands itself both scientifically and religiously as engaged and interrelated, churches that offer controlling and objectifying models of power attempt to meet religious and scientific perception with a secular and fragmented god. *The problem of "secularism" lies not so much in the culture as in the churches.*

When the churches emphasize a secular/sacred dualism by insisting that what is outside the organization is "secular," they are giving power and place not to what is secular, that is, morally neutral (constraint within the Christian ghetto does not make something or someone "sacred"), but to what is worldly, that which struggles for status and controlling power. By emphasizing a dualistic worldview the churches present us with a worldly god of status and power. The antidote to so-called "secularism" is not to make a ghetto of the sacred, thereby forcing the sacred to assume a stance of worldly power, but rather a sacramental view that reverences the humble indwelling of the divine in creation and all of life, particularly in those areas we instinctively shun.

While people living in the insecurity of life under the nuclear cloud or in a creation that allows for randomness may initially find comfort in the idea of a controlling Zeus-god, ultimately they discard such a deity because it is out of harmony with *what is*. We live in an age that desperately needs to acknowledge engagement with God as one single movement of eucharistic ungraspingness, and while this God may be received and communicated through the *experience* of the Trinity in still-prayer, too much emphasis on the *doctrine* of the Trinity not only gives the religious question a secular answer, but it also can be extremely destructive to the questioner's lived interdependence and seeking.

Even in areas of theology where there are hard data, such as biblical criticism, scholars increasingly recognize that we can be *more* objective by acknowledging and allowing for our interest or bias and for other elements we bring to the work, right down to the usually subliminal influence of the biochemical effects of breakfast (or lack of it). Within criticism itself we have long known that we need to acknowledge contexts, the matrix experiences of communities in which documents and doctrines have their sources. In other words, we need to have the kind of self-knowledge in scholarly work that is also essential to personal transformation.

Paradoxically, then, to deny that self-knowledge is necessary to objectivity is to blind ourselves to the unconscious and unattended forces that will emerge in our work one way or another. On the other hand, the more reflectively and critically "subjective" we become, that is, the more self-knowledge we have, the more "objective" we are likely to be because we tend to allow for what we know is our inherent bias. *However much*

response to secularism

denial we may indulge in, there is no way to avoid the reality of our engagement, the generative context of our existence.

When we realize that any kind of thinking that controls and manipulates its subject matter by ideas is *inherently* dualistic, that is, that merely by choosing something to think about, much is rejected and left out; when we realize that in thinking about the chosen subject, a hierarchy of ideas or priority of ideas is established, then the dangers of doing theology in an exclusively propositional way become even more abundantly clear. While most theologians would acknowledge this reality in theory, sad historical experience reveals that theologians and church officials frequently have confused their method with their content.

That is to say, we have wittingly or unwittingly moved from the assumption that because certain aspects of human relationship with God can be thought about in a controlled way, it follows that God or God's action can be directly described; or that power from God is bestowed on the thinker and can be directly wielded by the thinker; or in another distortion, that the thinker can so detach from God as to be "objective"; or, and this is the worst distortion of all, that because a theological construction can be made that attempts to unite irreconcilable opposites, as in the unfinished and reactive doctrine of the Trinity, that God must in fact be like the theory and no other model will do.

This philosophical trinitarian construction contrasts sharply with the *experience* of the Trinity in the early churches and in every age in prayer. While it may or may not have been the intention of early theologians, the philosophical constructs that make up trinitarian thought seem to communicate not a kenotic God engaged with the creation and experienced in prayer, but rather an oriental potentate god of "power and might" of a very worldly and self-perpetuating type, utterly happy and complete in self-contained three-in-oneness, concern for the creation and its transfiguration being confined to an entirely gratuitous afterthought.

The reasons for the churches' marked preference for this god should by now be obvious: such a god and those of us who worship such a god (and there are bits of our selves that probably always do, that need to be acknowledged and per-suaded otherwise) can be controlled, and in a closed system there are few surprises. The controlled and controller god rules by fear and needs begging and placating like the primitive gods of old. If we delude ourselves that all is under control, then we can ignore those bits of us that are unacknowledged and out of control—until they wreak havoc. The churches are afraid of a kenotic God; the consequences of worshiping such a divinity are too dangerous; the possibility of a social order transformed by mercy and reverence for the despised and the holiness of fools is too much to bear.

To be sure, the kenotic movement is inherent in the theolog-ical tradition of the three Persons' ecstatic self-emptying and finding completion in one another (perichoresis), and this movement is a profound model for human social relationships. In addition, according to some lesser-known mystical theolo-gians who emphasize the compassion of God, creation can even be understood to reside and be cradled in the Trinity's fiery heart. But these palliative qualifications do not change the fact that the *experience* of the Trinity is very different from the way the better-known aspects of the doctrine of the Trinity have developed and frequently have been taught. And these qualifications do not change the fact that the churches' teach-ing has been selective and that they have insisted on conveying an idea of God that is increasingly inaccessible to a holistic age as well as a distortion of Christianity's most ancient and essential message.

In sum, the kind of thinking used in much theological and doctrinal formulation is often precisely the kind of thinking condemned in the myth of the Garden, that is, that God's knowledge and knowledge of God beyond the capacity of our creatureliness can be wrested from God and exercised apart from engagement with God. The idea of a Zeus-god who is

Gen. 2 & 3   Garden

self-contained, whose power is exercised by mere condescending thought, who deals with creation as a gratuitous appendage, is utterly in opposition to the God revealed to us both in Hebrew Scripture and in the humility of Jesus the Christ.

It follows from this that to attribute a Zeus-like impassibility to the kenotic God is absurd (the idea that God is incapable of suffering; it is contradictory in any event to suggest that God is *incapable*). This is one of the points at which the trinitarian *doctrine* and kenotic models of God *cannot* intersect. This does not mean that one is "orthodox" and the other is "heresy"; they are simply two different, and at this juncture irreconcilable, approaches to thinking about God.

The words "impassible" and "immutable" are static and self-reflective. They are not words that relate to a kenotic living God who is unceasingly self-outpouring, compassionate, and engaged with the creation. Thus if we were to insist on applying an idea of "impassibility" to the kenotic God, we would discover that this God's impassibility is *not* God's being unaffected by passions (or, by implication, anything else) but whose *kenosis* is, in fact, *Passion*.

We would find that we have to understand God's impassibility as divine imperviousness to any effect we might think would alter God's inviolable vulnerability, God's unswerving commitment to suffer with and within the creation, to go to the heart of pain, to generate new life, hope, and joy out of the cry of dereliction, out of the pain of utter self-denudation, utter self-emptying, utter engaging love. Nothing, *nothing* will ever breach that commitment. To perceive this commitment is as close as we can come to describing the kenotic God's essence, because, as God has revealed in the humility of Christ, God's suffering is at the heart of God's outpouring.

One might then say, and perhaps it is only right to say, that if we were inappropriately to attempt to apply the idea of impassibility to the kenotic God, we would have to say that God's impassibility *is* God's suffering. We can speak of "total self-denudation," but we are speaking of the denudation that eventuates in the density of glory from which pours salvific love. God would also be immutable in this same sense: nothing changes in God's eternal outpouring commitment to suffer with and transfigure. But both these traditional words need to be laid aside.

Now, the exercise of power tends to disperse the energy of our being, whereas the exercise of self-restraint tends to concentrate, create density. There is an intriguing analogy here: to distract from its lack of density that results from its dispersion of being, its fissured self of which it is ashamed, a Zeus-god needs an artificial glory. It needs to decorate itself, to create false density by calling attention to a particular aspect of itself, and to insist upon its dazzling, extraordinary, super-human qualities (impassibility or immutability, for example).

By contrast, true glory, *kavod*, is the nonlocus, nonpositable density that is God's outpouring. What we can perceive of God is glory, especially the glory of the Cross, and that glory is continually outpoured and interpenetrates all that is. Nothing *can* be added to this self-emptying God.

We see this truth operating also on a human level. Those who are self-reflective, insecure, and self-aggrandizing, who flinch from the equipoise of conversion that is the gaze on God, need the trappings of success. Those who are self-forgetful, committed to the greater power of self-restraint, and self-emptying do not. Their glory radiates quietly forth from the gaze of their being on God, and that radiance of glory enables transformation all around them. This principle is operative across the spectrum of everyday life, in sports, intellectual work, interpersonal relationships, committed physical love-making, or other forms of prayer-that-is-life.

To make this point crudely, Zeus, that utterly self-indulgent deity, spends a lot of time mending fences, even when he has evolved to the stage where he controls things merely by thinking about them. Zeus is preoccupied with lust, that is, control, not sexuality. We might say that he goes around with his pecker on his sleeve instead of his heart. His various rapes are expressions of control, and it is no surprise that he evolves as the uncaring controller-god, the image later borrowed and projected irreconcilably onto the Christian God.

The model of God whose power is expressed in self-restraint, in seeming impotence, is in utter conflict with this caricature of Zeus. The reason the kenotic God has been sidestepped in history is not only because this model is impossible to integrate with the trinitarian model (which has often been raised to an idolatrous importance), but, more to the point, it is simply too damning for those who seek to justify their own lust for power and control in the churches.

By the end of the Middle Ages, the Zeus-god is three times controlling and separated from the creation: Father, Son, and Mother all need placating, pleasing, and "sacrifices." If we add clergy who exercise self-aggrandizing, worldly power in the name of this god's forgiveness, then there is yet a fourth remove. The declaration of papal infallibility is the last desperate reductionistic spasm of a church whose energies are collapsing with the effort to support its ego-inflation. I WILL BE creates out of self-denudation; and the divine Humility, giving the creation its freedom while still indwelling and sustaining it with the very divine life, does not control but rather coinheres and co-creates.

It should be clear, then, why the way we think about God is so crucial not only to the development and life of the churches but also to every aspect of our lives. If we are created in the image of God and our lives are spent struggling to aspire, to be willing to mirror that God, to partake more fully of the life of God, who creates and sustains us with that life, what are we going to be?

Are we going to build empires, control, intervene, coerce, dominate, and bully others into doing what we want without any regard for the mystery of their being—for we are untouched and untouchable by their sufferings, "impassible," exercising tyranny for the sake of a beautiful idea (or even "the beautiful") to the exclusion of goodness (or even the exclusion of "the good")? There is nothing wrong with worship of God in terms of beauty unless one begins to find less and less that is beautiful in the creation and to develop the idea that God who is Beauty will not indwell what we perceive as ugly. This line of reasoning leads us to find less and less tolerance for the diversity and foibles of creatures.

Or is our action going to be concerned first of all with the self-restraint of our own lust for power, ambition, and control? Are we going to be concerned with the eucharistic coinherence of our freedom with that of all creation, even to the point of acknowledging our participation in suffering and ugliness and sin? Are we willing to suffer, and by that noninterfering suffering-with, that is, the compassion that is eucharistic ungraspingness, thus give the strength and support that will release others (and therefore also, by confluence, our selves) into new life, hope, and joy, release them to find salvation, to be sprung from their trap?

At this point the question arises, what coerces us from the way through the self-emptying God to divine freedom? What makes us retreat to the Zeus-god and spiritual slavery? The answer is in the letters commonly attributed to Paul and in the Letter to the Hebrews. The coercive force is fear, fear of death, whether that death is mortality, or death threatened by another's claim to control our forgiveness and salvation, or the death of losing the power of self-aggrandizement. It is by magnifying fear that the churches have reinforced the centralization of their manipulative power, and it is fear—or the possibility of our being delivered from it—that determines which model of God we grow into (1 Jn 4).

We are always being pressured by our circumstances, and we have the choice of response in our daily successes and catastrophes. We can respond either by retreat from fear of suffering into the security of the reductionistic Zeus-god, using ours or others' suffering to further inflate our pseudo-selves that fall away from the pain that is inherent in coming to be. Or we can embrace and engage our fear and suffering

fear

in the darkness and unknowing that is our looking, with the humility of Christ indwelling, on the Face of God, life in I WILL BE FOR YOU. The direction of our response and our gaze will stunt our maturation—our coming to be—or enable it. And what is true of us is also true of our institutions.

A church committed to a Zeus-god will play upon our fears and keep its membership infantile in order to control it. A church committed to I WILL BE FOR YOU will support and encourage a faith that is the only security amid the insecurity of freedom that is life in the humility of Christ. This faith will be the ground, the humus, for growth, risk, experiment, pain, evolution, maturity, transfiguration, and joy.

The way we think about God is important because it affects the way we assume our responsibility in the world, and vice versa. Secretly, in our heart of hearts, there is a part of us that would *like* God to be a puppet-master. There is a hidden desire within us to emulate a god who is the unfeeling, immutable, and impervious tower defended against all contingencies. This was the meaning that some schools of stoicism gave to the word *apatheia* and that was disastrously mistaken by some Christians for our continual seeking the equipoise of inviolable vulnerability, of ready response, of conversion.

Dostoyevsky's Grand Inquisitor knows very well how part of us longs to give up our freedom to this cold idol. Much pseudo-Christian mysticism is based on this idea of slavery; the idea that union with God consists in completely abrogating our freedom in order to force our selves onto a rigid track that stretches before us that is known as "God's will." It is a slavery that includes abandoning to the domination of another not only our personality and mental faculties, but also our chastity, our inviolability, the integrity of the our relationship with God, the *pointe vierge* where no one else is able, much less has the right, to intrude. Inherent in this slavery is the consequence that we therefore also abrogate the chastity of our

Conference

relationship to the rest of creation and *creation's* inviolability, our reducing it to object for exploitation.

The temptation of the institution is always desire for certainty. Our hymns and prayers are often more full of the Zeus-god than I WILL BE. Even in the liturgy of the Eucharist, many symbols and prayers are subliminally, if not literally, appealing to an interventionist "god of power and might" in secular, worldly, human terms, in Zeus's terms. This god makes us feel certain and safe. When worship does mention the divine Humility, it too often interprets the weakness of God as languid impotence.

The truth is that the wounded God wishes to speak the Word through our particular gifts and personalities and lives— yes, and our mistakes and sins and neuroses. True Christian mysticism, true Christian life is willingness to engage God face to Face, to pay the price of the encounter of self-emptying love with Self-emptying Love. This confluence of Love takes us far beyond anything we can ask or imagine, and we cannot have any notion what will be asked of us; all that is sure is that we will journey where it is most certainly not "safe." But we no longer count the cost, because we are being so found in the kenotic Love of God that self-reflection burns away. The commitment of our lives to this kenotic journey is the baptismal vow, the beginning of our priesthood.

Can Athens and Jerusalem ever meet? Only if Athens is willing to admit that God is not complete until God is incomplete, because God's loving concern with creation is so essential to God that, as we are shown in the humility of Jesus the Christ, God is willing to enter the suffering and incompleteness of God's creatures. Athens and Jerusalem can meet only if we perceive God's power not merely as self-limiting but exercised in total self-denudation for the sake of the creation. God's willingness is to be subject to death and to harrow hell, each of our particular hells and the creation's hell, and to bring even hell itself into transfiguration.

This God meets us both in our aspiration that mirrors the

outpouring of divine Love, and in hell, in the failure of self-image we experience when our self-inflation has collapsed. God transfigures us into new life, hope, and joy when we acknowledge our powerlessness to save our selves and open to the divine indwelling.

Athens and Jerusalem can meet only if God's impassibility is understood as God's suffering, the constancy of love that is God's willing and inviolable vulnerability that commits God eternally to be for us in whatever condition we find our selves. This is God's priesthood for us, shown in the Cross, which spans every abyss in every age, and, with Christ indwelling, it is our priesthood for one another.

II. MODELS OF POWER AND SPIRITUAL MATURITY

You take a figger out of the bag nor it aint nothing only some colourt clof with a paintit wood head and hans. Then you put it on. You put your head finger in the head and you put your arm fingers in the arms then that figger looks roun and takes noatis it has things to say. Which they wont all ways be things *youwd* think of saying o no them wood heads the hart of the wood is in them and the hart of the wud and all. They have ther knowing and they have ther saying which you bes lissen for it you bes let it happen. 'I never look for my reveal til its ben.' That's what my dad said time back. My dad the connexion man. In my woal life Ive only ever done that 1 connexion which Ive wrote down here I begun with trying to put it to gether poal by poal only my reveal dint come that way it snuck me woaly. I wer keaping that in memberment now. Ready to cry ready to dy ready for any thing is how I come to it now. In fear and tremmering only not running a way. In emtyness and ready to be fult. Not to lern no body nothing I cant even lern my oan self all I can do is try not to get in front of whats coming. Jus try to keap out of the way of it.

RUSSELL HOBAN, *RIDDLEY WALKER*

4. Solitude: Becoming Priest

"A man would know the end he goes to, but he cannot know it if he does not turn, and return to his beginning, and hold that beginning in his being. If he would not be a stick whirled and whelmed in the stream, he must be the stream itself, all of it, from its spring to its sinking in the sea. . . . Now turn clear round, and seek the very source, and that which lies before the source. There lies your hope of strength."

URSULA LE GUIN, *THE WIZARD OF EARTHSEA*

Solitude is the womb from which we are born. Within our heart's solitude we find eucharistic confluence where God, community, and self suffuse one another with Love. It is a way of being in the world that coinheres with the transcendent God's willingness to be absolutely immanent within the creation. This being in the world in solitude gives shape to our existence. It is in solitude that we come to be for the sake of the community of creation. It is in solitude, Isaac the Syrian reminds us, that we become Eucharist.

When, however, we have found love, we eat the heavenly bread and we are sustained without labour and without weariness. *He that has found love eats Christ at all times* and becomes immortal from thence onwards. For whoever eats of this bread shall not taste death in eternity. Blessed is he that has eaten from the bread of love which is Jesus. Whoever is fed with love is fed with Christ, who is the all-governing God. . . . Love is the kingdom of which our Lord spoke when symbolically he promised the disciples that they would eat in his kingdom: You shall eat and drink at the table of my kingdom (Luke 22:30). What should they eat, if not love? . . . Blessed is he who has drunk from this wine. This is the wine from which the debauched have drunk and they became chaste, the sinners and they forgot the paths of stumbling, the drunk and they became fasters, the rich and they became desirous of poverty, the poor and they become rich in hope, the sick and they regained strength, the fools and they became wise [italics mine].[1]

When we fly from solitude, we fall away from being. We fly from solitude because we are afraid of our creatureliness and therefore of the creation. Readiness to respond to God both transcending and indwelling the creation is *apatheia;* its opposite is control, which stems from hatred of our creatureliness and in turn leads to abuse of the creation by attempting to dictate its response to us.

Our coinherence with the humility of Christ, our embrace of creatureliness arises only in solitude, and solitude is the human condition, no matter how crowded the world may seem. Solitude is not limited to wilderness hermits and in any event is a matter of the heart. The more crowded the world becomes, the more we are isolated, the more essential is solitude (the opposite of isolation) to survival and to the quality of life of the community.

The more obsessive society becomes about activity in order to feed its denial of mortality, especially under the guise of "leisure," the more necessary it is to redress the balance by growing into the solitude and stillness that give birth to action that does not destroy. The more darkly nuclear annihilation hangs over us, that ghastly fruit of our denial and fear of our creatureliness, the more urgent it becomes to be free of the denial of death and to understand the creative potential of human willing powerlessness where we meet the humility of Christ.

Many people spend their lives and their energy running from the pain and glory of solitude and silence from which energy is generated. We run from what is not tangible and controllable and self-reflective; we run from our self-forgetful selves found in God. Sometimes we dodge in another way: we grasp the pain of solitude and use it to decorate our egos to add to our heroic view of our selves. The evasions of solitude are as many as there are human beings.

When we will not turn and enter interior solitude, all our energy is preoccupied with controlling, inflating, and maintaining an illusory image for public and our own consumption. This image is the counterfeit of self-knowledge. When we fall from being in this way, we experience loneliness, fragmentation, and the despair that arises from seeking security in the closed system that helps us avoid suffering necessary to our maturation. When suffering comes, we are quick to turn it into a tool to make our selves feel good. We escape from suffering by creating a crisis so that we can function well in it. In this condition, we often will seek to help others in order to steal and feed on their suffering. We do this to assure ourselves that we are sharing their suffering and are compassionate, when in fact we are merely inflating our egos. In these ways and others we make counterfeits of intercession and the compassion that is eucharistic ungraspingness (2 Cor. 7:10 NEB).

By contrast, Isaac gives us the following picture of solitude-in-community. In the last line there is an interesting echo of the *Didache*:

Let this be for you a luminous sign of the serenity of your soul: when, as you examine yourself, you find yourself full of mercy for all humanity, and your heart is afflicted by pity for them, burning as though with fire, without making distinction of individuals,—when, by the continual presence of these things, the image of the Father in heaven becomes visible in you, then you can recognize the measure of your mode of life.[2]

It is right to allow God to turn suffering to our profit, but only *God* can effect this transformation; and God can effect this transformation only if we are willing to wait in the suffering, in darkness and unknowing. If *we* grasp suffering and turn it to our profit, it is mere technique and an escape from what must be incorporated in and through us if we are to come to be.

Without the balance of solitude, relationships become reciprocally devouring. Knowing how appropriately to leave others alone, that is, knowing how to have respect for others' needs both for physical aloneness and the inviolable vulnerability of the heart's meeting place with God, creates the matrix from which good relationships and creative unity-in-diversity arise. When we are terrified of what solitude will reveal, we are dispersed, enervated, exhausted by our frantic attempts at controlling ourselves, our environment, and others' behavior. We attempt artificially to recharge our flagging energies with drugs and distractions.

Acceptance of our aloneness is essential to our contact with reality. We are alone in time and in our birth and death; we are alone with our thoughts. When we are willing to embrace our aloneness, it becomes solitude, and it is only in solitude-in-community where we engage God, community, and self in a single movement of love. Only by embracing the fear of death can we, paradoxically, be freed from the fear of death. Only in solitude can we realize the experience that is common to humanity and creation. While we may be frightened at the prospect of the solitude that enables our true human existence, it is precisely our engagement of the vulnerability bestowed in solitude that frees us from our fear of our creatureliness and reveals it as our glory.

True experience and energy are available to us only when we work at being awake in the heart's solitude. When we use activity to flee, when we are busiest and therefore most truly slothful, we are seeking instead for artificial and illusory experience with which to decorate our selves, to hide from our selves the dispersion of our being. Without solitude at the heart of all we do, our very being becomes diffuse.

Our fear of appropriate suffering and our desire to isolate ourselves from solitude permeate all of Western culture, whether it is American desire for conformity and anesthetic activity expressed as individualism (the counterfeit of authenticity), or British addiction to and preoccupation with hypocrisy, gossip, and wondering what, in fact, was meant. Solitude is our religious question, and the techniques of flight are too often our secular answer.

In both countries we fly from solitude and deny our creatureliness by use of alcohol and drugs to create a surrogate
behind which to hide. One hallmark of addiction is the compulsion to attempt to control everything and everyone to keep
ego-inflation going. Whether or not every one of us drinks or
takes drugs, the thrust of our culture is addictive. Our collec-
tive political mind seems preoccupied with control and greed
and generates grandiose, shortsighted priorities that are implemented according to the criteria of expediency and superficial pleasure.

We are solitary no matter what our exterior living conditions;
we are solitary in a crowd. Only in solitude can our shattered
selves give up the illusions created in isolation and alienation,
illusions that make us feel omnipotently controlling and immortal, the very illusions we project onto God, who, contrary
to this illusion, is kenotic and immanent. Solitude is the matrix
out of which communion and community are born.

Some people find their true solitude through good learning
relationships, noncontrolling relationships, which give rise to
a maturing community, and some find true community through
exterior solitude. The need for the balance of solitude and
community is vital no matter what kind of community is in
question: a marriage, a housing estate, an urban parish, a
college community, a contemplative religious order. Because as
unique creatures we vary in the degree to which we are willing
to enter solitude, community is always full of tensions and
demands on different levels: demands of dependence and control; demands of people asking to be helped to grow out of
making demands and controlling in order to find their solitude
and their own true being.

At the heart of a maturing community are people who have
begun to find their balance in solitude, their equipoise of
conversion, of ready, eucharistic, ungrasping response, of
apatheia. By discovering what they must do to find and maintain this moving balance and repose, they have begun to find
true community; they have realized interdependence that is
focused beyond itself.

They have discovered eucharistic sacrifice that is the humility of Christ. Rarely will such people be the ostensible leaders of the community. Rather, in the stillness at the heart of solitude, where, in the Silence of God, they enter both the agony of the first moment of creation and the glory of its final transfiguration, they become its sacrifice and *therefore* its priests. They answer the religious question with the engagement of their being.

By contrast, people who seek leadership roles, even those who seem to have altruistic motives, do so more often than not out of a need to create a sense of self through their ability to manipulate others or the environment. They wish to grasp their gifts, and so they fall away from their potential greatness of being into the closed system of their own perception of these gifts. They are unwilling to go through suffering, and the more gifted these people are, the greater the danger for themselves and those around them. They are unwilling to surrender to and be changed in an unforeseeable and often imperceptible way by the suffering that is the weather of their lives[3] not realizing that it is only in this way that God may use their wounds to transform themselves and others and bring their gifts to fullest maturity.

Instead, they use their often profoundly inspiring gifts to convince themselves and others that they have given themselves over to the mystery of suffering when in fact they have wrested control and are trying to determine its outcome. It is almost a cliché that the greater the gifts given, the greater must be the willingness to let go of them, to allow God bring them to fruition in *God's* way, which may at times seem to involve their abandonment or destruction. But the gifts are not destroyed. Rather it is the inflationary perception of them and our using them to control others that is destroyed.

It cannot be too strongly emphasized that this maturing process cannot be entered by any person other than the one who has the gifts. It is the utmost presumption for one person to order another to abandon or destroy gifts, a practice that

Wounded   Healer

was once common in religious communities. The most another person can do is be a companion who encourages and cautions and most often is silent. It is particularly important for gifted people to go through ordinary, garden-variety suffering and humiliation *in appropriate circumstances,* such as waiting in line at the supermarket, driving within the speed limit, or steadying through the misery of learning fundamentals in a new discipline without pleading exception or dodging.

If gifted people are excused from the weather of ordinariness, they often become pharisaical; they begin to feel they are humans of a special and privileged order and that their gifts exempt them from petty suffering or the mundane gestures of compassion and courtesy and caring that are vital to everyday life. Without this discipline, they move toward elitism and control. The key word is appropriateness: it is sadistic to insist that in school gifted people must learn at the pace of the less gifted when what they need is greater challenge, stimulation, and undistracted time for reflection.

A desire for leadership is a desire for worldly, self-seeking power, no matter how admirable the predominating motives. The word "self-seeking" is ironic in that the would-be leader is not seeking the self, that is, being-in-God, at all, but rather an inflationary pseudo-self. Even our language helps the camouflaging process. A community composed of people in various stages of dependence and maturity (as most communities are) will enable such a leader's desire to manipulate and use the leader to do their own manipulating. This kind of "church" creates and feeds on co-dependence.

When we seek to use other people for achieving status, privilege, or other ends, we are self-reflective; we point toward, instead of away from illusion. When we seek leadership or membership in community as a distraction or as anesthesia, our self-aggrandizing manipulation disperses our energies. We draw on everyone else's reserves to keep the individual and group illusion propped up. In this way, we create ministry and community that are diabolical and idolatrous, spiraling inward, devouring everyone. The illusory security such a community and its leaders frantically seek ends in the very living death they are trying to avoid.

The human tendency to support illusion by devouring others is the weakest point in a democratic or any other political process, and those who engage in liberation theology need to be aware that there will always be those who seek power in this way, biding their time, waiting for a vacuum or perhaps even creating it, aided and abetted by the human tendency to leave responsibility to someone else. Any political ideology that does not see through human limitations and put checks on the lust for power will invariably end in tyranny. Revolutions seem almost always to end in tyrannies that offer less freedom than the regimes they have superceded.

Most of us in the West immediately think of Russia when we think of tyranny, and certainly a communist ideology that refuses to look beyond itself, its propaganda, and its limited human perspectives is doomed to the dead end of a closed system. *Glasnost* is perhaps a sign of Russia's awareness of the need to break out of its trap, which would offer a possibility of readjustment worldwide.

However, when we think of tyranny we must also look to the West. The United States is moving toward the same dead end. It has lost its vision of individual freedom *for the sake of* the common good and instead has grasped the secular Old Testament attitude imported by puritanism that says the rich are especially blessed by God. This is hardly a Christian notion, but in the United States today we have further twisted it into the idea that greed and expediency at the expense of everyone else is the only human goal worth pursuing. This goal operates on individual, national, and international levels. We seem to fall farther and farther from being, and we seem to have no sense of reality beyond our self-made self-image and the heedless pursuit of secular and worldly answers provided by technology. We are quite literally trying to buy being. The religious question has been secularized, anesthetized, forgotten, or ignored—except when technology fails.

Americans not only do not seem to know how to leave one another alone, we no longer seem to know how to relate to one another without having a self-aggrandizing motive, a "subtext" lurking in the background. Discussion no longer seems to be a means for airing views with an eye to enabling everyone to break into a larger perspective. Discussion, if it occurs at all, now seems to be conducted for the sole purpose of ensuring that everyone has the same opinion or to coerce or persuade those who differ. The United States is moving rapidly toward a new kind of tyranny, a dead end.

The move toward uniformity in the United States can be seen at every level of society. Anti-intellectualism, devotion to solipsism and the sloth that demands easy answers, is behind the collapse of its educational system; behind the ennui, which it attempts to relieve with bread-and-circuses technology; behind the low comedy of television evangelism and the power-mongering of Christian denominations so-called; and behind the lunacy of its foreign policy that is unable to allow other nations their self-determination, arms enemies for war, flaunts military might that frequently fumbles, and ultimately promotes xenophobia.

And at the core of all these problems is the cancer of nuclear weapons that maintains the illusion of absolute power. The United States is not only falling rapidly away from being; it is putting pressure on the rest of the world to fall away from being as well.

The current situation in the United States is a particularly clear example of the dangers attached to having a prodigality of riches, gifts, and *power*. To outsiders, on one level, it is a country with much to envy. For those who see more clearly, it is a nation that has lost its reality. Its sole preoccupation seems to be flight from the creatureliness that haunts its spectacular national celebrations of itself. It is haunted by the homeless on its streets, the tens of thousands of names on the black wall of the Vietnam memorial, its fiscal house of cards.

Worst of all, what other nations have often perceived as national virtues of openness and honesty are now being exploited for deceit and disinformation; its medical technology seems more interested in self-perpetuation as an industry than healing; its religious leaders lust for political power and preach a gospel of wealth, exclusion, and destruction; its democratic ideals are vaunted as an excuse to establish and support tyrannies abroad. And most blasphemous of all, its "Christian" leaders invoke the Holy One of Ungraspingness to give credence to their ruthless greed for money and political control. Christianity, the Christianity of the humility of Christ, is hardly to be found.

If those seeking leadership of any kind would also truly desire to find solitude, to enter its suffering and self-knowledge and its glory; if leaders were willing to live in the paradox and conflict of at once seeking being and falling away from it, of transformation and failure, then and only then would there be possibility for relationships to take the form of true ministry that creates a maturing community.

Seminaries try to make their students aware of the dangers of the human desire to control others, but these warnings often are contradicted by the kind of leadership skills the seminaries consciously or unconsciously teach and by their refusal to nurture commitment to spiritual maturity, which is *not* the same as "personal growth." In any event, seminarians' awareness of these dangers seem to fade after ordination. If seminaries are to discover their purpose of enabling the maturity of the churches instead of destroying it, their priorities will have to change. Maturity based on self-forgetfulness is not an option: it is our being.

Solitude; even more, stillness within that solitude: everything in our culture mitigates against it, from the first pre-requisite of the ability to stay in one room, to overcoming *horror vacui*, the terror of space or time that is not filled up and overflowing. But it is only in solitude that we discover the depths of our self-delusion, and this discovery alone already benefits the community of creation, and not our selves only. In solitude, if we are willing, we become aware of our motives that spring from unacknowledged wounds, and we are led to enter these wounds. Isaac the Syrian shows us the cosmic significance of this movement, which is our repentance:

Better is the person who has perceived his sins, than the person who profits the world by his appearance. Better is the person who has once sighed over himself, than the person who raises the dead by his prayer while dwelling among many. Better is the person who has been deemed worthy to behold himself, than the person who has been deemed worthy to behold angels; the latter partakes of the eyes of the body, the former the eye of the soul. Better is the person who has clung to Christ in mourning all by himself than the person who celebrates Him in a congregation.[4]

In solitude we learn to mirror God's self-restraint; in solitude our being is generated, gathered, concentrated even as it is spent, for it is in solitude that we meet God's *kenosis*, that we become willing to be emptied out, poured-out-through, self-forgetful. It is in solitude that we find Christ indwelling and the Name of the Father and our own name written on our hearts (2 Cor 3:3). It is in solitude that we find we can no longer look at or point to our selves, but only gaze on and through God as God gazes within and through us. Our being and our lives' actions no longer communicate control and imprisonment to the community of creation but open to others the freedom of the children of God. We have learned no longer to flee the pain inherent to life and transmutation but at the heart of pain to find God's new life, hope, possibility, joy, celebration. This is our priestly task.

Solitude contains within itself the universal level of all experience that unites the creation, bad and good, sinful and holy, sorrowing and joyous. Yet because each individual is a unique expression of the love of God, no two experiences are identical. The meeting of solitudes in communion, which may or may not involve physical encounter, and the meeting of solitudes in the physical gathering of the eucharistic community provides support and is enhanced by what is unique and fresh that has come to be in each solitude.

Physical meeting in community does not require full disclosure of solitude or concerns. Indeed, the deepest meetings of community and its greatest opportunities for healing rifts and forging bonds are in the silence of liturgy, liturgy composed in such a way that words emerge from silence; liturgy that focuses through and beyond itself and its celebrants; liturgy that focuses the community outward. Such liturgy becomes the silence of creatures' solitude confluent with the Silence of God out of which the Word, the First and Last, is spoken.

Liturgy is the gathering of priestly solitudes whose desire is to gaze on and meet only God outpoured, suffusing our being poured-out, so that, paradoxically, the distinction between love for "God" and "neighbor" becomes blurred and finally disappears, yet without confusing God and creatures. Christ's priestly indwelling pours this stream of Love through our being alone and in community. Each of our priestly solitudes in Eucharist embraces all of creation: its loneliness, its struggle, its despair, its fear of death, its encounters with hope and joy, with thanksgiving that burns with the Love of God. Priesthood is hidden and, like the God who indwells, self-effacing.

The Shamanic Background

In the early days of the world, everyone was a shaman. So say the legends of nomadic peoples scattered over the world. Everyone lived without clear distinction between seen and unseen, between individual and community, and everyone's life was open to the holy coursing through creation, engaged in the divine exchange. We are speaking here of the traditional shaman who is the sacrificial heart of community, not the individualistic narcissistic neoshaman of the contemporary religious supermarket.

But as time passed, people became distracted. They began to seek security in the material world, and soon they designated particular members of the tribe to be shamans for them. Even today, these designated individuals go through an initiation designed to develop keen awareness of the unseen and training in the self-restraint demanded of all who would encounter the holy. Frequently the shaman tradition expresses androgony in dress and behavior. Shamans were—and still sometimes are—individuals who undertake the perilous contact with the holy to be bearers of blessing and healing or, when they attempt to grasp the holy and use it for their own ends, cursing and sickness.

Shamans have too often been associated in our minds with the magic that is control. While some shamans do perform what we would regard as magic, a close reading and deeper penetration of ancient rituals often suggest something quite different, something that is highly consonant with the kenotic tradition in Christianity. In realizing the shamanic vocation, the shaman commonly goes through a transformational experience of death, dismemberment, and rebirth. It is through this experience that the shaman is freed from the fear of death in all its forms and comes to self-knowledge, deliberate engagement with the universal level of communal experience, and conscious engagement with the interpenetration and infusion of the holy throughout creation.

A shaman's specific questing for the holy often receives help from relationship to a spirit-guide—an animal or natural object. The spirit-guide instructs the shaman in the particular aspect of the holy in which the individual is adept for the sake of the community and at critical moments provides counsel. The relationship of shaman to spirit-guide and creation is *not* always what has often wrongly been perceived in the West as pantheism, but much more closely resembles the Judeo-Christian notion of God's immanence often referred to as pan*en*theism. To put this distinction simply, people from the Western European tradition have a tendency to label any unfamiliar notion of the holy indwelling the natural world as "pantheism."

The distinctions between animism, pantheism, and pan-entheism all come out of the Greek philosphical inheritance filtered through Western European civilization. Once we have had the humility to experience a non-Christian, non-Western tradition from the inside, these distinctions often seem inaccurate, inappropriate, and patronizing. In panentheism the energy of the deity is neither confined to nor exhausted by that with which it coinheres. Bishop Kallistos Ware beautifully describes panentheism in *The Orthodox Way*.

As creator, then, God is always at the heart of each thing, maintaining it in being. On the level of scientific inquiry, we discern certain processes or sequences of cause and effect. On the level of spiritual vision, which does not contradict science but looks beyond it, we discern everywhere the creative energies of God, upholding all that is, forming the innermost essence of all things. But, while present everywhere in the world, God is not to be identified with the world. As Christians we affirm not pantheism but "panentheism." God is *in* all things yet also *beyond and above* all things. He is both "greater than the great" and "smaller than the small" . . . "everywhere and nowhere, he is everything and nothing." . . . "God is at the core. God is other than the core. God is within the core, and all through the core, and beyond the core, closer to the core than the core.[5]

No shaman is expected to know and to practice the entire body of ceremonial knowledge. In Navajo culture, a medicine man may be able to retain only two or three chants and ceremonials. If there are not enough initiates, some of the chants are lost. The shaman is engaged with the holy not for solipsism, but on behalf of every member; all members are latent shamans whose power needs only to be awakened. The shaman is engaged with the community at so deep a level that the community is contained in the shaman's being (in Western tradition this community-in-solitude is described by St. Peter Damian in *The Book of the Lord Be with You*; he describes each solitude as an *ecclesia*[6]). As evidence of this latent power, each person's coming-of-age involves an initiation, often some sort of vision quest that mirrors in a short time span the shaman's necessarily longer education.

While the foregoing is a truncated, idealized, and eclectic account of the way of the shaman, there are also many stories of shamans who have in some way betrayed their trust by grasping power for their own ends or who, refusing the advice of their spirit-guides, lose their transparent vision and revert to a nonspecialist life in the community. Some form of the shaman commitment exists in most world religions: it is not unlike the deepest understanding of the Christian commitment of baptism, Eucharist, and ministry (especially intercession).

Today there are still peoples who are not hierarchically oriented; they still retain a mythopoetic sense that "all are shamans." In *The Mountain of Names*, Alex Shoumatoff suggests that the development of hierarchies and elitest systems is relatively recent.[7] Other authors conjecture that they arise with the development of agriculture. Whatever the answer, there are places today in which the tradition of religious egalitarianism still survives, and even allowing for cultural differences they offer us hope. At the same time, we must remember that egalitarian does not mean individualistic, and that we Americans are isolated from the rest of the world in our insistence that egalitarian means "do your own thing" (although it is ironic that in our approach to foreign policy we seem to feel only the United States has the right to do its own thing at the expense of others' autonomy).

Kenosis and Worldly Power

The Judeo-Christian heritage echos the primitive "before time" vision of each person's responsibility for direct engagement with God. In the New Testament, personal responsibility before God becomes unequivocal.

While for many contemporary Christians personal responsibility before God in itself is not a conceptual problem, when it comes to its practical living out in churches, it seems to find little expression. An alien little voice seems to whisper that the minister is somehow closer to God or has privileged access

Priesthood of all believes

to God. The congregation and its leaders acquiesce and fall into the confusion that is the false synthesis of two models of power, the open system of direct responsibility and engagement with God, on the one hand, and the co-dependent, self-contradictory hierarchical system, on the other. In this situation, people do not seem to mind how flawed or mistaken are the assumptions on which they are operating. And because the congregation's idea of itself excludes solitude, it is rarely possible for it to discover its fundamental errors.

Without a sense of reverence for the equality of the true priesthood given to each creature, the best-intended ministry becomes a way of control and self-aggrandizement and creates a situation that makes people aware of their status or lack of it (Mt 18). We frequently see this mystique at work in parishes; in a disagreement, the pastor's opinion is sought as the correct one, as if being ordained bestowed God's perspective on every matter.

We see this behavior with particular clarity in groups of women who have been subjected to a patriarchal society or a church that has devalued the priesthood of their being and forced them to find their authenticity outside of themselves. As a result they spend their energy trying to enlarge the tiny scrap of earth on which they feel they teeter by devaluing those around them. Only by devaluing others do they feel they can have a sense of self-worth, however false. Most of us have seen this syndrome at work in women *and* men or taken part in the process ourselves, whether or not we were aware of what was going on. A member of a group will share a profound insight, which is ignored, discounted, or mocked by the members. But the same remark coming from an ordained person takes on scriptural weight.

A monk tells the story of another of his community returning from an assignment as chaplain to some nuns. "Lots of little notes, Father?" he asked.

His discouraged companion sighed, "I'm afraid so; they seem to find even my sneezes inspiring."

This is hardly the atmosphere in which a community of any sort can come to the maturity of ungraspingness. In such a system what passes for religious adoration is not awestruck wonder aroused by eucharistic engagement with a self-emptying God but rather the worship of an idol of control that points toward itself and desires to be pleased. When clergy and congregations engage in the idolatry of control, it is often excused by the notion that those who exercise ministerial functions through ordination or vows are in some way living out a vocation that is closer to God than the life of the poor little nonordained person in the pew. Therefore, many nonordained people reason, why make the effort to engage God ourselves when we can hide behind such people or get them to pray in our stead?

Thus do the tendency to power and the tendency to evade responsibility converge; both are flight from humanity discovered in solitude, and both contribute to our descent into the fragmentation of falling from being. When we create a clerical mystique of deliverance, we camouflage the ontological trap that lies before us. When we encourage this mystique, it provides us with entertainment; we enjoy the *frisson* it engenders, little realizing that we will later find ourselves in the very trap we have helped to conceal. Romans (8:15) is specific in telling us not to return to the slavery of fear in the interest of shoring up our sense of omnipotence, that is, becoming once again subject to a magical system of illusory control of "sin and death." Such a closed system *is* pagan.

In a recent essay in *The Christian Century*, Don Coville Skinner exposes one reason it is so difficult to help congregations break out of an infantile mentality. He writes of Rosa Parks, who, thirty-two years ago, tired from a long day's work, tired of the tyranny that negated her humanity, refused to move to the back of a Montgomery, Alabama, bus. She was arrested, but by her simple act she ignited the civil rights movement. Recently she was given an award by Allegheny College.

The Allegheny College students' attitude appalled Skinner.

They were unable to comprehend the significance of who she was or what she did. After an initially electric welcome, they became bored and wandered away because she failed to dazzle them.

For those who remained in the chapel that evening, there was at least the possibility of seeing beyond hype and illusion to the redemptive potential of common things. Those who walked out may never understand. Awash in a sea of images at once artificial but marvelously entertaining, they have no tolerance for that which does not shock or distract or amuse.

It is difficult to be hopeful about our future . . . until we learn to appreciate a historical fact: the power of social change and the glue of social cohesion reside in the conviction of common people, not in the influence or rhetoric of charismatic leaders or cosmetic heroines. Leadership is vital, and I do not underrate it. As sunlight through a magnifying glass sets the grass ablaze, so leaders focus and direct the energies of a community. But the people are the sunlight, wherein resides the energy. . . .

History knows no more awesome power, nor tryanny a more fearsome opponent, than ordinary acts of courage. In her stubborn refusal to be the victim of a degraded and degrading system, she provided an example for others, and the combination of these people's energies ignited the conscience of the nation, engulfing the institution of segregation.[8]

It is no wonder that Christianity seems to flounder in an age whose despair is covered over with hype. In an earlier age, the matrix of annihilation and despair were the very conditions under which Christianity flourished, nourished by the blood of its martyrs. The difference today is that we seem to have lost any sense of the life-enhancing sacrifice that is at the heart of Christianity, Christ's sacrifice within our lives that creates our being. Many Christian communities gather not for worship that expresses the awe of solitude-in-community, the nurture of solitude in each member, and therefore the bonding of the community's being-in-God. Rather they come together for entertainment mounted by those who have become unwitting sycophants of an idol.

At such services silence and mystery are nervously kept at bay, and there is no space for reflection. A congregation that insists on the noise of entertainment to make its members feel good about themselves and to distract them from the reality of their solitude is trapped in the very illusory and power-oriented thinking from which the gospels (ironically read week after week) offer salvation. Does anyone ever really *listen?*

The Confrontation with God

It is a terrible thing to fall into the hands of the living God.

While we can be glib about "personal responsibility before God," it is quite something else to commit our selves to have the totality of our being focused in confluence with God's outpouring love. The dark light is searing; nothing is hidden from God, and sometimes God seems to show us more about our selves and more about God's love and therefore more about the hypocrisy of our communities and the blasphemy of our worship than we think we can bear. And we cannot bear it, unless we are willing to be emptied of our idolatry so that God's indwelling may transform us.

It is through the fiery compassion of our priesthood discovered in solitude that we communicate God's salvific love to the world no matter what the cost. It means a commitment to bear the evil and pain that are invariably attracted by such a commitment; it means to be willing to acknowledge that we are as united to one another by the evil we do as we are by the resurrection from death God offers to us.

We forget that the only sin of which we have to repent is looking away from God's Gaze, for this Gaze *is* our equipoise of conversion. In that illumination we cannot but realize that all of us sin all the time. Only Jesus the Christ was able to gaze with the totality of being, for Jesus was God gazing at God out of our humanity. It is in us that the Christ gazes at the Father through the eyes of our heart as we receive the power of Holy Ghost who, as we become willing, empties us of illusion and pseudo-being and gives us back our true being.

The extent to which we are willing to allow this humble Gaze upon Gaze from within our selves is to the extent to which we are priests.

A life committed to mirroring God's self-denudation is entirely incompatible with the exercise of secular-become-worldly power, the kind of power too often wielded in the churches' dealings with the world and, sad to say, our dealings with one another. Thus it is doubly absurd to say that those who undertake such functions are priests by reason of their ordination and no other and to attempt to justify this contradiction by claiming that the ordained have somehow undergone an invisible ontological change effected by human agency that authorizes them to wield their un-Christlike, often anti-Christlike power. For any church to insist that we must support the conceit that the ordained alone have the fullness of Christ's transforming humility and that their worldly domination is in fact a mirror of the self-emptying God is perhaps the ultimate blasphemy.

A life that mirrors God will use secular, that is, minimal organizing power with enormous discernment and self-restraint. However, clergy, like the rest of us, suffer fragmentation from being, and sometimes precisely because of the added burden of the illusory ontological elitism that attaches to ordination, they are more divided than the rest of us. They struggle with the temptations of secular power eliding into worldly power, which is an extension of a competitive instinct that is the counterfeit of competition for survival. And at the same time they struggle to mirror the self-emptying God. To try to combine the two kinds of power in one person is unfair, unfair most of all to the clergy.

Solitude, Transformation, and Sacrifice

The priestly commitment to meeting God in our humanity, to being part of the divine Gaze within God's life that releases God's life in creation, is joy born of inconceivable pain—

inconceivable because it is unlike what we normally think of as pain—and endurable only because it is part of the gift of transfiguration. The pain is forgotten in the joy, which directs our attention away from our selves; but the pain is there nonetheless, and it is there in part because sometimes only pain can penetrate our awareness. The life, death, and resurrection of Jesus the Christ shows us what life willingly lived in the humility of God is like.

As is natural and healthy, we all seek to avoid pain, pain that tells us our fingers are too near the fire; pain that tells us to take care, that it hurts to fall from a step; pain that tells us we are ill, that our appendix needs removing. Our minds, too, respond to pain and have protective mechanisms that keep us from exposing our selves to too much reality all at once. Shock and numbness help us through terrifying experiences and personal sorrow and gradually wear off as, little by little, we are able to absorb what has happened to us.

Living in the Gaze of God rejects none of these healthy mechanisms; only our grasping puts us in jeopardy. It is when we want to take on the heavy burden of control of the situation, to deny the willing readiness of solitude that admits pain and joy as we are ready to receive them and is at the heart of life in God that we create suffering for our selves and everyone else, suffering that is more difficult to bear than what we would have experienced in solitude. It is when we fall into denial, when we insist on deciding for our selves how much of God we can receive or how much pain we will refuse to bear, that we fall away from the fragile equipoise that constitutes true solitude and therefore true community and find our selves in isolation. Or, in reverse, it is when we decide that the body inhibits our life in God and that its willful abuse can force the relationship that we counterfeit self-emptying and the equipoise of response to which God brings us when we become willing for whatever and let go our lust for dominance.

We interact with the pain and joy of life in God by means of symbols. They help us to communicate among our solitudes and within our solitudes, within our consciousness and what lies beyond consciousness in our "unconscious," in preconceptual and superconceptual engagement, and in the heart (all of which are different one from another). Symbols become crucial in the work of salvation because they have the potential to spring us from the traps we have made for ourselves by our secular techniques. Symbols can illumine solitude and draw us toward the density of glory where all creaturely experience coalesces.

However, symbols equally can trap us and make solitude inaccessible. The magic with which we support our self-images is as black as any sorcerer ever practiced and wreaks havoc on those who live around us. Symbols in the service of making our selves feel safe can thus be instrumental in narrowing us and trapping us in the real hell of isolation. Or, if symbols are manipulatively employed in the service of our lust for "religious experience," they can summon horrors that overwhelm us. Hell is not other people but rather choosing to allow in our existence only the illusory self-image and experience we substitute for our selves, others, and our engagement with God in order to avoid embracing our own darkness.

The choice of salvation or hell depends on the kind of power we seek, and the power we seek determines the symbols we employ. If we use symbols in the service of salvation, of embracing our darkness so that God can bring forth light from it, of springing from traps, of opening-out, of bringing us to the security of faith alone amid the insecurities and contingencies of responsive creaturely life in God; if we use symbols to point beyond themselves to the outpouring of Love within the creation, then we use them in a kenotic way.

If, on the other hand, we use symbols to shore up shaky defenses, to imbue a sense of security-by-control, to assure our selves that the Zeus-god is absolutely manipulating everything, and thus to assure us of our own self-importance; if we use symbols as part of the worship of hierarchical and therefore dualistic power; if we surround our selves with ritual as an end in itself, then symbols are diabolical and entrapping, not saving. The popular contemporary slogan "God is in *control!*" can be taken two ways. It can mean we are superimposing the Zeus-god, the projection of our lust for control, onto God; or it can mean that we are in fact willing to let go control so that our self-emptying meets God's to create new possibility out of seeming hopelessness.

We see humanity continually wavering between these two uses of symbols throughout history. While ritual sacrifice can be a way of expressing interior sacrifice, or *kenosis*, it is more often true, as the prophets and Paul note, that ritual sacrifice becomes a surrogate for interior sacrifice and is therefore impotent. Sacrifice becomes a means of distraction from and avoidance of the pain-in-joy of the heart's sacrifice. When ritual sacrifice becomes externalized, it puts at arm's length the pain of encounter with God. The painful struggle of the sacrificial animal becomes a way of distancing our selves, of denying the solitude, pain, and struggle—and the joy—proper to transformation in God. Our "lower nature" (Rom 8:3) reverts to a primitive pain-avoidance reflex and fear blocks from our hearts the divine vision inherent in our createdness.

Being aware of subjective reflexes does not mean that we ignore our own survival. As we shall see, self-care is the first order of entering our solitude, a movement sometimes called asceticism. God does not give us the creation to abuse. What we must transcend is false competition, the survival instinct we interpret in techniques of ambition, control, and self-inflation, the illusions we can maintain only at the expense of others' survival and growth, which the New Testament collectively calls "the world." Isaac the Syrian sums up the vicious cycles of "the world" succinctly:

These are: love of riches; the gathering of possessions; fattening up the body, giving rise to the tendency toward carnal desire; love of honour, which is the source of envy; the exercise of position of power;

pride and the trappings of authority; outward elegance; glory among men, which is the cause of resentment; fear for the body.[9]

Worldly, that is, self-aggrandizing, ideas of survival are often shortsighted and self-defeating both for the individual and the community. To maintain illusion requires enormous dispersion of energy, and the effort going into short-term survival may make long-term survival impossible because the controller has exhausted all available spiritual, if not material, resources. We have only to look at the warning signals our fragile planet is giving us in response to our heedless exploitation to verify this notion.

When we control and objectify sacrifice by creating a sacred class, we no longer find ever-new possibilities for co-creation in the circumstances of life. Rather, circumstance becomes evidence of the greed or hatred of a god now perceived as the great Controller looking down on the ragtag people; disaster is strictly a matter of cause and effect: improper sacrifice has been made, the magic has failed.

What we *should* be enabled to hear at the words of institution over the elements on the altar are not only resonances of the life, death, and sacrifice of Christ echoing eternity through time, but simultaneously an inclusive reference to *my* Body, yours and my flesh and bone, Reader, and *my* Blood, yours and my life, Reader, because that is in fact what we mean by our souls and bodies being a *living* sacrifice holy and acceptable to God (Rom 12:1). Our lives coinhere with Christ's indwelling sacrifice, and the liturgy reaffirms our lives' commitment to be that sacrifice.

The concept of a sacred class leads to the mistaken notion that the gift of engagement with God in the solitude of the heart cannot be as "special" or as "holy" or as "true" or as "close" in those outside the sacred class as it is in one set aside to wield power over the sacrificial victim's life and death (and by conscious or subliminal extrapolation, over other human beings as well). Thus, vamping by the clergy on the theme of clerical control over forgiveness—and therefore life and death—introduces worldly power to the picture; awe becomes fear, and worship becomes magic.

Under these conditions we try to fix our selves up so the magic will work. The Greek inheritance stresses the perfectability of humans by human effort—a perfection that ultimately denies creation—whereas in the Judeo-Christian inheritance God transforms and transfigures the creation *as it is* into its maturity, its being-in-God, revealing the divine life that is immanent within and sustaining it at every moment. There is the further problem in Greek philosophy that the beautiful must not be violated by what is considered mundane or ugly. This notion is a direct contradiction of the humility of Christ, Beauty who for love of the creation became marred and broken.

The idea of a god who is untouchable and detached beauty leads to the debasing and dehumanizing of our creatureliness, of the poor, the sick, the sinner, the ugly, the outcast, the disgusting, the useless, whom in Christ we see not only external to our selves but also as parts of our selves. It is pressure from the Greek inheritance in Western Christianity that makes us feel we need to deny our wounds and our creatureliness, that we need to fix up our selves or others to be acceptable to God. This cosmetic process is a counterfeit quite different from transformation by grace, and to coerce the many into the abstract aesthetic categories of the few is an insidious form of psycho-spiritual rape. Contemporary Christianity condemns brainwashing in other cults and yet seems to condone and even encourage it within itself.

The word "rape" is not out of place here, for physical rape is not an expression of sexuality but of control that is sexually expressed. Control is not always sexually expressed, and it is arguable that the most insidious and destructive forms of rape are those that have no physical expression.

Discernment and Direction

It is certainly true that we need people with particular gifts and training to help focus our selves and the community on the Gaze of God, to help us recognize pastoral gifts, to enable discernment and transformation. And it is also true that we need people to help us distinguish the subtle ways in which we exercise the tendency toward self-deception that leads us to try to grasp our heart's engagement with God, which we can in fact glimpse conceptually only in tiny amounts.

But while we need some kind of check on our potential to wield self-seeking power in the name of God, it is certainly *not* true that those who help us in these movements toward the equipoise of conversion have privileged access to God, or that only those visibly set aside and ordained are able or have the authority to authenticate our relationship with God, or that authentication must be external to our selves. No one has that authority.

This is one reason the term "spiritual *director*" is so destructive and misleading, because it encourages abrogation of responsibility on the part of the person seeking help with discernment and encourages not only a dependent relationship, but also spiritual infantilism. We need to find another term, especially as discernment relationships have become so fashionable. People new to spiritual relationships are often ignorant of even the basic patterns of spirituality and often expect a spiritual *director* to give them a formula for experience, a technique for holiness that is internalized from the outside. Equally, the discerner bears the burden of terminology that reflects the Zeus-god and violates the individual's gaze on God. Such a co-dependent relationship destroys any possibility of spiritual maturity.

One of the most poignant and destructive examples of the confusion of the two models of power in discernment relationships is found in arguments over contemplation. Some of the most popular writers throughout Christian history have been victim of the Zeus-god in one form or another and have insisted that "pure contemplation" is not only limited to an elite but also requires special living conditions, such as being bricked up in dank, spider-infested caves, or in overheated, middle-class, politics-ridden monasteries. This view of still-prayer is a perfect example of the creation of mystique and is consummate romantic rubbish. In addition, the person who makes such distinctions not only presumes to have God's point of view by attempting to evaluate prayer, but implicit in such a claim is an attitude of superiority, self-reflection, and spiritual masturbation.

Unfortunately, generations of Christians who have truly engaged and found their being in God have been brainwashed to feel that, if they do not have the luxury of living under special conditions, their prayer and engagement is always second-class and they have not offered the whole gift. Nothing could be further from the truth. To insist that the "right kind" of living conditions are a prerequisite for contemplation renders prayer mere secular technique. Further, the setting up of such criteria implies a static and mechanistic uniformity of human nature that is in contradiction to the way we are in fact created—each of us is unique. Grace builds on nature, and God does not create the nature that finds fulfillment in a monastery holier or of greater value than the nature of a working mother.

To live in today's world and within it offer the solitary witness of staying unentangled, uncompromised by its power-struggles, unviolated by its attempts to corrupt is what will, in fact, change the world. The resonances of *kenosis*, the power of transformation, are just as potent when radiating from those in the marketplace who rise in the night and pray in the dark, as from those who have made some sort of formal profession who rise in the night and pray in the dark. It is simply a matter of becoming willing.

This brings us to an even more important aspect of solitude, one that is the prerequisite for disengagement from the world on any level (not from the community of creation) and that is what Pascal hints at when he remarks that all our unhappiness arises from our inability to be alone in a room. In his hilarious study of American (and now, ironically, British and European) culture, *Travels in Hyperreality,* Umberto Eco puts his finger on the disease at the heart of the Western world, which is *horror vacui,* the terror of space or time that is not filled up and overflowing, whether it is our plate at the restaurant, the clothes cupboard, the two-car garage, the image in the mirror, or, most terrifying of all, interior solitude.[10]

The incarnate, creaturely *fact* is that within our hearts we gaze on God *all the time,* and this is true no matter who we are or what our state of life: married, single, monastic, drunk, lunatic, fool, rich, poor, sick, well, prisoner, prostitute. Under *any* living conditions we can seek our being by turning to and becoming willing to focus on and be focused by the Gaze of God. For each person the ideal conditions for this seeking differ. If they are doing their job, discernment relationships can help us find out the ideal conditions for each of us to seek this Gaze. The *only* condition required for "pure contemplation" is a heart broken by the resonances of Mercy.

Ideally, discernment relationships test experience, help us keep from being trapped by our own illusions, educate us to be able more and more to make discernment on our own. A discernment relationship does not teach us someone else's method of discernment. Rather, it enables us to perceive what is authentic in each unique engagement with God and to be able to risk being in the world from the ground of this authenticity. This frees us from measuring our selves by the standards of worldly power—or of those who claim to have spiritual power.

To learn discernment is part of freedom from the fear of death, and most of the work is done not in the discernment session, but in solitude. Solitude is the matrix of our humility because it is an encounter with the humility of God. It is the unflinching and immediate face to Face engagement that we can seek *only* in the heart's solitude.

When we hear people confirming an action or decision by saying "my director says . . . " it is a sure sign that the discernment relationship is being abused by one or both of the parties involved. Either there is a co-dependent *de haut en bas* power relationship or the discernee is using the relationship to abrogate responsibility, to hide from solitude and transformation. Such an attitude on the part of the discernee assumes god-like knowledge on the part of the discerner. No one can know the experience of another; there is common ground in the experience of the holy, to be sure, and there are common failings, but in the end, the solitude, the discernment, the decision, the action is the responsibility of each of us.

A discernment relationship, like sacrifice, can become an externalization and dispersion of the sacrifice of the heart, so that the heart is no longer impressed by Mercy. Instead we become sidetracked and dazzled by the experiences and concepts and processes of transformation we discover, so that interior solitude is no longer painful and joyous waiting on God in the dark, but rather a film in which we are the star from which we can clip stills to show to our spiritual companions. Sometimes we even start having experiences to have something interesting to talk or write about, in the same way that we may "dream to order" in a therapeutic relationship.

The second and third chapters of Isaiah cry out against this bowing down to the work of our hands (or stony hearts) and the guides who lead us astray. While, on the one hand, we have the danger of authoritarianism that attaches to the term "spiritual *direction*," on the other, we also have the contemporary problem of *laissez faire*. Today, those who communicate the elements of interior exploration place emphasis on ego-enhancing experience: sensing, feeling, listening, resonating, encouraging, affirming. This is all very well and good for those who need healing from self-negation. The problem is that some schools of discernment so emphasize feeling and the person's own perception of feeling that discernment boils down to "if it feels good, do it."

If this is all that discernment relationships amount to, then they are little better than affirming one another's consumption preferences. While none of us in our right minds would return to the pre–Vatican II bad old days, at the same time there is something to be said for the Nathan-element, for the prophetic voice willing to risk the displeasure (and even the relationship itself) to humbly point out to someone who is living in self-deception that there is danger in the way. As Robert McAllister writes, "Everyone at some time needs the strength of a friend who says, 'Please don't do that. It is not good for you. It is not right for you.' If instead the friend says, 'Let's talk about it over the weeks to come but in the meantime I won't give you an opinion and you do what seems right for you,' perhaps that friend gives the cold stone of counseling to one who needs the warm bread of concern."[11]

In discernment relationships there needs to be an element of challenge, of vision that provides the aspiration necessary to motivation and focus. As the person grows, the vision necessarily becomes less idolatrous and more profound. As transformation takes place on ever-deeper levels, there will be fewer demands for "answers," because the religious question is being answered by self-forgetful engagement.

This is not to say that experience is not important; it is important to feed the "out of sight" processes with all appropriate intellectual, liturgical, and relational richness and to embrace, as we are able, what irrupts from the depths. But the time comes, quickly for some, more slowly for others, when what was once appropriate experience, discussion, even liturgy all turn to dust and ashes, when all these once-profitable activities become something of distraction, when one's "spiritual life" dies. When this happens, the deepest journey begins, and if we have not had the conditioning of making hard choices and undertaking hard tasks to prepare us, if we have not the commitment or aspiration, we will quit: the journey will end before it truly begins. McAllister concurs:

Mature individuals possess a sense of personal worth independent of the successes or failures of daily living. . . . The mature layperson and the mature religious use their emotional conflicts as motivation for change, not guilt, as a source of self-appraisal, not self-doubt, as a measure of the distance still to go, not a signal to avoid the journey. . . .

They seek to improve their relationships with others but recognize that all their communication skills cannot prepare them for their face-to-face meeting with God. They grow in their appreciation of community liturgies, but they do not lose their attachment to silent prayer, which foreshadows the loneliness, the quiet, the abandonment of death. They know that, no matter how much they discuss their problems or with whom, the resolution of emotional conflict comes as a private achievement, not a public victory.[12]

This means that very early on in a discerning relationship the discerner-midwife must help the discernee to learn to distinguish processes of self-deception, the way an ascetical exercise becomes an ego trip or an act of charity a prop for inflating self-image, or how emotional self-indulgence has become part of the discerning relationship. The discerner must help the discernee discover when it is better to endure a seemingly destructive relationship, not only because there are elements that the discernee may be missing, but also because it is a hard saying that it is only in difficulty and suffering that the deepest relationships are born and the deepest transformation takes place. The shortsighted "therapeutic" nature[13] of much spiritual midwifery tends to cultivate self-indulgence by being too quick to establish the norm "if it feels bad, get out" or to recommend avoidance of all conflict—and therefore its resolution—by "you don't need that."

Of course this is not a recommendation to stay in destructive relationships or to have emotional conflicts on principle. Rather it is to question whether we have listened and endured enough in situations we have labeled destructive or at an impasse, whether, beyond our inclination to get out of the mess, we have waited on the insight that comes only from deep listening in pain in the dark, the insight, clarity, and new perspectives that may begin transfiguration for all involved. To wait in the dark is a process that means suffering, but it is vital. If we "get out" every time we have a conflict or a seeming failure, we will never be able to receive or enable the gifts of reconciliation, of fortitude, of endurance, of courage, of commitment to Christ's humility that will enable us to risk our lives for what we believe. We will never develop courage to risk the faith whose fruits may not appear until long after our own sacrifice is complete.

It is important here to make a distinction between aspirations and expectations. An aspiration is not a norm of behavior but a religious question of coming into our true being. Aspiration is not an idea into which we are trying to force ourselves. It may happen that we discern at some point that we have been fooled by self-deception and that we have had the wrong aspiration, which needs must change. An aspiration is rather an ideal to fling our hearts at, a goal that changes before us even as we wonder if we will ever reach it and are willing to die in the attempt. Aspiration is the direction and thrust of our being in solitude in the world. Therefore, our expectation is not grandiose but is tempered by humility.

If we have grandiose expectations, we have opted for the Zeus-god, we have chosen to internalize an external and illusory self-image that we have initially projected—for the potential to grasp controlling power and its technology of blame lives in each of us. The constraint we impose on our selves by grandiosity focuses our attention on the self-image that dissatisfies; aspiration, on the other hand, elicits self-forgetfulness; constraint is the crushing burden of the law; aspiration is Elijah's whirlwind. This falling away from our solitude that results from grandiosity, this displacement of our creatureliness by projection of an image, this mistaking of technology for the divine engagement only reinforces our fear of death and therefore our hatred of creation.

This is the Fall.

In falling away from solitude and being we lose the ground of our beseeching and, having lost this ground, we seek an artificial and external place on which to stand. But this synthetic ground is illusory, and to make the illusion seem secure we lock ourselves into a closed system of technique and appearance.

Our struggle to maintain this system results in envy, illusion, and their bitter, empty fruits. There can be no envy in self-forgetfulness; if we seek the Gaze of God in still-prayer, we cannot but seek it in one another. If we seek the Gaze of God, we are enabling God to empty us of seeking for our illusory selves. Our real selves are thus increasingly exposed, and with barriers of illusion down, we cannot help but penetrate beneath illusion in others. If others are seeking that Gaze, our relationships can be a fiery mingling of pain and joy, for they too will see beneath what remains of our illusions. If we are not mutually seeking that Gaze, then exposed truth may cause an explosive and destructive reaction, but destructive only in the short term if it drives us deeper into our seeking.

All of this discussion of discernment, distancing, elitism, and envy applies to all of life but most of all to life in the churches. If we could see clearly how we use the sacramental life of God to avoid God, our shame would render our careful posturings unnecessary. Fortunately there are many people who are true priests (ordained or not) who *do* see clearly, and by their tears and their living-out of God's self-emptying they keep the faith of the humility Christ alive, transcending hierarchical political power-struggles.

To be politically effective we must be politically uncompromised. As Arthur Hertzberg has written of Brian Urquhart's forty years in the United Nations,

In one political crisis after another, successes happen when people act with decency and disinterest; the failures have most often been brought about by the narrow-minded "realists." . . . After forty years at the United Nations, he is more persuaded than he was at the beginning of his career that virtue is its own reward; even for the selfish, it is a far more effective political principle than self-interest. . . . [but] He was to live with the knowledge that human vanity and ambition would always be stronger than wisdom and principle.[14]

In Urquhart's own words,

Reason, justice, and compassion are small cards to play in the world of politics, whether international, national, or tribal, but someone has to go on playing them. If you hold on to your belief in reason and compassion despite all political maneuvering, your efforts may in the end produce results. A determined effort to do what seems objectively right may sometimes eventually transcend the vicissitudes of politics. . . . I also learned that *immediate success often has very little to do with lasting achievement, and that the judgment of history on many controversial issues will be very different from the fashionable judgment of the time.* [italics mine][15]

In seeking solitude, we return to the humility of openness within which we can hear the resonance of *God's* beseeching in our own heart. This is our true union with God, in which we are found and find our being (Ps 42). Our task is not complete; we are only beginning afresh, freer, in a universe that has suddenly become enormous. In the union of beseeching is the Word; in the resonance of beseeching the new creation is brought into being. Our steadfastness before the awesome Face of God intensifies our engagement; our awareness of being changed fades into the background as transfiguration continues unnoticed out of our sight. Under this Gaze and by this Word of beseeching, the mists of our illusory self-image dissolve.

Priesthood and community are constituted within the solitude of each created being. Priesthood costs no less than life itself in the direct and willing readiness of engagement in which God's eucharistic ungraspingness is received, focused, and outpoured. No human rite can make or unmake this priesthood. No one but Christ can mediate for us, and Christ's mediation is not *between* us and the Father but *within* us looking on the Father, writing the Name I WILL BE on our hearts in our solitude from which community is born. Each of us has the task of mediating in community the Love that bridges the abyss of our falling from being.

5. *Kenosis:* Becoming Sacrifice

Haven, harbor, peace, safety, all that was behind. They had turned away.
They went now a way in which all events were perilous, and no acts were
meaningless. On the course on which they were embarked, the saying of
the least spell might change chance and move the balance of power and
of doom: for they went now toward the very center of that balance, toward
the place where light and darkness meet. Those who travel thus say no
word carelessly.

URSULA LE GUIN, *THE FARTHEST SHORE*

We respond to the humility of Christ by allowing it to transform and change and indwell us. Becoming willing to be
changed by this humility is a process of *kenosis*, of emptying
out, of allowing the Consuming Fire to burn from us desire
for status, self-aggrandizement, control, and our compulsion
to fix our selves up. We try to fix our selves up by accepting
part of our selves and rejecting the rest, and thus begins the
chain of fragmentation that ends by fragmenting creation. The
humility of Christ allows us to live in the paradox of being
creatures who also are enabled to mirror the God whose costly
love suffuses all that is.

Christ is sinless and we fall from being, but the divine
humility assumes our sin and effects our transfiguration through
the life-enhancing sacrifice we are invited to share; that is,
what we regard as worst in us is not to be repressed or killed,
but made part of our offering and the vehicle of our transformation. It is through our wounds that we come to desire to be
emptied of all that comprises our illusory world, our bastion
against the fear of death; and it is our wounds that become
Christ's through which healing is poured upon the world. And
the seeming polarities of this paradox that shows us to be both
creature and divine heir are held in communion by Love itself,
by the Holy Spirit.

The Judgment of Zeus

Our projection of control that is the Zeus-god leads invariably to the "wrathful God" of unevolved religion, religion that grows out of a cramped vision of immediate, short-term survival-by-control. The god of control shows us the self-seeking that disperses power and becomes diffuse, as opposed to the self-emptying that generates power from the dense glory of I WILL BE.

Since the Zeus-model lacks immanence yet may choose to intrude, the believer sees this distant god as an implacable judge who has impossible and rigid standards. According to this model, the inevitable failures and sins of creatures bring them before his terrible eye, which looks down on creation from the other side of the unbridgable abyss. Sins must be punished, and all of creation thus needs to be "redeemed," bought back from hell. The implacable judge needs to be appeased, so the Son becomes a blood sacrifice to appease the judge. When we project wrath onto this insensitive idol, the fear it elicits from us can rule all else.

The first step, then, is to become willing, to come to an understanding of our fear of our creatureliness, our unacknowledged or perhaps all-too-explicitly acknowledged fear of death, and how this fear cripples us. Fear is a way of being in the world that provides us with a mask of self-importance. If we despise our creatureliness and flee from it to the illusory shadow-world of denial, we *need* to fear the remote Zeus-god to reassure ourselves that we are important enough to attract his attention.

This masking, this rejection of our createdness means that to find a substitute for being we use techniques of mastery over self and the community of creation and even over the judge on whom we project our fear/self-importance. This barter in control counterfeits our being, our self-offering, our life-enhancing sacrifice, and hastens our dissolution.

When we regard death as a punishment for sin, we reflect this dualistic, reductionistic god of control. To regard death with clear-eyed humility, to understand death as the mysterious completion of this phase of the sacrifice of our lives that is offered on the altar of our bodies, reflects life in I WILL BE. To insist that judgment means some will end in hell is a subtle bid for control and a presumption of knowledge proper only to God.

Quite contrary to this notion of the implacable judge, God reveals in the humility of Christ that judgment is given from the perspective of the Cross, and that we "have . . . been appointed . . . to ask for mercy for the world, to keep vigil for the salvation of all, and to partake in every man's suffering, both the just and the sinners." "For this reason," continues Isaac the Syrian,

even on behalf of the irrational beings and enemies of truth, yes even on behalf of those who do harm to it, [he—the one whose life is God's] offers prayer with tears at all times that they may be protected and spared . . . on account of his great compassion infused without measure in his heart, after the likeness of God.[1]

While hell may exist for a time, even the devil may be saved in the end, and there continues in some of the most ancient Christian churches a tradition of praying for the conversion of this metaphor for evil. To enter into compassion with such intensity conveys to the world something of the vastness of God's prodigal gift of divine life, love, and humble mercy. The humility of Christ has condemned condemnation.

The rule of fear is subtly self-perpetuating because the closed system the Zeus-model offers is "safe," however terrible it may be. There often seem to be cause-and-effect relationships in our lives, and to extend this perception, to bend it into a closed system, gives us a sense of control.

The first presumption implicit here is that we know (that we *can* know) from God's point of view what sin is, and the second presumption is our insistence that sin deserves punishment. We can be "justified" in this "divine" accounting system by hiding behind the mediator; or, to use another version of the same attitude of control, we can be "justified" by "doing penance" for our sins (or paying for them with money).

Whatever the variation, the idea of control is still there; we can *do* something about our sins. When we think in this way, sin takes on a concrete and static nature, as if sins were "things" to be moved around like beads on an abacus, instead of propensities that are ever with us and through which we may be brought to the feet of Christ. The attitude that sins become spiritual objects and our claim to presumptuous "knowledge" of their manipulation gives us the illusion of control under this rule of fear. Thus the rule of fear can in some ways subtly provide more "comfort," cold and ruthless as it is, than the rule of radical love and freedom of God.

If it were not enough that we have projected the Zeus-god onto I WILL BE, if we look into the wound of Christian history we see that even the crucified One begins to be merged with the Zeus model, as if the redeemer also needs to be placated. The "triumph" of humility that is the resurrection gradually gets separated from the humility of which it is a sign, and its meaning, the exaltation of *humility*, is lost entirely.

A violent shift takes place: the King whose rule is humility suddenly becomes a potentate, the controlling king and lord of creation, and therefore the judge of creation. Forget the humility, the image of the humble Christ becomes the projection of naked, controlling power. The rule of fear again takes over. The inevitable reductionism to which this kind of thinking leads is a real hell, a trap created by the very churches that purport to offer salvation from it. The rule of fear is totally at odds with the Gospel, and its only conceivable purpose is an attempt to control people, to take away their freedom and to elevate the self-importance of leaders.

The demands for "penance" (the subliminal message of power over life and death) by those who "sacrifice" or "mediate" only reinforce human desire for security and control and lead deeper into the fragmentation of a no-exit situation. And if the action of redemption is all "out there," effected by a clerical elite, and if we take refuge with them in condemning others, then the solitude required for learning *kenosis* is too terrifying to contemplate, and death becomes an inevitable horror that we must endure as the beginning of our punishment. Isaac is clear on this point:

> But if we become castigators, chastisers, judges, investigators, vindicators, and faultfinders, in what respect does our life differ from the life in the towns? And if we do not give up these things, what could be more miserable than such a life in the desert [interior solitude], falsely quiet?[2]

The Judgment of Love

But in spite of the predominance of the Zeus-god projection, particularly in Western tradition, living engagement with the kenotic God has survived, and from time to time through the ages, a few courageous individuals have spoken out, even though to speak sometimes cost them their lives. The kenotic judgment of Love, in Love, is the message of the Gospel. Isaac points out that the Incarnation has nothing to do with "redeeming" us but is solely God's concern to show us how much God loves us. If, Isaac says, we had needed to be "redeemed," God could have gone about it in a much less grisly way.

> Why did God the Word clothe himself in the body in order to bring back the world to his Father by means of gentleness and humble manners; and [why] was he stretched out on the Cross for the sake of sinners, handing over [his] sacred body to suffering on behalf of the world?
>
> I myself say that God did all this for no other reason, but only the love that he has, his aim being that, as a result of our greater love arising out of an awareness of this, we might be captured into love of Him, when he provided the occasion of [this manifestation of] the

kingdom of heaven's great potency—which consists in love—by means of the death of his Son.

The whole purpose of our Lord's death was not to deliver us from sins, or for any other reason, but solely in order that the world might become aware of the love God had for creation. Had all this astounding affair taken place solely for the purpose of the forgiveness of sins, it would have been sufficient to deliver [us] by some other means. For who would have made an objection if He had done what He did by means of an ordinary death? But he did not make His death at all ordinary—in order that you might realise the nature of this mystery. Rather, He tasted death in the cruel suffering of the cross. What was the need for the outrage done to Him and the spitting? Just death and in particular His death, without any of these other things which took place, would have sufficed for our salvation. What wisdom, filled with life is God's! Now you understand and realise why the coming of our Lord took place, and all the events that followed.[3]

To live in forgivenness, to sin in the Face of unalterable Love, is much more painful than to sin in the face of an implacable authority. To return, having sinned, to gaze on that Gaze, to be powerless to conceal or to rectify sin within that loving exchange, burns every vestige of control from us. This Love is so great that we know that even the effects of our sin, not only our selves, are transformed. Our turning to God enables the resonances of even our most evil and fragmenting choices to be stilled in the Silence of God, wherein we find the first moment of creation and our re-creation in the pure fire of self-emptying Love.

We cannot be justified by "works" alone because they focus us away from that gaze on Gaze, the core of solitude in which we find our equipoise of response. Works that do not derive their energy from solitude are destructive and fragmenting and generate yet more frantic attempts at control.

We can be justified only by letting the illusion of control be burned away by the Gaze of God's loving-kindness. The fires of love are infinitely more painful than the fires of so-called hell, which at least we can "control" by telling our selves we deserve them. The uncontrollable fires of Love are what we meet when we turn from our frenzied efforts to create enough noise and hot air to sustain our inflated illusions, to the silence of looking once again at God. We are powerless before this Gaze and must acknowledge our powerlessness to return to ever-moving repose, the stillness and solitude of responsive being, the restoration of covenant, the equilibrium of eucharistic ungraspingness.

This Love will neither force itself on the creation, nor be forced by it. We live in the radiance of this Light whether we acknowledge it or not, and all we can do—"all," yet the cost is everything—for our selves and our sins is to turn toward it and be cleansed by it. Forgivenness, the solitude of our openness to possibility in the freedom of the love of God that enables our re-creation, is a condition of our existence. Paradoxically, in forgivenness the finitude and woundedness that is our creatureliness becomes the vehicle for infinite forgiveness, re-creation, and transfiguration, not only for our selves, but for the whole creation.

But to live in and from our forgivenness, for it to be poured through us in forgiveness, requires our opening to it. Even if we seem hopelessly trapped in our closed systems, Love will seep in whatever chinks and cracks we leave in our self-made hells and dwell there with us until we become aware that *it is in our very wounds that we find the solitude and openness of our re-creation and our being.* It is in our wounds that we become aware that there is no existence outside the divine Gaze of Love outpoured and that hell is the attempt to live disengaged in our pseudo-selves. It is this pseudo-life that is destroyed when we see God's Face, the life that we must lose to be given true life.

The myth of the Fall reminds us that our control of the knowledge of good and evil is only partial. If we take a dualistic view of evil, if we make evil into a kind of god set in opposition to God, a god that we can control or defeat or do battle against, then we not only compound our futile grasping at knowledge that is beyond our creatureliness by choosing to be trapped in this false dialectic, but we also create a hierarchy in which evil must be assigned to material creation. Even more insidious is that we end by pitting our willfulness against the willfulness we perceive as evil. What is evil in the mystery of God we can never know. We can only be wounded by it as we choose it, do it, and suffer from it, and even then we must not presume that we know what is and what is not evil from God's perspective.

Who are we to call evil what God has called good? We do make wrong choices—sin is a reality—but God weeps for us and with us and within us; and when we have returned to forgivenness and the pained recognition of our responsibility for our acts and choices in the world, we have returned to the forgivenness that is the eucharistic Silence of our solitude. Sin is behovely, says Lady Julian, by this word meaning not "necessary" as we commonly understand it, but "part of the package."[4] Sin is part of our freedom, which paradoxically is both finite and infinite. Freedom is finite in reference to our being in time as we experience particular acts and choices; freedom is infinite in the Silence from which the Word who is First and Last is eternally spoken. God's anguish in creating comes in part from knowing and suffering through the mess we make of our freedom and the potential of salvation inherent in it, which is God's very kenotic life.

Our individual choices—choices consciously made, choices made on the littoral of consciousness, choices we hide from our selves in our hearts—are important, and we hold not only the means to destroy creation, but also the means for God to enter, to offer us possibility and save us. If we are found in God, our being sounds a clear note, the resonance of which elicits harmonics throughout a universe seeking consonance. We have only to choose our solitude. In this way, incredible as it may seem, God asks us to call God into being. It is only in this loving and generative context of the Silence of God that we can be freed from the fear of death.

Freedom from Fear

Once we begin to be free from the fear of death (fear that paralyzes and confuses, as opposed to awe or dread that arises from clarity and calls forth response), once we no longer run from mortality, we begin to see how the fear of death is operative at every moment when we are asked to give up control, whether this loss is as simple as giving away a favorite book or as complex as setting another person or other of the creation free from our desire for domination. While our control is illusory, the death attached to giving it up is very real, and we weep.

We soon realize that these tears are not tears of self-pity for our loss, but something quite different. We have glimpsed something of greater value than what we have lost, and the pain is as real as the desire. In this seeming polarity of love our tears become holy tears, and their salt lights God's fire upon the earth. The choice to return to God's Gaze brings us to tears, for it is only in stillness that we become aware of what is unacknowledged and unconverted in us, and it is only when we weep—with or without physical tears—that we have any sure indication of changes occurring on a level beyond the merely conscious, beyond an escape into yet more hyperreality. Tears are a sign that we are struggling with power of one sort or another: the loss of ours, the entering of God's. By tears the unseen wildness in us is tamed for God, the wayward found, the compromised made inviolate. Isaac the Syrian describes the role of tears:

Tears are the border, as it were, between the bodily and the spiritual state, between the state of being subject to the passions and that of purity. As long as one has not yet received this gift, the labour of his service is still in the outward man, and this is to such an extent that he does not even perceive anything of the hidden service of the spiritual person. Once he has begun to leave the bodiliness of this world and steps into that territory which lies beyond this visible nature, then he will immediately reach this grace of tears. And from the very first staging-post of that hidden mode of life these tears will commence, and they will convey him to perfect love of God.[5]

Most of all, tears arise from stillness and lead us to deeper stillness.

From stillness a man can gain possession of the three [causes of tears]: love of God, awestruck wonder at His mysteries, and humility of heart. Without these it is unthinkable that a man should be accounted worthy to taste of the wellspring of flaming compunction arising from the love of God. There is no passion so fervent as the love of God. O Lord, deem me worthy to taste of this wellspring! Therefore, if a man does not have stillness, he will not be acquainted with even one of these, though he perform many virtuous deeds, he cannot know what the love of God is, nor spiritual knowledge, nor possess true humility of heart. He will not know these three virtues, or rather these three glorious gifts.[6]

As we turn again to gaze upon Gaze, our experience of tears changes.

Some tears cause burning, others provide a kind of unction. All tears which flow out of compunction and "anguish of heart" [2 Cor 2:6] as a result of sin, dry up the body and burn it. And often when these tears are shed, a person will even feel that some harm has been done to his brain. A person will necessarily encounter this order of tears first of all. Then by them the door leading to the second order will be opened for him, an order which is by far superior, because it constitutes the sign of the receiving of mercy. What is this? Those tears which pour forth as a result of some insight provide the body with a kind of unction; they flow spontaneously and there is no compulsion in them. They also anoint the body and the appearance of the face is changed. For a joyful heart renders the body beautiful.[7]

Tears become a sign of our transformation:

A constant flow of tears comes about in a man for three causes: [firstly,] from awestruck wonder arising from insights continually revealed to the intellect and replete with mysteries, tears spill forth involuntarily and painlessly. For with the vision of the intellect a man considers these insights, being held fast with wonder at the knowledge of things spiritually revealed to the intellect through the same insights and, (at the same time) tears flow effortless by themselves because of the strength of the sweetness that confines the intellect to gazing at the insights. The Fathers call such tears the type of the Manna that the sons of Israel ate, and the outpouring of water from the rock, "for that rock was Christ," that is to say, insights both mystic and spiritual. Or else, constant weeping arises from the fervent love of God that consumes the soul, and because of its sweetness and delightfulness a man cannot endure not to weep continually. Or [thirdly], constant weeping comes from great humility of heart.[8]

And tears are a sign that we are being born into the "new age" of sacred time, which means not only the interpenetration of time and eternity, but even a reversal of time as we know it. The "new world," the world to come, is now, not merely an apocalyptic moment; the "now" has all the echoes of time that is being fulfilled with the promises of God.

Once you have reached the place of tears, then know that the mind has left the prison of this world and set its foot on the road towards the new world. Then it begins to breathe the wonderful air which is there; it begins to shed tears. For now the birth pangs of the spiritual infant grow strong, since grace, the common mother of all, makes haste to give birth mystically to the soul, the image of God, into the light of the world to come. And when the time of birth is come, then the mind will perceive something of what belongs to that world, like a faint perfume which an infant receives inside the body in which it has grown. Then, unable to endure what is unwonted, it [the spiritual infant] will set the body to weeping mingled with joy which surpasses the sweetness of honey. Together with the growing of this interior infant there will be an increase of tears. The stream of tears occurs when the mind has begun to become serene. I am talking about the flow of tears belonging to the stage which I have described, not that partial one which takes place from time to time. This consolation which takes place intermittently occurs for everyone who serves God in solitude; sometimes it happens when the mind is in contemplation, sometimes while reading the words of the scriptures; sometimes when the mind is occupied with supplication.

But I propose to speak of that total kind, which continues night and day without a break, and by the sincerity of his behaviour, when the eyes become fountains of water for a period of nearly two years. This happens during a transitional period; I mean mystical transition. At the end of the period of tears you will enter into peace of thought; and by this peace of thought you will enter into that divine rest of which Paul spoke, rest in part, according to [our] nature.

From this place of peace the intellect will begin to see hidden things. Then the Holy Spirit will begin to reveal before it heavenly things, while God dwells in you and promotes spiritual fruits in you. Then you will start to become aware of the transformation which the whole nature will receive in the renewal of all things, dimly and as though by hints.[9]

The new age has a profound identification with the days of Adam and Eve in paradise, but given to us is a greater gift than theirs: compassion.

The burning of the heart on behalf of the entire creation, human beings, birds, animals—even all that exists; so that by the recollection and at the sight of them the eyes well up with tears as a result of the vehemence of the compassion which constrains the heart in abundant pity. Then the heart becomes weak [from the force of compassion that pours through it] and it is not able to bear to hear or to observe the injury or any insignificant suffering of anything in creation.[10]

It is as if the angel guarding paradise with a flaming sword lowers it in wonder at the sight of our tears, and as its cruel blade falls before us, it is extinguished and dissolved by the flood of our pain and joy. So may we enter an innocence more precious than our first parents'.

In the new age, we see our mortality in a different light. We are able to look upon death as the most profound mystery of life. It becomes, in a quixotic and capricious world, one of the few solid truths we have, though we do not know its time or season. We are no longer victims of fear of the unexpected, building walls and fortresses of illusion to protect our selves, walls within which only more suffering and fear and death are bred. We can *choose* the inevitability of mortality and even celebrate it as did Charles Wesley in his hymn that begins, "O thou who camest from above":

> Jesus, confirm my heart's desire
> to work and speak and think for thee;
> still let me guard the holy fire
> and still stir up the gift in me.
>
> Still let me prove thy perfect will,
> my acts of faith and love repeat;
> till death thy endless mercies seal,
> and make the sacrifice complete.

Choosing Life and Choosing Death

Memento mori, like everything else in Christianity, is subject to distortion. To remember death is to remember the reality of our mortality, not to use death for coercion or punishment, on the one hand, or as a romantic never-never land, on the other. Our culture externalizes death and dresses it up as a ghastly fantasy of pseudo-life, a public occasion removed from our creaturely condition, extraneous and an embarrassment to humanity. Only in solitude can we discover death and find our re-creation, the darkness that brings forth light; only in stillness can we choose our death and, in the Silence of God, hear the Word of salvation.

Any of us could be hit by a bus tomorrow, and if we have kept death properly in perspective we do not wait until the end of our lives to live rightly and fully; and we can live rightly and fully only from the glory of our creatureliness that we discover in our heart's solitude. This rightness and fullness is not subject to other people's opinion, but rather is the commitment, in what time we are given, to freely make an offering of our lives, to have aspirations we can fling our hearts at, to have choices, to take risks, to make use of the gifts we have been given, to acknowledge where we have gone wrong, and to weep over the tragedies of which we have been part.

And we are at peace knowing we have made amends as best we can, knowing that God holds all impossibilities in reconciling love. Death, properly understood, reveals to us our freedom and the resonances of our being. To be able to come to this kind of serenity is only possible when, at some point in time, we consciously choose the death that waits for each of us.

A candle can be seen only in the dark. Death is the dark from which our lives shine, the cyclorama against which all tears, laughter, pleasure, play, joy have meaning. Death gives life its tensile quality; it is why artists are artists—and each of us is an artist if we choose to be, painting our lives boldly on a scrim. If we do not wish to be, if we abandon our choice, then we have chosen by default to be used by something outside us. Our life will be painted out by someone else or by fear and another kind of darkness.

Yes, there is pain. We, like artists, cannot be artists without suffering. In the West we have lost or abandoned the wisdom that some suffering is necessary to life and maturity. Suffering is not "good" but it cannot be seen in isolation from the personal transformation that is wrought in us by no other means—not by avoiding death but by wrestling with it as Jacob did, not by seizing suffering and exploiting it to inflate our selves, but by embracing it so that it can bring us to being in the humility of Christ.

Our lives are promethean and the kenotic God rejoices; Christianity is audacious, but not presumptuous. We steal our light and the intensity of our lives from death, but we may not presume to sidestep death itself. I would rather choose that my taper shine brightly, penetrating the darkening edges of the unknown; I would rather that my taper be blown into a perilously bright flame in the Silence of God at risk of being extinguished by the force of the divine Breath, rather than have it gutter low and safely in still but dead air, where it finally goes out without having illuminated anything but its own closed space.

In an interview with Carolyn Coman, Helen Caldicott said,

I didn't get to be a good doctor until I developed severe depression myself. I used to hand out drugs and say, "There, there, this will fix you, come back next month." After I got severely depressed an old woman came in to see me, terribly depressed, and I told her, "I know what it feels like—you'd rather have cancer," and she put her head on my shoulder and wept and said I was the first one who had understood. You only get to be a good doctor by living life. You only grow emotionally when you are in pain. I welcome pain, although it's unpleasant, because I always grow. *And I am not here not to grow.*[11]

What Caldicott describes is true death and resurrection, not the endless, monotonous, limp, living death of so-called "immortality," which is a projection of our unwillingness to admit there is much we do not know and cannot control. What Caldicott is talking about is true healing.

In *Arctic Dreams*, Barry Lopez writes a fugue on the theme of edges:

The fear of being hunted is vestigial in us, a dim memory from the open savannas of southern Africa. For a man waiting alone at an aglu [a seal's breathing hole] for a seal on a winter afternoon, looking around in the half-light, alert at a subconscious and primitive level for the triggering sound of the bear's footfall, the fear must have been palpable. . . .

Bears approached men as though they were a kind of resting seal. Some of these encounters must have ended with a pounce, a single blow, a man dead. But some of them were finished with a seal harpoon or a knife, a bear dead of fatal miscalculation. Of the latter, some were encounters deliberately courted, by men on the verge of manhood. These were not simply terrifying moments but moments of awe and apotheosis. These were moments that kept alive with the culture the overarching presence of a being held in fearful esteem. *Tôrnârssuk*, the Plar Eskimo called him, "the one who gives power."

To encounter the bear, to meet it with your whole life, was to grapple with something personal. The confrontation occurred on a serene, deadly and elevated plane. If you were successful, you found something irreducible within yourself, like a seed. To walk away was to be alive, utterly. To be assured of your own life, the life of your kind, in a harsh land where life took insight and patience and humour. It was to touch the bear. It was a gift from the bear.[12]

Reflecting on this passage, a woman writes,

Isn't there an apotheosis of a very subtle kind when we learn, after years of suffering, to come out the other side of one of these attacks of fear and depression? Haven't we been hunted by the bear, who silently pounced, and we became aware only as it was crushing us? And hasn't that plodding through the icy, stygian tunnel, putting one foot painfully and breathlessly in front of the other, been stalking the bear in return? Something astonishing quietly happens after years of this: if we live through the fear (never a sure thing, no matter how skilled at survival) we afterwards become aware of the moments when we are alive, utterly: I don't mean being manic. And we become aware that underneath the surface of the ordinary there is this being alive, utterly, and we face fear and depression with a kind of grim, taunting laughter the next time we go through it, carefully *not* engaging as it stalks and tries to possess and crush us in the ice-cave.

In other words, the pain of transformation is morbid only if we choose it to be, only if we do not want to look beyond and through it. If only we allow, the pain itself is transformed and becomes Eucharist; and Eucharist deepens us until we burn with Love in God's very heart. If we spend all our time trying to block out pain with illusion or to twist it to inflate our egos, we will stagnate; we will cause in our selves the destructive pain of disintegration. The inescapable truth is that, for each of us, there is pain we must choose to embrace if we are to grow. If we dodge, we get tangled and stunted; we fall from our being.

The kind of pain we are discussing is inevitable; it is the "weather of life." It is not self-inflicted, which would simply be another attempt at control; neither is it an excuse for hurting others, or failing to alleviate the suffering of others. Nor is it a recommendation that we avoid asking for painkillers after surgery or seeking support in the darker passages of life. It is the willingness rather to receive the pain that brings us to maturity and deepens in us the compassion that is in communion with the heart of all human pain.

Paradoxically, by receiving, choosing, allowing, and embracing the pain that comes to us, we can take true charge of the parts of our lives it is given us to be in charge of which we are then able to let go. We can be responsible for controlling our own lives in this kenotic sense, because the constraint is to keep our selves open instead of allowing our selves to snap shut when confronted with pain. We do not have to be subject to the vicissitudes of our lives in the sense of being forced into submission or domination either by slavery to fear of death or slavery to those who would control us by fear. But there will be pain.

One very practical reason to choose what is inevitable is so that we are not at the mercy of the emotional blackmail of honest and well-intentioned but insensitive doctors. I mean insensitive in the deepest sense. They coerce patients with the promise of "life," which is the ultimate illusion, the ultimate denial of death. An AIDS patient has commented,

Doctors are playing God. They're working in the dark, using the patients as guinea pigs. They're taking away the responsibility and control from the patient. They don't have time to answer your questions. It's "You'd better take this chemo- or radiotherapy because what's the alternative?—Death." And that is why people give up. They then unconsciously collude in the game. I've seen AIDS patients bargaining with the doctors: "If I take your drug, if I'm a good patient, will I live?" I've been the ideal patient myself, turning up on time, always smiling. And I saw it was a load of crap. I think the answer lies with the patient. . . . I can't say that AIDS is the best thing that ever happened to me, but it gave me a challenge, a purpose, a meaning for my life. Because suddenly it could be taken away.[13]

This patient knows that true healing—even though we die—occurs by choosing and exploring and taking responsibility for what frightens us. Hospices report that when patients' pain and fear are reduced by the right combination of psychological support and pain medication in a loving environment, few ask for euthanasia.

A sensitive doctor confronting a patient with mild depression that is a natural consequence of major surgery might say something like this: "I can give you some medication, of course, but in the end it would be better if you can simply go through what you have to go through, rather than postponing it. What do you want to do?" Such an attitude puts the depression into perspective as part of the normal postsurgical healing process, the reality of the sense of the body's having been invaded and violated. The sense of violation must be acknowledged and gone through. Why mask it, risking not only a larger crisis later on but also dependence on drugs and emotional self-indulgence? The physician should offer clear, noncoercive options, but leave the final decision up to the patient.

Worldly society tells us in its untruth that if we give up our lives unthinkingly into the hands of the medical idol, if we surrender the lives that we can choose and for which we can be responsible, if we yield them up to technological hocus-pocus, death can be conquered. That is the biggest lie. Becoming aware of the fact of our death and thus choosing it means we can live on the most honest and transforming level *now*, that we can choose the quality of our lives, whether we will be victims and live in fear and let others control us, or whether *we* will choose what our life and death (whenever it comes) will mean.

To put this notion in equally significant and more day-to-day terms, if men and women are no longer afraid of death, their relationships will improve, as will their respect for one another. When a woman says *no* to a man, she subliminally looks death in the face. Men have not only more physical strength—and the threat of that strength is always there, consciously or unconsciously—but in today's society of inequality, men usually have more status and power than women. If women learn not to be afraid of death in all its forms, they will not hesitate appropriately to say *no* and stand firm. If men learn not to be afraid of death, they will not feel castrated or threatened when women oppose them.

Choosing means we may, by entering the humility of Christ, have the capacity to disturb the universe, each of us in our own small way. We can change it, transform it, not by exploding bombs or creating space stations, but by who we are, by finding the equipoise of being that is gaze on Gaze, by the resonances of our interior choices—morphic resonance on a cosmic scale.

Morphic resonance in creation is more than a change in the charge on a particle that causes all particles around it to change their charge, or rats learning mazes more easily after one has learned it, or monkeys washing fruit without having seen the original monkey who first washed hers. We may speak of the resonances of our being helping (or hindering, depending on our choice) Christ's transfiguration of all that is.

That we can disturb the universe is evident not only on the level of the unseen, but also in practical, visible ways. If in the mystery of God and in the privilege of my relationship with God I choose my life and my death and refuse to let others choose it for me, their attempt to dominate is rendered impotent by the unexploitable integrity of my *being*, not by my violence. They cannot but allow me my freedom, which means they must change as well. They may not like it; they may kill me for my freedom, but they cannot take away what my life signifies in time or in the eternity of God (Lk 8:26–39).

It is this freedom that the humility of Christ teaches us. Each year the entrance into the dread of Holy Week becomes more profound and humbling. What gives us the courage to begin? It is grace. The power of Holy Week lies not in Christian borrowings from pagan mystery religions for its own convenience. It is rather that the journey through the darkness that ends in more light than we can bear is the way the universe is made, is what we must live and do and be. It is the power of the humility of Christ portrayed in the New Testament, not in the religiosity of our time or any other time. Jesus the Christ also chose, chose to disturb the universe on an ultimate level, chose death, a death that seemed to be meaningless in its cruelty and dereliction, and it is *that* choosing of which we are a part in the resurrection.

The particle, the rat, the monkey, each of us, Jesus the Christ—if we are willing to be fully who we are in the equipoise of solitude, in the Silence of God, each of us is testing the edges of darkness, of unknowing, of death, testing the edges because only *there* is life. Faith is not assent to doctrines or surrounding our selves with props and propositions. It is trust that God—as Christ shows us—has been there before us, goes within us, waits to find us beyond the edges of utter dark. And, found by God, we become aware that God is closer to our being than we are.

We no longer need the bastions raised by fear, the fortress of self-reflective and illusory security. Faith brings us to the equipoise of conversion, gives us the security to live in insecurity, to make our sacrifice, to explore the darkness with no safe holds. We find our selves free-falling in eucharistic ungraspingness; and in faith we choose to continue to go on disturbing the universe, co-creating with God by our life and by our death become prayer in the mystery of grace. Isaac the Syrian sums up our life in God:

Q. What comprises all the labours of asceticism, in this way of life, so that when someone has reached it, he will recognise that he has reached the limit of his course?

A. When he is deemed worthy of constant prayer. When he has reached this, he has touched the limit of all virtues and forthwith he becomes a dwelling-place of the Spirit. Unless someone has indeed the gift of the Paraclete, it is not possible for him to accomplish constant prayer in a restful way. Once the Spirit has taken up her dwelling-place in a person she does not cease from prayer, because the Spirit prays constantly. Then, neither when he sleeps, nor when he is awake, will prayer be cut off from his soul; rather, whether he is eating or whether he is drinking, whether he is lying down or doing something, yes, even if he is immersed in sleep, the fragrance of prayer will exhale effortlessly in his soul. Henceforth he will not possess prayer at limited times, but at all times; and when he has outward rest, even then prayer ministers in his hidden person. For the silence of the serene is prayer, says one of those who are clothed in Christ. For their thoughts are divine stirrings. The movements of the pure mind are still voices with which they change psalms in a hidden way to the Hidden.[14]

*   *   *

At this point I have to make a qualification to all that has gone before in this book. I hesitate to do so because it is possible to make this qualification the thin end of the wedge of abuse. Nonetheless, there are times in our lives when we are so beleagured, under so much emotional and spiritual pressure, that we need to take refuge in more structure, and in our pain we need God to be for us a God who is willing to organize and intervene, to be a Magic Cookie, to make plain obedience we can blindly follow.

What saves this retreat from taking refuge in the Zeus-god is that the kenotic God meets us in our poverty; we *know* we are taking refuge; we *are aware* that it is a temporary situation, and, above all, we are not imposing this idea of God on anyone else or fooling our selves that it is the only way God relates to the world. Further, it is a retreat into the protecting love of a Mother's arms, not seeking condemnation so that we may judge our selves and others. And in the end, our divine Mother, having caressed and kissed our hurts, opens her arms at our slightest move to venture forth, ready to comfort us again if we have need. God does not require us to hang glide if we are just recovering from a road accident.

The Reciprocity of *Kenosis*

It is only against this background of awareness of the models of power and their effects, especially in terms of the fear of death, that we can begin to know what the humility of Christ means in our lives. The Beatitudes, and the evangelical counsels of poverty, chastity, and obedience, which are derived from them, explain this humility to us. The Beatitudes are at the heart of our baptismal vows, which do not confer a result but commit us to our priesthood that is inextricable from our sacrifice. As priests we are committed to be caught in God's Gaze in solitude, to go, with Christ indwelling to the heart of creation's pain, of suffering, of hell, to find new life, hope, and joy, to celebrate God's life in our own and convey it to the world.

"How blest are those who know their need of God; the kingdom of heaven is theirs." In the first Beatitude we find the source from which all else proceeds. How blest we are when we understand the ways in which we fall from being, from the salvation of possibility, from the community of creation, from co-creation with God. How blest are we when we allow the technology of control to fall from our grasp. How blest are we when we can give up the need to control, to fix up, to compete, to seek status and put down others, to be self-reflective and have all other eyes on us, when we can stop running from death and simply look at God. How blest are we, for we know the glory of our wounds in that Gaze of Love, by which we and the creation around us are transfigured by Christ's indwelling.

"How blest are the sorrowful; they shall find consolation." How blest are all tears of loss, for ultimately they set us free: tears for loss of loved ones, because we finally begin to accept that there is nothing we can do to bring them back, and more, that their gifts can now be manifest in us; tears for loss of our sense of omnipotence, because we no longer need to reject our creatureliness, to struggle to be larger than life; tears for loss of the security of our sins, because, trembling in the insecurity of possibility, we may begin new life in eucharistic engagement; tears for loss of denial, because we can stop decorating our lives with vapid illusion; tears for loss of idols, because we are freed into the vastness of the humility that is the love and glory of Christ, whom we reverence in the poor, the sick, the sinner, the ugly, the outcast, the disgusting, the useless, who are both created beings and despised parts of our selves; tears for loss of bitterness and hatred, because this loss leaves a fallow field in which tears may be sown and joy reaped; tears for loss of the scales from our eyes, because we can see with clarity what our tears magnify, not only the paradox of failure and glory we are as forgiven humanity, but the Face of God, which our tears magnify as they fall unceasingly in joy.

"How blest are those of a gentle spirit; they shall have the earth for their possession." No one, remarked St. Thérèse, fights for the lowest place. How blest are we when we can take no notice of status at all, when we look at nothing created with eyes of exploitation. How blest are we when in each moment we can receive creatures as they are, pregnant with laughter and tears; how blest are we when we can truly listen, truly see, truly smell, truly taste, truly touch and be touched, when we can have our senses impressed by the Eucharist of creation, when we can reverence and contemplate what we no longer need to dominate and put to use; how blest are we when little children and wild things laugh with us and invite us to play, when plants breathe to us their secrets, when we hear the stars sing and reply, when earth breathes the Word of life.

"How blest are those who hunger and thirst to see right prevail; they shall be satisfied." How blest are we when we realize that the cure for social ills begins with our selves in solitude, with reverence for others; how blest are we when at last we can look beyond our senses, beyond color, beyond sexual orientation, beyond illness, beyond poverty, beyond class, beyond degradation, beyond ugliness, beyond wealth and see the glory that shelters in each frightened and categorized creature, a glory that arcs across the abyss in recognition and kindles us into a single flame; how blest are we in that moment, for we know that this is true right prevailing in eternity, though our struggles to transform the social order may seem to fail.

"How blest are those who show mercy; mercy shall be shown to them." "They are merciless, totally without pity," wrote Etty Hillesum from her concentration camp, "and we must be all the more merciful ourselves. . . . Each of us must turn inward and destroy in himself all that he thinks he ought to destroy in others. And remember that every atom of hate we add to this world makes it still more inhospitable."[15] How blest are we when we no longer need to take the role of the accuser, the evil one; how blest are we when we know that every sin is our sin and our forgiveness unites us with the other; how blessed are we when our hearts are broken by compassion and become unflinchingly honest because we see that the sin of the other is the sin we do not wish to face in ourselves; how blest are we when our wounds open us to the Silence of God, which creates in us the context of forgiveness, the environment where others no longer feel the need either to oppress or rebel, the moment when condemnation dissolves and, embracing, we wash one another with tears.

"How blest are those whose hearts are pure; they shall see God." How blest are we when suddenly the struggle to become single-hearted has begun to be born in us, when we realize that nothing, not even life itself exists outside that Gaze, when we realize that it is in stillness that we come to be; how blest are we when all the false polarity of our lives begins to come to convergence, to the density of glory, when we are still free creatures, yet transfigured; how blest are we when the silence of obedience comes to live within us, so that the ear of our heart receives the whispered Word that is First and Last, and our action is tempered by its wisdom; how blest are we when every where we look we see the Face of God.

"How blest are the peacemakers; God shall call them the fruit of divine love." How blest are we when we bring forth silence amid the noise of conflict and illusion, when we find the common ground, when we make the connection; how blest are we when the self-effacing Spirit breathes through us the spirit of peace; how blest are we when rage and annihilation are transformed by tears of reconciliation; how blest are we when we are so found in God we have nothing to defend; how blest are we when our suffering gives birth to greater love; how blest are we, waiting in the dark, in the still-prayer that is our being that silences the blasphemous and the debaters.

"How blest are those who have suffered persecution for the cause of right; the kingdom of Heaven is theirs." How blest are we, for persecution is the sign that God's justice and holiness radiates from Mercy indwelling; how blest are we, when slander has brought us to the freedom to see that we cannot control what others think and say and that, no matter what is said about us, their slander will not change us; how blest the freedom then to act with integrity and responsibility, for cursing and lies cannot touch us; how blest are we, for in the face of fearless humility, tyranny senses the crumbling of its empire and the feebleness of its energy that wildly and futilely grasps for support; how blest are we, for the leaven hidden in the loaf has begun to transfigure; how blest are we, for we know that all that is and will be now resides in the silence of the priestly sacrifice of our lives.

Practice and Counterfeit

For most of us, the Beatitudes sound so utterly impossible, so fantastically untenable and unlivable, that we shake our heads and turn away in sorrow like the Rich Young Man. But they are impossible, untenable, unlivable only if we insist on making them static ideas of self-mastery required to placate a cold perfection external to us. *The seeds of the Beatitudes are* *already within us,* and we have only to become aware of this latent potency, to desire them to grow, to water them with the tears of our desire as we search for the Face of Christ our Sun, whose warmth will mingle with our tears and bring us to being; whose light will disperse confusion and illuminate the darkness; whose love will transform and sustain for all eternity.

To help us recognize and enable this growth, the early churches condensed the essence of the Beatitudes to three evangelical counsels. Under the mismatching of desert monasticism and the state (and later, feudalism), these counsels became political tools for controlling people and placed power in the hands of a monastic theocracy. Monasticism is still suffering today from this *mésalliance*. The monastic habit became the successor to the philosopher's robe, philosophy being the provenance of the elite.

But fortunately there is an alternative monastic tradition that is periodically revived by those society thinks mad and calls saints, not political saints declared by an institution decorating itself, but holy fools like Mary of Egypt, Francis and Clare, Lady Julian of Norwich, William Blake, Seraphim of Sarov, Etty Hillesum, Dag Hammarskjöld, and Dorothy Day. These are some who were known; there are many more unknown. Their lives show to us that there is no distinction among people who live the evangelical counsels in the humility of Christ. They show us that the stifling strictures of control that still politicize monasticism need not keep us either in the illusion that we are second-raters in the eyes of God, if our vocation is in the world, or that we need be intimidated by yet another form of "religious" institution that attempts to use secular techniques to bring us to religious engagement.

The changes in contemporary monasticism so far have been cosmetic; religious life needs to see the problem that is at its root, which is that about the time of Constantine's conversion, many of its leaders abrogated engagement with the kenotic God and set up monastic authority to mirror a Zeus-god.

While monasticism sometimes needs organization (more often it does not), both men and women, but especially women, often experience monastic control by men as psycho-spiritual rape.

Without wisdom, without allowing that we can and must grow into the freedom of spiritual maturity, monasticism leads to the opposite of its intended goals. It does not make us single-hearted, it fragments; it does not bring us to being in the glory of creatureliness, it makes us hate the creation; it does not bring us to spiritual maturity, it makes us infantile; it does not bring us to the humility of Christ, it sets up competitive self-mastery; it does not bring us to solitude and stillness, it brings us to politics.

If the evangelical counsels are meant for all Christians without exception, how do we translate them into ordinary twenty-first century life? It is not difficult, as long as we are willing to ignore those whose status and control we threaten, who insist that there are two levels of obedience, that ours is a lesser path to holiness, and who take every opportunity to slander and belittle us. We must then recognize that the first responsibility we have is to cherishing, not destroying, what God has made and called good and that what may appear to be "inside" and "outside" are integrated, engaged, and focused by Love. To seek our being in this Love, in the solitude where we engage the humility of Christ, is the only reason to undertake the journey in the first place.

Ihidayutha

In the Author's Note, I briefly mentioned the Syrian ideal of *ihidayutha*. It is difficult for the tidy Western mind to enter the vastness of interior territory through which *ihidayutha* permeates. *Ihidayutha* is the focus of the whole creation coinhered with the single movement of love that is God. Subsumed under *ihidayutha* are virginity, chastity, integrity, inviolabile vulnerability, wholeness, solitary, single—unity with God and creation, unity of inner and outer, unity of man and woman, unity of image and what is imaged. It is as if light is focused into a laser, or our humanity into a pillar of flame. It is the uncompromising, joyous wildness of undistracted longing and love for God who is worshiped as both Father and Mother and also without the use of any personal pronoun.

Perhaps the absolute essence of *ihidayutha* is singleness of heart, the desire for God alone that, even given the vision of paradise, ends in the often terrifying abandonment of all images of God, all notions of God, all notions, even, of what prayer is, all in religion with which we comfort our selves, and which ultimately creates a barrier between us and the divine fire, if not allowed to fall away. Isaac speaks of the person "who in his mind clings to nothing visible," of imageless prayer, of prayer beyond prayer. This iconoclasm in prayer is, of course, a form of death because we give up the security of our pet ideas of God and religion; we abandon all the ways that encourage us to self-reflection, all the ways that enable us to tell ourselves that we are good and are becoming holy.

Isaac is rather concerned to communicate the prayer that ignites when the self-emptying of God meets the self-emptying of the creature in the solitude of the heart:

I think that, if one were to come to an exact understanding, it would prove a blasphemy if anyone among created things were able to say that spiritual prayer can be prayed at all. For all prayer that can be prayed lies on this side of the spiritual realm. And all that is spiritual is a class that is free from movement and from prayer. . . .

As soon as the mind has crossed this boundary of pure prayer and proceeded inwards, it possesses neither prayer, nor emotions, nor tears, nor authority, nor freedom, nor petitions, nor desire, nor longing after any of those things which are hoped for in this world or in the world to come. . . .

Therefore after pure prayer there is no longer prayer; all prayer's movements and forms by the authority of their free will, conduct the mind thus far: for this reason struggle is involved; but beyond this limit there is wonder and no prayer. From here onwards the mind has ceased from prayer; there is sight, but the mind does not actively pray.[16]

Yet Isaac's imageless prayer in no way denies the created order; his is not the sort of spirituality that demands we shun the creation.

The humble person approaches beasts of prey, and as soon as their gaze alights upon him, their wildness is tamed and they approach him and attach themselves to him as their master, wagging their tails and licking his hands and feet. For they smell from him the scent which wafted from Adam before his transgression, when the beasts gathered to him and he gave the names in Paradise—the scent which was taken from us and given back to us anew by Christ through His advent, for it is He who has made the smell of the human race sweet.[17]

Asceticism is a word that makes people flinch when they do not know that it is *not* a technology of self-destruction, but rather a name for entering our solitude where we engage God, community, and self as Eucharist. Its first rule is *self-care* for the sake of the community of creation, because we may not presume to abuse the creation God has called good. Self-care is not cultivation of self-image, of the pseudo-self that springs from fear of our wounds. It is not even cultivation of a monastic self-image, or an ordinary self-image, or the self-image of not having a self-image.

If we enter the solitude of our wounds, we are too caught by the Gaze of God to look to see where we are in relation to others on some imaginary scale of holiness. Status again: it has to go; all geometry and measuring has to go. We must allow it to fall away; we must examine our selves for this greed that ravages the most religious of circumstances and that is the most devastating temptation of life in God. If we are to begin to find the balance of responsiveness to God, of ever-moving repose, we must give up all coordinates in human terms—up, down, inside, outside, progress, failure, achievement—and respond, in our watchfulness, only to the coordinates of grace.

Self-care: when speaking of the evangelical counsels of

poverty, chastity, and obedience we have first of all to realize who we are and how deeply we are wounded. It is not only a matter of asking, "Where do I hurt?" but realizing that because of the particular combination of wounds and gifts each of us has, that what is self-care for one may be self-indulgence for another, what is purification for one may be polluting for another. Discernment is important, but imposition is wrong, which is why the woes of Matthew 5 and 18 in regard to despising the "little ones" are so forceful and absolute. If we try to impose the ways of God on others, if we coerce, condemn, accuse, rage, or sneer, we distract them from the mystery of their own gaze on God, who alone can do the transforming; we disturb their equipoise; we fall from our own.

When we look down on others or are made aware of our status, we are thrust into a boiling maelstrom of fear, insecurity, and the struggle to survive being devalued and dehumanized. All of these reactions push us toward immaturity. We become aware of those things around us that have not seemed to matter before, and we stumble and fall from the exquisite balance where we gaze on God alone.

If we are distracted and made to look at our position, if we are forced to compare our relationship, our journey, our living-out of the divine reciprocity, we fall away from being, we are plunged into a sea of chaos, lostness, inadequacy, perhaps even envy, jealousy, and vengefulness that cause us to gasp and clutch and forget that it is only by letting go and allowing that Gaze once again to be our only focus that we can recover our being and responsive balance. We are the little ones, no matter how remote from that image we may, in our arrogance, feel. It is that Gaze that draws the fragments of our lives together, that inspires the seeking that focuses our energies and gives us our density, our glory, our virginity that makes us *ihidaye*. When in the old texts we read about "control" or "subjugation" we need to remember the hubris that is the illusion of self-mastery; we need to enter again the glory of our wounds; all is gathered and transfigured in the Gaze of

God, and nothing is repressed, rejected or wasted. Morality is *not* an immutable, merciless moral structure imposed by a Zeus-god on humanity to mold it into a static, artificial, and fragmented idea of perfection. Rather, constraint is transformed into self-restraint in our self-forgetful aspiration toward Love.

Morality becomes ontological when it is no longer merely veneer for public consumption pasted over a commitment to "self"-aggrandizement, but rather proceeds from our being-in-transformation. On the most mundane level, we do not shoplift not because it breaks the law, or we might get caught, or because no one else does it, or because we value someone's opinion, but rather because it would violate the focus of our gaze on God. It is only with this ontological aspiration that we can live out the evangelical counsels, which are the wisdom that bring us to the equipoise of *apatheia*.

Poverty

Poverty in itself is not a virtue. To be materially poor can be destructive. The aspect of *ihidayutha* that is poverty of spirit, knowing our need of God, can be ours under any conditions, though material simplicity of life often frees our concentration. Underneath a literal reading of the story of the Rich Young Man lie insights that have little to do with possessions as such. While some people, like St. Francis, have acted literally on Jesus' words with great profit, it would be destructive for most of us to try to emulate him. This does not mean that St. Francis is more "perfect" than the rest of us because of his literal interpretation; holiness does not attach to literalism.

It is obvious that the Rich Young Man is already devout: he knows his need of God, he has great hunger for God and has sought God as best he knows how. Jesus' radical suggestion confronts him not merely with the material insecurity of being poor and homeless, but, more significantly, with the much greater insecurity of knowing that if he follows the suggestion, he will have so clear a vision of the world that he will be pierced to the heart. He will no longer have the luxury of imagining that everyone loves him for himself; perhaps in his vast army of sycophants there might be one or two who in fact do. He will no longer be respected; people will no longer leap to serve him; he will lose all status and recognition; he will be laughed at and considered a fool.

But he will also be free to engage God most intimately in the solitude of worldly poverty, that is, giving up self-aggrandizement, that bestows ontological wealth. The gospels do not tell us what his final decision was; he went away sad, but we do not know what aspect of the proposal was the final cause of his sadness. However, if we are honest, it is not difficult for each of us to know what makes *us* sad on hearing this story.

The most essential factor in learning our need of God is to understand that it does not depend on material possessions or lack of them, but rather on the degree to which we are willing to enter life-enhancing powerlessness that is the stripping of our self-image. Next, we need to acknowledge how much we pretend to ourselves that we know when in fact we do not know, how much we pretend that we have or feel we ought to have God's perspective and control of all we survey. And how much we use our possessions to shore up this illusion.

The reason that self-care, finding out where we hurt, is the first rule of asceticism—doing what each of us must do to put on the humility of Christ—is to be clear-eyed about our humanity. We must find out which wounds are the doors to solitude, and, on a practical level, we must know what our bodies and minds need and what they can do without. It is absurd to ask a one-legged woman to run a marathon on her feet and equally absurd to say that a man is not holy because he looks fat (look at the portrait of roly-poly little John of the Cross).

Thus there are two traps in this matter of finding out what

we need and where we hurt. There is the presumption that tempts us to do more than the grace of our creatureliness allows—which means we are attempting something to inflate our conceit instead of increasing our focus on God. And there is the equal and perhaps worse presumption that we judge holiness in a way that denies God's salvation through our bodiliness.

In *Sayings of the Desert Fathers* there is a story in which one monk, an Egyptian, criticizes another for having more than other monks have and asks him to explain himself. The man responds,

"I, the poor man whom you see, am of the great city of Rome and I was a great man in the palace of the emperor." When the Egyptian heard the beginning of these words, he was filled with compunction . . . [and] came to his senses and said, "Woe to me, for after so much hardship in the world, I have found ease; and what I did not have before, that I now possess. While after so great ease, you have come to humility and poverty."[18]

We might translate this story into modern terms. Each person's needs are different from another's. An artist needs certain materials to speak the word God has given. Some writers need to write or they will lose their emotional balance. Some writers write happily with typewriters, while others, sometimes because of physical difficulties, find using typewriters so oppressive that they cannot break their writer's block without the help of a computer. This is true of me. If I do not write, if the mechanics of writing are so difficult that I cannot face my writer's block, I become slightly more unfocused and crazy than I may ordinarily be.

My computer is a need. I can and have lived without plumbing, in a canyon so isolated as never to have known power lines. I have cut cords of wood to fuel my only source of heat in winter. I have lived in a tent on the side of a mountain in all seasons. You may take away from me most of what people would consider comforts, even needs, but, whatever you do, for the sake of my solitude with God, do not—at least for the moment—take away my computer.

On the other hand, a writer has to be confrontive about the computer. Perhaps a laser printer or a scanner is not a real necessity. They might be wants, but they are not needs. Yet needs can change. There may come a time when a writer no longer needs to write; there may no longer be the pressure of a word to be spoken on paper. Then what now is a need may become merely a want.

The point is that there is nothing fixed about all this. The process of becoming focused on the Face of God is different for each one of us. There is no possible way to legislate this process. We can catch ourselves looking enviously at someone who walled herself up and lived on three prunes and a locust a day for seventy years, but for most of us to live like that would be destructive to our creatureliness and to miss our own mystery. Better to find out what our own minimal and shifting true needs are. We must always be evaluating in a distanced way, always aware of what will bring us closer to mirroring the self-emptying Love of God.

What we have to learn is to start where we are and be who we are and do what we are able in a particular moment, and we have to consider carefully how our efforts affect others, all of this in the light of aspiration and obedience to the word God wishes to speak through us. Sometimes there is the moment for the grand gesture, but it is better to beware of grand gestures. Often there is a more obvious and mundane demand on our love that is costly because it means we must go against the grain and expectations of society. A costly act like this is more to the point—but we must also beware of doing costly acts to feel virtuous, or to indulge in self-pity, or to rock society's boat as a mere exercise of our own power. Often in the initial stages of being wildly in love with God the greatest penance is to simply stay where we are. This is how Bishop Anthony Bloom's *abba* started him off in monastic life. He insisted Bloom carry on as a busy

London physician while secretly a monk until well after he made his monastic vows.

The point is not that we all have to become monks in an institutional sense (the word "monk" derives from a tantalizing word meaning many different kinds of singleness, similar to *ihidaya*): the point is that regimentation or rigidity in any part of the journey into God is destructive to the person and the community of creation and a travesty of the ready response of conversion. There are many different ways to poverty of spirit, and it is for each of us to find out how we are poor and how we are rich. It is for each of us to discover how we need to enrich our lives spiritually in order that we may become poor or vice versa; sometimes we need to become more simple in our living conditions, sometimes not. Sometimes the greatest poverty is to realize that we must simply go on with the burdens given us.

Some people are given other kinds of burdens. There are some people who seem to arrive naturally at positions of power and status and who, conscious of the gratuitousness of these gifts, use them to promote kenotic attitudes in the churches and the world. While these people may be outwardly wealthy and powerful, the primary focus of their wealth and power is not self-aggrandizement but compassionate transformation of the society in which they live. People who have taken this stance open themselves to envy, abuse, and criticism (which is not to say there are not counterfeits whose morality is a pious veneer for worldly success at any price).

This sense that privilege entails responsibility used to be called *noblesse oblige* (not to be confused with *droit du seigneur*). It is part of the European heritage of the United States that seems now to have disappeared, especially in the churches, with a few notable exceptions such as Bishop Paul Moore of New York.

Whatever one thinks of Moore's approach or policies, by virtue of his independent economic and social position, he has been free to serve as the conscience of his church, to care for those condemned and outcast by the rest of society. He has taken risks with people and is an extraordinary pastor. He is not only willing to take chances; he offers comfort and resources if they fall or fail, and, almost unbelievable in this day and age when we treat failure as leprosy, he is willing to help pick up the pieces so that those involved can continue on the way with renewed strength and deeper wisdom. There are doubtless others in the churches who are less visible and equally effective, but their occurrence seems to be increasingly rare.

Noblesse oblige is an attitude we need to recover. By the humility of Christ we have become heirs of God, and by our baptism we have taken on responsibility to be the world's conscience and, even more, its compassion. This is our *royal* priesthood. In the past, this ideal has been counterfeited as paternalism and patronage, but it is a vital element in our aspiration.

It takes all our life to give up power-games, to give up the power of blame for the power of weeping. By comparison, it is relatively easy to give up addiction to materialism. We need to live on a material level that leaves our hearts free to know our need of God, so that our gaze on God holds us in equipoise for the sake of the creation. We need to understand that what we do materially on a personal level, as well as spiritually, affects the whole web of creation. Self-care for the sake of community of creation has taken on a new and desperate meaning, for the community reaches far beyond our small planet.

To discern what we need is subtle, very difficult, very delicate, and more complex than we can ever realize. We learn discernment by trial and error, by slipping into judgment, and then being embarrassed by how wrong we are. But gradually, if we are not obdurate in our mistakes, we learn. Sometimes we can evolve criteria for discernment, and sometimes it seems as if we must simply operate on an educated hunch. What we must always be prepared for in our readiness is surprise.

What surprises us, and what we least like about poverty is the demand that we let go our pet religious idols, idols to which we retreat when religion has sunk to solipsism and a desire for security. There are big idols like the inviolable ghetto mentality of Zeus-god institutions of every denominational stripe, and there are the little idols into which controlled projections of the Son and the Holy Spirit have been made in recent times. The institution idol is the subject of this book; the idols of the others are instantly recognizable. Sometimes the Son is referred to as "my buddy Jesus," and often it seems that the self-effacing Holy Spirit has been turned into "a bottled gas that will produce specific manifestations when you push the right button." One idolatrous hymn of the blackest magical variety begins, "Blessed assurance, Jesus is MINE!"

Chastity

Poverty is the willingness to enter the richness of our creatureliness assured by the humility of Christ. Poverty is embracing who we truly are in the Love of God, which we discover is abundance beyond imagining. Poverty and chastity engage. Chastity is, no more, no less, the degree to which we are willing to be focused, to be brought to being by our gaze on the Face of God.

Virginity in this landscape is a much larger notion than mere genital intactness, the degrading technicality to which, over time, it has become reduced, or celibacy, with which chastity has often been confused. In Syrian Christianity virginity is rooted in resurrection, paradise not only restored but transfigured. Virginity is received in part at baptism, and in fullness in the *parousia*, both beyond time and interpenetrating time. We grow into virginity, which mirrors God's inviolable vulnerability.

Ephrem celebrates virginity in his hymns:

> See, people being baptized,
> becoming virgins. . . .
> having gone down to the font,
> been baptized and put on
> that single *Ihidaya*.[19]

Isaac of Antioch—another Isaac—records an encounter with a pagan:

I heard a young man singing one day,
"Would that someone would pull me down and rebuild me, and make me a virgin once again,":
and I told him that "this request of yours is possible with Jesus."[20]

Virginity is associated with wakefulness, the equipoise of reciprocity with God. Ephrem is particularly acute on this subject of wakefulness, and in *The Luminous Eye*, Dr. Brock writes:

At baptism the baptized "put on the Wakeful One in the waters" (Epiphany 4:8), and so themselves become, in potential at any rate, "wakers"; and at the Eucharist, as we have already seen, they are continually being recreated as angelic beings by means of Fire and Spirit (Faith 10:9). Furthermore, spiritual wakefulness means to be single, to be in harmony, whereas if the soul is in "sleep" it is "divided" (Heresies 19:35).

The ideal of wakefulness, characteristic both of the angels and of the wise virgins, together with that of singleness, would thus seem to be among the most important motivating factors that lay behind the ascetic vision and orientation of early Syriac Christianity. It was a vision which, if interiorized, Ephrem saw as being applicable to all Christians, the married just as much as the celibate.[21]

Dr. Brock denies that *ihidayutha* is a dualistic or Manichean view, at least in Ephrem's circle, for Ephrem "specifically disassociates himself, and the Christian community to which he belongs, from Marcionite and Manichean views of marriage as something 'foul.' "[22] Dr. Brock's position is supported by a new reading of early Syrian documents, one that differs from that of earlier scholars from the West who have gone looking for dualism and found it.[23]

This reading suggests that far from attempting to eliminate sexuality, early Syrian spirituality recognized it as an integral part of the creation God has called good and with which God is united. What it meant for relationships between men and women was that they may no longer be exploitive, that men might no longer use women merely to satisfy their pleasure (1 Peter 3:7). Rather, the partners are to reverence each other, their love, and love-making, thus helping them further along toward the interiorized goal of becoming *ihidayutha*. Translated into plain language for today, kenotic love-making in committed relationships mirrors the love of God and increases your virginity. We will look at celibacy in a moment.

If this new reading is correct, the implications for us are most exciting. I have long felt than one of the primary reasons for contemporary moral collapse is directly related to our degraded idea of virginity as genital intactness, an attitude that expresses hatred for our creatureliness. This debased idea of virginity has created a great, gaping wound in us. Men particularly have lost their sense of virginity; they seem to feel that they never in their life actually have virginity, because of their impression that genital intactness—and therefore virginity—applies only to the female. For both men and women, our culture's thinking seems to go like this: "If penetration means loss of virginity, means that it is no longer possible for me to be whole, or perfect, if I can never again find innocence, why bother with morality of the most ordinary sort? Any integrity I might seek would only be a sham, a pale echo of what once was and cannot be again."

If we can change this sort of thinking; if, in our age, we can restore the wider sense of *ihidayutha* to virginity, that our sexuality is caught up in aspiration, part of our all-encompassing focus on and in the Love of God, then morality might once again become viable. It would no longer be confined to the strictures and platitudes of constraint, platitudes that not only sicken us but lead to the opposite effect than they intend.

Chastity asks the question, *what do we really want?* It is a process of continual *self-confrontation* (the second rule of asceticism) and vigilance over the temptation to compromise, to use expediency to avoid the suffering necessary to our maturity. It is vigilance for attempts by others to exploit us for their own purposes. Chastity is not confined to the area of sexual activity any more than sexuality is confined to sexual activity. Chastity and sexuality are linked, but the linkage goes far beyond the criteria by which we cherish our bodily relationships.

Chastity is the particular ground of the Holy Ghost—*Geist* because of the nuances of wildness that attach to the German root. Chastity is a self-restraining, self-emptying, other-oriented inviolate wildness the freedom of which is the freedom of listening obedience to the Word of God spoken out of Silence, from whom it cannot be distracted.

The energy for inviolable vulnerability arises from our sexuality, through which we relate bodily to the creation. We are incarnate in the world. Sexuality affects everything we do. It affects equally the writing of this book, relationships of all kinds, and prayer. It is rarely entirely focused, and as well as being the source of creativity at all levels, it can also be the energy that stimulates the mental chatter that fractures silence and the restlessness that makes physical activity a vital balancing factor in a life of prayer. When we violate our chastity or are caught in situations where people attempt to violate us, to change us into their own image, our chaste sexuality responds to attempted rape with incandescent fury.

While all of these effects of sexuality are natural and morally neutral, to come to equipoise the mental chatter needs to be coaxed into a single Word sounding that is left behind in the silence; the restlessness needs to be channeled so that it swirls around a still center; and the fury—the fury can only be wept over and offered in the burning light of God. There is too much healing to be done when we are violated to know what rage is necessary psychological glue and what is willfulness. It is a matter for God in God's time to slip this fury from our fingers, which are often stiff and twisted from the effort of willingness to be unclenched.

Sexuality, for better or worse, is *in* everything we are and do, but it is not *all* we are and do. This is an important distinction. When we categorize people by artificial sexual groupings, not as men and women but as "heterosexual," "homosexual," or "bisexual," not only are we using biologically, psychologically, and spiritually inaccurate language, we are also reducing people to the sum total of their presenting body type or predominant orientation.

We are both our sexuality and are more than our sexuality. When we talk about chastity, about virginity, we are talking about everything we are and will be. And everything we are and will be invariably entails our sexuality.

The first premise in regard to sexuality is that there is no such thing as a casual relationship, whether or not it is sexually expressed. In our sexuality we enter into the realm of the numinous and the creativity that is part of our engagement, part of our being in the image of God. Thus, without getting overly serious about it, without losing the sense of play and pleasure and joy and simple fun, we need to realize that *every* encounter is significant whether or not it is sexually expressed, and that we need to exercise self-restraint not simply to be in conformity with someone else's ideas about morality or to avoid disease, but because we affect the focus of our entire being and the being of others by what we do or do not do with our selves, particularly with our feelings and bodies, in relationship.

Celibacy is something else again. There is nothing holy about celibacy *per se*, and celibacy without chastity can be very unholy indeed. In the past, celibacy often has been used as a mask for hatred of our bodies and the creation and denial of and flight from the death of surrender that is part—sometimes the most awesome part—of kenotic sexual love-making.

The choice of lifelong celibacy cannot be imposed by law. It is a gift, and its bestowal lies in the mystery of a person's unique life in God in the creation. All the mystique and high-flown language that for centuries has exalted the confusion between celibacy and chastity and implied that to be celibate is to love in a "higher" state is simply a cover for institutional attempts to justify control. Perhaps this mystique is a distortion of what Dr. Brock observes, that "for those who opted to live a consecrated life, as *ihidaye* following the example of Christ the *Ihidaya*, this vision was doubly meaningful." Thus, celibacy is significant in terms of personal meaning, not in terms of value on an absolute scale of holiness.

People receive the gift of celibacy for any number of reasons. People with communicable diseases can choose and be gifted with celibacy not only to be sexually responsible, but also as a way of offering their unique life's sacrifice. Some people choose celibacy simply to avoid distraction from the vision of God—they are more easily distracted than others. People often receive the gift of celibacy who can think about only one thing at a time—they *need* to be celibate. The vast majority of people, however, find their equipoise of responsiveness to God without being celibate.

One of the saddest and wickedest policies in the history of Christianity has been its effort to control people by means of isolating sexuality, making it object and killing it; by defining sexuality as the sexual act alone; by condemning sexual feelings that arise in response to biological and psychological signals too subtle for us consciously to perceive. At times, prelates of the institutional church have even declared that sexual expression in marriage is mortal sin, e.g., Gregory the Great.

Gregory's Manichean horror of sexuality lingers today in the exalted position some of the churches still wrongly give to celibacy, an attitude that degrades the creation God has called good and in which God dwells in the humility of Christ; an attitude that degrades those for whom celibacy would be an abuse of the creature God has made them. We need to throw out nearly all of the writing we have on chastity, celibacy, and sexuality and begin all over again.

If we are chaste, we can look upon the Face of God whether we are married with children, in a committed relationship with another person, or celibate. This is a general rule of thumb for middle-class people in Western cultures. This does not mean that those whom we regard as the poor, the sick, the sinners, the ugly, the outcast, the disgusting, the useless do not look on the Face of God; they nestle with particular closeness in the love of God.

In addition, chastity can take forms that are wildly divergent from what we might ordinarily think of as normative, interpretations that most middle-class people in Western cultures continue to find scandalous. For example, the woman at the end of Steinbeck's *Grapes of Wrath* who feeds the starving old man with her breast-milk, now useless for her stillborn child, is one of the purest examples of chastity in all of American literature. A more recent example in England is *The Harlot's Room* by "Melissa," the story of a woman raped psychologically and spiritually by government and mental health authorities and well-meaning religious idiots, who finally finds her integration and chastity, recovers her virginity, by going into solitude (she uses the word *retreat*) and exercising a ministry to herself and others from her seclusion most would call prostitution. When her retreat has done its work, she leaves it.

Contrary to the aspiration of *ihidayutha*, the Zeus-god demands a constraining, materialistic, empirical virginity. In contemporary culture, virginity is a value placed on women by measuring a membrane: either you have it or you don't, and once it's gone, too bad, it's gone forever. It is easy to see where this attitude leads theologically. If the god we worship is the Zeus-god, then the Annunciation is rape. This may seem an outrageous statement until we become aware that there are many women who have been raped by their fathers or brothers and relate to Mary precisely because they perceive that she was raped by god her father. This is not a rare or even an occasional devotion. To change the image to God her Mother does not help: there are also women who have been raped by their mothers and other female relatives.

However, if God is I WILL BE, then Mary is a pillar of flame, the first perfect, kenotic priestly mirror of God, who, in courteous and kenotic exchange of love and co-creation with her, becomes incarnate in her womb. Her virginity is not genital intactness but her life that is totally focused in God.

The way we perceive the story of the Annunciation reveals the way we relate to God. The great unease many people feel about the Annunciation stories in Luke and Matthew arises in part from the introduction of the idea of a controlling and intervening God and our debased ideas about virginity. In addition, to make a special case for Mary's conception of Jesus is the first dangerous vitiation of the enfleshment of God. The Evangelists Mark and John feel the story is irrelevant. Unfortunately there is not room in this book to pursue this line of questioning further.

Feminist concern with biblical, liturgical, and theological attitudes and language is not only rage at inequality. The attitudes we have toward women and the body, the cultivation of Manichean dualism throughout the history of Christianity right up to the present is reinforced by phrases in some of the churches' most significant and universal prayers, such as the *Te Deum:* "When thou tookest upon thee to deliver man, thou didst not abhor the virgin's womb." While this phrase may originally have been intended to mean God's willing involvement in the creation, the assumptions these words communicate today are foul.

Why should a womb—any womb—be abhorrent to God *or* humanity, since it is the source of our life, just as the humility of God who took flesh in Mary's womb is the divine womb in which we find our being? The thinking behind such phrasings is not merely a denigration of creatureliness: it is blasphemous to the humility of I WILL BE.

The notion that chaste sexual relationships can increase virginity is not mere mystical moonshine but based in concrete reality. Right love-making in committed relationships is mutually kenotic. We embrace the other, warts and all, in self-emptying and self-forgetfulness, and by this embracing we also embrace God's forgivenness of all we cannot bear in our selves. In this love-making all roles disappear because the lovers are not self-reflective, and each is striving for an equipoise that is complete readiness of response to the other. But in any love relationship whether or not it is sexually expressed, we have the opportunity to mirror the kenotic reciprocity of the humility of Christ.

Obedience

The humility of Christ is obedient, even to the death of the Cross, and *therefore*—how much we would like to forget this *therefore*—God has highly exalted . . . Obedience asks the question, *what price are we willing to pay?* The third aspect of asceticism, to which chastity is the key, is *self-forgetfulness*. Self-forgetfulness cannot be a rule because it is a gift of *ihidayutha*, a gratuitous gift of God.

Self-care and self-confrontation prepare in us a greater capacity for self-forgetfulness. The predominance of self-forgetfulness in our lives can be hoped for, but it cannot be sought, because if we look at our selves to see if we are self-forgetful we obviously are not. Like other forms of unitive experience, self-forgetfulness is noticed—if it is noticed at all—obliquely, in retrospect, and with astonishment.

If we are willing to pay the price that is not less than everything, then we are opening our selves to receive self-forgetfulness. We watch and listen not to our interior monologue but to God. Obedience is our listening response to God from the equipoise of *apatheia*. And the Face of God is worth the ultimate price; in its Gaze we know ineffable self-forgetfulness, *ekstasis*, literally, "to stand outside" our selves. Or, better put, to stand outside the closed system of our preoccupation with our pseudo-selves that is our fallenness from being.

Obedience; *ob audiere:* from listening; being and action from listening. In the New Testament churches, obedience is to the Word of God revealed in Christ in the Scriptures, in prayer, in the breaking of bread. Obedience is a simple attentiveness to a fathomless mystery that may cost the disciples their lives. But they give this price not a thought; the kingdom of their Christ is worth everything they have to give and more.

In the desert, the solitaries also learned from listening to one another, listening not so much to speech, for it was exceedingly difficult to get a word out of the Old Women and Men; they were forthcoming only under conditions of great need. Rather, the disciple would come and live with the *amma* or *abba* and learn by imitation when to pray, when to eat, when to sleep, when to work, making the necessary adjustments that physiology and psychology demanded. By this silent teaching the disciple entered the Silence of God and began to hear the Word that sounds in that Silence. Learning what the desert-dweller had to teach was thus a slow process of questioning, analyzing, reflecting (because often learning seemed to mock analysis), and finally, illumination. It was for this Word that the solitaries went to the desert, a Word that made words superfluous.

St. Ephrem understands obedience, its profundity, its kenotic reciprocity, and its playfulness. He tells us quite rightly that Mary conceived the Word through her ear:

> Just as from the small womb of Eve's ear
> Death entered in and was poured out,
> So through a new ear, that was Mary's,
> Life entered and was poured out.[24]

Ephrem's suggestion that we conceive the Word, Christ's indwelling, through our ears, through the Word both silent and spoken, has essential relevance today. Too quickly did the obedience of the desert solitaries become twisted into a kind of spiritual slavery that exalted the head of a monastery. Too soon did the word of earthly obedience come to be considered semi-divine, no matter how ill-considered. Too quickly did the self-effacement of the *abbas* and *ammas* become monastic nobility, both monks and rulers taking the title "Lord" that properly belongs to the Servant-Savior. Too rapidly did the leaders of the churches not only seek self-aggrandizement, but the power of secular government as well.

Today in some churches we still see "obedience" that exalts the ill-considered words of hierarchical autocrats, words used to break people, to violate their chastity, to tell them what they must believe, to force entry into the dwelling of the Holy, where no outsider has a right to enter, much less rule. Whether this counterfeit obedience is demanded by the Vatican, a parish or monastic council, a board of presbyters or a "spiritual director," it is a travesty of what listening to the Word is meant to be.

What is often conceived through our ears today in the churches is not the transfiguring Word that is Christ our Serpent lifted high as medicine for the serpent's sting. What is conceived more often through our ears in the churches today is a cockatrice: the worm is within, and unless we let go our idol of power quickly, Christianity—what is left of the institution—will surely come to a quivering, whimpering end.

The price of obedience to the Word is everything and more than everything. Those who know the Gaze of God wish they had ten lives to give; those who know only the Zeus-god, the projection of their own greed, are reluctant to give even a fraction of one self-reflective life.

One Rule of Love

While there are ten beatitudes and three evangelical counsels, and while I have added three questions for discernment—self-care: *where do I hurt?*; self-confrontation: *what do I REALLY want?*; self-forgetfulness: *what price am I willing to pay?*—there is only one rule of love. The beatitudes are one beatitude; the counsels are one counsel, and all divisions are subsumed into the humility of Christ, the *Ihidaya*, whom we put on. Even one movement of love may seem impossible unless we keep in continual remembrance that the goal of our struggle is not to achieve but to become poised in willing response to the love of God.

It is grace alone that can accomplish the imperceptible transformation and integrative focus that God works in us out of our sight. Often nothing seems to happen. And yet if we persist through our failures and rebellions, we *are* changed. It is not change we expect to be able to see often, or even usually. But sometimes, in a flash, in the very shadow of death, we become aware that we are changed and given new life.

Even so, even when this miracle is accomplished in our selves, when we have to deal with the institutional churches we are brought very nearly to despair. Our efforts to effect the smallest change in the face of institutional inertia makes us feel about as effective as hunting a mammoth with a fly swatter. But maybe, just maybe if enough of us grit our teeth and get on with it; if we can endure the slander and persecution; if enough of us continue to erode the closed system of the Zeus-god and insist on the primacy of Christ's open and saving humility; if enough of us can inspire only a *little* vision and a *little* generosity, then maybe, just maybe, Christianity could begin to fulfill the deepest meaning of Jesus' great high-priestly prayer (Jn 17). While it may be beyond even Christian hope to think that the institutional churches might one day make the first steps toward the responsive balance of Christ's humility, those of us who know that our only existence derives from that humility needs must try by the persuasion of our being.

In the end, the criterion for institutional discernment is noise. God's Word comes out of Silence and brings us to Silence. Institutions of any kind, when they can no longer coerce and deceive, tend to retreat behind deafening, shattering, trammeling, numbing noise. On the Eve of Pentecost, 1987, according to Rowan Williams, 750 people gathered at a United States Air Force base in Britain. It was an open day at the base, which meant that visitors were streaming in and out to watch the big planes display their power. Outside the fence, the motley group of protestors could not have an "official" Eucharist, but they prayed prayers of thanksgiving and they broke bread together. During this and other liturgies of the day, the prayers and hymns were dimmed and drowned by the roar and thunder of the bombers flying low over their heads.

In the backwash of the jets' howling, the prayers seemed themselves to be silence. Hour after hour, mile after mile, the procession continued through rain and hail, lightning and thunder, as its members tied small white crosses to the fence posts around the base. Hour after hour the display of two kinds of power did battle, each in its own way: one overwhelming by the sheer force of violence, the other coinhering by the self-outpouring of the Love of a humble Christ.

At the end of the day the machines of war grumbled into the distance, and the tired marchers handed a cross of flowers through police lines. And suddenly in the silence, being of one mind and heart, they burst into the joyous chords of *Ubi Caritas.*

6. Eucharist: Envisioning the Future

> "But when we crave power over life—endless wealth, unasailable safety, immortality—then desire becomes greed. And if knowledge allies itself to that greed, then comes evil. Then the balance of the world is swayed and ruin weighs heavy in the scale. . . . Death and life are like the two sides of my hand, I said, but the truth is we do not know what life is or what death is. To claim power over what you do not understand is not wise, nor is the end of it likely to be good."
>
> URSULA LE GUIN, *THE FARTHEST SHORE*

It should be apparent by now that the model of power on which an individual, a community, a church institution—or any other institution—operates will determine the spiritual maturity of its members, that is, whether or not eucharistic community is formed, whether the community finds its being in equipoise of ready response or whether it creates self-image to mask power politics. Nowhere is the perception of power more critical than in the formation and life of the eucharistic community through which the vows of baptism, of commitment to become part of the salvation that is the humility of Christ, and of its day-to-day living-out are strengthened and renewed. In the Eucharist the community not only realizes its life in Christ but comes to know itself as the Body and Blood of Christ.

We should not be surprised at the situation in which we find ourselves, given not only the dualistic hierarchical polity of our inheritance but also the wounds of Judeo-Christian history. Although salvation was to come to the world through the people and in spite of the reiteration of this vocation by the prophets, the Jewish tradition became more and more a closed shop to preserve identity in dispersion and a pluralistic world. Devout Gentiles were tolerated around the synagogues, but they were not "real" Jews, just as in the Christian past devout people could make deep commitments to God, but if they were not ordained or monastics they were somehow leading a "lower" life, or if they were non-Christians, they were "heathen," outside the love of God. This mentality persists both on the part of those specially consecrated and those not and within the continuing narcissism of the Christian ghetto.

This mentality must change. We need to recognize once and for all that *the whole creation* is the Body of Christ and that when we talk about the humility of Christ, of Christ's sacrifice "for all" and our participation in that sacrifice, the whole creation is included in the "all" and has the choice of finding being in that sacrifice. In spite of the testimony of the author of John's gospel and of Paul and the writers of other letters attributed to him, only today are we beginning to discover this reality in all its grandeur. We cannot help but wonder if some of those first baptisms were eager intuitive acknowledgment of the cosmic Christ. But the simplicity of the early days of Christianity was short-lived; too soon the nonbaptized were forbidden Communion; technique replaced vision, legalism replaced ardor, the desire for a false reality diluted the scandal of the divine Presence in history, in time, in creatureliness and the role of creatureliness in transfiguration. Today we are bogged down by additional centuries of power politics, controversy, theorizing, and control.

Each bit of the creation is sustained by the life of God, is sacrament, and is engaged with the whole of creation. Each moment of life can be and, if we are committed to the humility of Christ, *must* be Eucharist. The early Syrian church recognized this fact and allowed all who wished it to receive the Eucharist, whether or not they were baptized. This church understood that in Eucharist sacred time and linear time coincide here, and the *parousia* is *now.* Sacraments of the Christian churches must not be allowed to exclude or devalue our interrelatedness with the creation. On the contrary, sacramental life should enhance reverence for and relatedness within the creation.

Thus the eucharistic community includes all of creation. The Body of Christ is the fundamental resonance of humility, of self-giving, that is, sacrificial *kenosis* that leads to creation and re-creation, no matter in what sphere. It is the cohesion of creation. Perhaps we can image this notion as resonant densities refracting Christ's generative context of forgivenness. To recover our humility within the whole creation as the Body of Christ means radical, practical changes in Christianity. If we come to engage the whole creation as the Body and Blood of Christ (succumbing to neither monism nor pantheism), then our sensibilities have been re-created, and this transformation of our being necessitates a transformation of the means by which we order our eucharistic community.

How can we enable the institution to put on the mind of Christ? Over the centuries there have been many attempts at reform. Some wrought gradual changes in structure; some caused radical breaks and established new paradigms of organization. But a new organizational paradigm is useless and its implementation reverts to former ills unless its foundation rests in the humility of Christ, of *kenosis,* of eucharistic ungraspingness, unless the people of God are educated to cherish self-forgetful, awestruck wonder before the humble God from the beginning of their coming to the community.

What we need today, then, is not only to separate the two conflicting models of power that presently reside in a confused and confusing way in the clergy, but also, and vital to restore Christianity's foundations, we need a fundamental revision of our theology and practice of baptism. Our attitude toward baptism determines all other elements of the organized community. I would now like to sketch out some possible ideas for the radical reorganization of Christian institutions. I am not offering these suggestions to be voted on. They are simply an attempt to get us to think in different ways about the organizational structure that too often seems sacrosanct (it isn't). No system is going to be perfect, and the suggestions I make here are by way of transition. There is no question that we need something much more radical.

But for the purposes of this book, I am trying to suggest ways in which we might move in new directions without being too threatening to people who have profound personal investments in older perceptions of church polity. We need to reverence their commitment and their notions of God, while at the same time not perpetuating the ills of the past. As with everything else, it is a matter of finding responsive balance.

Baptism

The implications of abandoning the false synthesis that attempts to unite the Zeus-god with the kenotic God means that our experience as a worshiping community will change. If we commit ourselves to mutual *kenosis,* our experience of self, community, and the divine are commingled in the confluence of Love's humility. It is here that we discover the ground of our beseeching, the foundation on which the institution may be ordered, and the equipoise of conversion that is its source of action.

Baptism is the commitment to become a living sacrifice; Eucharist is the kinetic icon of our moment-by-moment living-out of this sacrifice in the ministry of our daily lives. Thus baptism is the commitment to be both priest and sacrifice; to be willing to be enabled to bear God's Gaze and to gaze back, Face to face; to be changed by it, to seem to be annihilated by it as our illusory and worldly power-oriented self-image is consumed; to be returned to the glory of our creatureliness as we are brought back to our being, to our equipoise of ready response from which we have fallen away; and to communicate this love to the world, to illuminate and to celebrate it no matter what the cost.

If we accept with any seriousness that the creation is Christ's Body and Blood, that within creatureliness God willingly indwells with radical immanence and glory, then any living, any action has the potential of being eucharistic. Interior choice and action no longer can be separated, compartmentalized, externalized. All actions and interactions have the eucharistic reciprocity of coinherence, which is the Love of God. If we are committed to the priestly transformation that is the sacrifice of our lives, the resonances of all life, of all actions, even those of which we must repent, become part of the living sacrifice of mutual *kenosis*, in which and by which the resonances of the Word, spoken First and Last from the Silence of God, enable the transfiguration of all creation.

Within the humility of God, the eucharistic community may no longer be self-reflective. We may no longer be inward-looking, ghetto-oriented, searching for the noisy technology with which to wrest from the depths of our ontological fissure the synthetic secular answers that are unrelated to our religious questions. We may no longer be concerned for status and control. We may no longer engage in power-games; our life has sacramental coherence. If our energies are generated by kenotic self-restraint because our gaze is fixed on God, the community is not dissipated by its efforts to maintain its own inflation, to keep its fragments from flying apart. Instead, our response may become timely and appropriate to the level of need. We disclose and enable kenotic engagement.

As human understanding has changed, so baptism has changed. It has been treated legalistically as "forgiveness of sins" once for all; it has been treated as admission to an elite; it has been treated as magic, so that the fate of those who died unbaptized was uncertain if not dreadful. Baptism has enormous and complex symbolism too great even to survey in this short book.

In theory, baptism should mark commitment to the priesthood we have been discussing. In practice, those within the Christian community who take this commitment seriously usually come to their seriousness after the fact: they are already baptized. They often come to an awakening not because someone has finally told them that seeking the Face of God in the humility of Christ's sacrifice is what baptism is about, but more often through an illuminating shock that can leave them bewildered and angry at having been deliberately or ineptly hoodwinked out of their birthright, their being, that they have been kept ignorant and immature. And having finally realized what baptism in fact is about, they find little support in the unawakened, if legally baptized, community in which to live out the vision of life in God they have been newly given.

Any concrete realization of their baptism seems to have a price tag attached to it, requiring that they become part of an explicit or implicit hierarchy. And it is often precisely because of their new awareness of the contrast between the controlling hierarchy and the *kenosis* of baptism that such people have awakened in the first place. In short, there is nowhere they can turn to find support for their return to being-in-God, to the proper ordering of solitude and community, within their church. It is this dilemma that originally gave rise to solitaries and the monastic life, and the rise of monasticism is directly linked to the devaluation of baptism and shift of power models in the church.

People who take seriously the priesthood I have been describing have few options. They feel there is no support for their struggle to offer the sacrifice of their lives, no recognition of the real meaning of baptism, and no way of consecrating or committing their being in a permanent way to eucharistic engagement with the numinous in the community of creation. Until we can sort out what baptism means and administer it only after extensive preparation and only to those who are willing to make the kind of priestly commitment this book describes, we will need to find new ways of consecration— vows on top of vows.

It may seem sheer lunacy to suggest such a thing, but the churches have been doing it for centuries in the vows of monasticism and ordination. It might be argued that to allow still other ways of consecration would create the danger of a gnostic network of the elect—to which the only possible response is, what have we already got in the clergy club and the religious-life ghetto? At least this network would broaden the base and point of view; at least its orientation might have a better chance of being self-emptying rather than self-serving. In any event, the two traditional ways of consecration have served only a tiny fraction of those with this willingness, in part because those with kenotic vocations have had too much spiritual maturity to play power-games.

In the United States, the Episcopal Church has hundreds of people inappropriately seeking ordination because they need some way of consecrating their lives, and although they know better intellectually, the present-day trivilization of baptism means that their baptismal vows do not signify the life-and-death commitment they wish to make. Baptism is cheap these days. What rector is not happy to have another dues-paying member on the rolls or a larger body count to report to the bishop at the end of the year? The average member of a congregation seems to have made the haziest sort of commitment—if there is any sense of commitment at all—and is quite happy to remain in the role of a second-class citizen. But this basking in ecclesial sloth is not what Christianity is about.

The two options the churches have traditionally offered have become entirely inappropriate for the kenotic Christians who take their commitment seriously. The clerical club of the ordained, with its ideas about precedence and career orientation, and its dedication to the dualistic abyss it perpetuates between itself and the nonordained is the last place to grow into kenotic life. Religious life has its own inheritance of power-games, as well as a dismal history of anti-creation dualism. In addition, today people want to be consecrated *where they are*, in "ordinary life"—often married, with children, continuing in their chosen career in the world, and working out their part in transfiguration through it. In today's culture everyone is always leaving home, and a stability in ordinariness (which has itself become extraordinary), much less a stability in the humility of Christ, is a precious icon for the whole community of creation. Far from being the nuisances they are often regarded as by their bishops because they don't fit into a convenient slot, these people are the lifeblood of Christianity.

Throughout history, the inescapable fact that when two or three are gathered together there is politics means that religious communities are often very poor places for simple prayer, solitude, and the committed living that is balance of ready response to the rhythms of God. This is not true of *all* communities, but the exceptions are few and far between.

This is not to say that we must abolish religious life or clergy, but rather that we need to look again at baptism and how we administer it. And most especially we need to reconsider what the "teaching authority" of Christianity is and where it resides. It certainly does *not* reside with those whose formulation of doctrine is compromised by money or the desire to rule others. And given the freedom of God, the churches must be ready to recognize a true Word wherever it arises—which most often is from among the humble.

For all of the churches' study about baptism, for all the change that has taken place in the last twenty years, today in many Christian churches baptism still has about as much significance as a club pledge or a fraternity initiation. Ordained people or those in vows—in spite of disclaimers—are still regarded by vast numbers of the nonordained and nonvowed as the "real" Christians, those with a "real" relationship with God or a "real" commitment.

For all of this, there are those who take their baptismal vows seriously and who wish the gifts they have been given by God for the sake of the community to be taken seriously by those people they perceive as holding power and making decisions in the institution. They do not want power; they want to be authorized to get on with their commitment and its ministry. Without authorization they will probably get on with the ministry in any event—outside the institution.

Whether the people with "authority" are ordained or vowed, those "merely baptized" are rarely taken seriously by the institution unless they are parish officials or have great financial clout. Even so, the wardens or parish council members are at a disadvantage when clergy are around, and often their practical, canny wisdom is ignored for the perhaps ill-advised preferences of the cleric who feels personally threatened by nonordained expertise. It is not just a matter of "prophets without honor"; the prejudice goes much, much deeper.

The Church Club

A local church today is often a more or less friendly club of people who try to feel good, perhaps try to be good, and, rather more unusually, try to support one another through the hard times, using the simple weekly formula they understand as Christian liturgy and the social milieu of the parish. It is comfortable and comforting, rather like keeping God for a pet or having God keep us for pets.

The ordained clergy do the God-business, saying the right prayers, making the magic each week, organizing charitable works, ensuring that no one rocks the boat. God is a distant and frightening, or indifferent, or cozy figure, and the weekly group confession of sins soothes whatever vague discomfort there is, followed by the assurance of forgiveness and, sometimes, the magic Bread of Communion. In a specialized society, religion is the business of the clergy, and God is better left to the professionals. After all, that's what we hire them for, isn't it? Baptism is the little service you go through to become a member of this cozy club.

The church club is like any club. There are officers, and there is a social hierarchy, and you are known by being a supporter of Mrs. A who is always in competition with Mrs. B in terms of putting on events like the parish festival or the rummage sale. You are a crony or hanger-on of the rector and his senior warden (who is almost always one of the rector's drinking and card-playing buddies) or else you are classified as part of the disgruntled minority who are shoved to one side. Or, more likely the group is indifferent, and after a few half-hearted efforts to get you involved on their side (after weeks of ignoring you), you are written off.

For those readers who instantly react that this description is an exaggeration, I suggest they visit parishes outside their normal round, and more than once to get beneath the superficial jargon that sounds very committed and self-forgetful but is in fact P.R. and self-inflation. It might be objected that a little self-affirmation is harmless, which may be true on a merely psychological level, but in the commitment of the humble Christ, of coming to be, there is ultimately no such thing as harmless self-inflation. It must be let go as we mature.

In the church club, young families have their moment of glory when their infants are baptized in elaborate private christenings (for social cachet) or publicly (often over protests). Training of godparents is rudimentary if it occurs at all, and often the baptism is more of a seal of an agreement between parents and godparents about the care of their mutual children, should one set of parents die, than it is a seal of the living God on the child.

Older children who are baptized usually have little choice whether or not they make their own commitment, though children are often ready to make serious commitments at a far earlier age than we give them credit for. There are some eleven-year-olds who are able to make a deeper and more permanent commitment than middle-aged adults. Yet often, and in spite of their school records that provide some empirical proof of their ability to understand baptism, they are forbidden to make their own promises because the adults think the little ones "can't possibly understand what is going on." This kind of unthinking betrayal and belittling by adults can be devastating for preadolescent children and for them puts religion into a lifelong adversary role.

Baptism of adults often occurs after only the crudest

elucidation of Christianity's creedal propositions, instruction given by clerics many years removed from seminary education who often have only dim memories of passionate, self-forgetful commitment (if they ever had it), and who are interested only that the catechumen "believe the right way" and know enough not to be embarrassed or embarrassing in church. Or else an elaborate catechumenate is devised that more closely resembles a kind of extended religious bank holiday than the communication of matters of life and death.

Suggestions for Change in Initiation

What follows is no guarantee of improvement. And even with improvement, the churches must always be ready to change and to reform themselves in response to changing conditions. Any changes will be futile unless the fundamental model of power to which we are committing our selves is reexamined and until the focus of our commitment is rooted in the humility of Christ. Our rites of initiation are unsatisfactory and we need to change them. Further, we need to emphasize that the rite is only the first sign of a lifelong process on which the authenticity of the community depends.

Since parents have every reason to celebrate the entrance of their children, and adults their own entrance, into the Christian community, the first step might be a naming ceremony. There could be rites appropriate for infants, children, and adults depending on the age at which they enter the community. The naming ceremony would provide an initial bonding with the community and make the person named a catechumen.

At the time of becoming a catcheumen, a child might receive not only godparents, but a spiritual nanny as well. An adult would have the opportunity to develop a discerning relationship with a member of the congregation (see below). The nanny could be male or female as appropriate. This spiritual nanny or auntie or uncle would be someone specially gifted in relating to children and helping them with their questions about God, about life and death, about the way the world works. The spiritual nanny would not take the place of religious classroom education, but supplement it.

The spiritual nanny would be an adult outside the family in whom children could confide, someone who is not personally obligated to the family (and therefore someone who will not be likely to betray secrets). The spiritual nanny would be an adult who not only could share the enormous questions and terrible secrets that haunt children, but who also would help confirm them in their often extraordinary sense of the numinous at which less sensitive adults often scoff. A spiritual nanny would be able to help a child become appropriately articulate and communicative on a one-on-one basis about relationship with God, so that later in life, problems of religious self-consciousness, embarrassment, and posing would be less likely to arise.

The relationship of the child to the nanny might change; the child's or nanny's external circumstances might change. Each situation would have to be adjusted according to circumstances, but the role of spiritual nanny could provide children with a sense of security and stability in the eucharistic community wherever that might be.

Admission to Communion would be the next step, but this has always been a matter of controversy as regards children. Because the ghetto mentality still prevails, admission to Communion of the nonbaptized would be even more controversial. Yet if we accept that the whole creation is the Body of Christ, we Christians have to admit that we do not have privileged access to God, as much as we might think we do. Under appropriate circumstances, anyone desiring to acknowledge the living reality of our unity in Christ in the Eucharist should be allowed to receive it whether or not they are even catechumens. The first steps toward acknowledging the mystery of God often begin with an inarticulate longing that eucharistic silence alone can express and nurture, and Christians should reverence these first stirrings by sharing this most fundamental Food.

Communion would be appropriate before baptism because baptism would no longer signify initiation into the Body of Christ. We are already members of the Body of Christ; we are already engaged with Christ because we exist. To allow the nonbaptized to receive Communion turns a lot of tradition on its head, but we no longer live under the mental, political, or geographical conditions to which this tradition was a response. Today we have a more profound knowledge of the processes of the creation of which we are inherently a part, as well as a sense of our limitations before its mysteries, and we are more aware of our unity as a global society.

Baptism would be reserved for those who live a conscious commitment to the kenotic, eucharistic ungraspingness of Christ's priestly humility in every facet of life. The baptized are committed to be, with Christ indwelling, the Bread that is offered to sustain the community of creation. It is a commitment to focus all that we are, no matter what our social status—married, single, job, no job, sick, healthy, respectable, destitute, holy fool. Admission to the Christian community as catechumen would begin the process of articulating this reality that resides inarticulately in each person. It would signify a commitment to worship and to grow, perhaps to the point of making the kenotic commitment, perhaps content to remain a catechumen.

Such changes in our attitudes toward the creation as the Body of Christ, toward Communion, toward catecumens and baptism might create a strong Christian community that could in turn more effectively reach out to a religiously hostile or indifferent world. Equally, a eucharistic community that is focused away from itself, sharing its Body and Blood outside its ghetto could go a long way toward eliminating many of the negative attitudes that still linger inside the churches, attitudes that are aimed at other human groups as well as the rest of creation. Today we often exclude from Communion the very people—the poor, the outcast, the sinners, the despised—who are closest to the heart of God. God offers Bread without price. If we do the same, mirroring our Lord's humility, people may then come to understand why the commitment to become that Bread of Life is so important.

The next stage in initiation might be a puberty rite that recognizes the adolescent's special status of one in transition. Adolescence is a singularly inappropriate time for making baptismal or any other commitments. Thus the churches would not demand Christian adulthood from young people before they know what adulthood is. At this time, the spiritual nanny would be exchanged for a discerner who has special ability with young adults. There might be a third rite as the adolescents pass into the working world of adult responsibility.

As the catechumens deepen in their engagement with God and in desire—desire not for climbing some kind of sacramental or ecclesial ladder, but for in-depth instruction and maturity that can come only from personal commitment to prayer, they might take further steps toward baptism. Education for baptism might take years, no matter at what age the catechumen was initiated, and responsibility for this education would be part of the commitment of the baptized. This continuing education could be modeled on the lay academies or schools for deacons some churches have set up, and those with special gifts of ministry might go to seminary or theological college whether or not they were to be ordained.

The primary focus of this further education before baptism would not be primarily book knowledge (though it would be for some for whom intellectual work would deepen their love of God) so much as deepening engagement with the self-emptying God and the implications of the kenotic commitment. It should be obvious that education in kenotic living could *not* be taught by those in the churches—ordained or not—who are in positions of administrative power. Discerners, who have themselves learned something about the kenotic life of Christ's indwelling, who have been through the entire baptismal process and who have the teaching gift, would be responsible. Spiritual nannies, discerners, and those who exercise pastoral ministry would also be drawn from this pool of baptized adults.

In adult education for baptism, the mere intellectual qualification of the catechumen would be the least consideration. Baptism should be the sign of a deep experiential understanding of and commitment to a kenotic life, what it means to be willing to look at God gaze on Gaze. It would mean a serious confrontation with the fear of death. Some few people might be ready for and desirous of baptism early on, even as preadolescents; others might reach this passage only on their deathbeds. Some might never be ready. But if what Jesus says in the parable of the workers in the vineyard is true, whether or not one receives the rite of baptism makes no difference on an ontological level; baptism is not magic, and God seals whom God will with or without human agency. This may sound shocking, but there is no reason to make people feel guilty— as often happens today—about the implications of a commitment they only vaguely understand and are unable or uninterested to make, for reasons for which they are not necessarily responsible.

Catechumens could be full members of the *organizational* structure of the Christian community and possibly could provide unique perspective in an office whose function is primarily administrative, such as warden or member of the vestry. But baptism would entail serious lifelong commitment, undertaken only after years of education and testing.

Ideally, the rite itself would be performed only once a year at the Easter vigil by the local bishop. This would eliminate the need for confirmation. We badly need to restore the sense of awe, the confrontation with death and life, the symbolic renunciations and turnings, and the light in the darkness that were once a part of the "awe-inspiring" (literally, "hair-raising") rites of initiation. We need to act out the seriousness of the commitment in a significant and unforgettable way.

Baptism should be the moment in life that surpasses all others and is burned into our memory as the focal point from which the fullness of life takes its inspiration. But we have a long way to go in the transformation of our attitudes before we are able to create liturgy and rites of passage full of awe and mystery that do not degenerate into credulity, magic, and ritualism. Today's worship too often trivializes. We need worship that is a corporate movement of the people of God that expresses reverence both for God invisible and inaccessible and reverence for the mystery of immanence, the glory of God indwelling creatureliness.

To revitalize Christianity; to bring deeper awareness of the meaning of baptism to our consciousness; to make possible this kind of nurturing and commitment will require the churches' looking at themselves and stripping themselves with a kind of relentless honesty, committing their resources to an educational process the reorientation of which will take decades and generations. Even if the churches were able to bring themselves, by grace, to begin this program, there is always the danger of the baptized becoming counterfeit, becoming an elitist in-group such as many clergy and monastics are now. There must be safeguards built into any system to guard against this distortion and to ensure that the baptismal commitment emphasizes constant vigilance. The baptized are watchers.

Nonordained, nonstipendiary members of the core community of the baptized, properly discerned and properly trained, would have full exercise of gifts given by God as confessors, teachers, healers, and discerners. Many of these people would seek advanced training in theology in seminaries and theological colleges that specialize in enabling theological, religious, and *spiritual maturity.* Nonordained ministers would be authorized by their local bishop-discerner (see below) to preside at the Eucharist if they lived in a geographically isolated community, at times of retreat, or at times of singular pain and transformation. In most situations, such celebrations would be authorized ahead of time, but discipline among the baptized should be such that they are able to discern true appropriateness for nonordained presidency at the Eucharist.

Clergy would be drawn from the ranks of the baptized, nominated by the baptized. People desiring to be ordained could make themselves known, but all those ordained as deacons or presbyters would have to be called by the community before any internal call came under consideration. Within such a church, individuals who insisted they should be ordained would be regarded with greatest suspicion.

In addition, the community would designate those called as either stipendiary administrators or nonstipendiary discerners and liturgical specialists, and the candidates would receive training that emphasized one or the other sphere of activity. In parish life, in order to reflect the model of kenotic power primary to the eucharistic community, the paid administrator would organize celebrants from the pool of nonstipendiary clergy in the parish but, because of the controlling nature of administration, would not be permitted to preside at the Eucharist except under emergency conditions. At the main Sunday Eucharist, the administrator would have a role in the liturgy, but it would be a subordinate role. The parish would ordain as many nonstipendiary clergy as it needed, so that no one would have too great a work load, but the bulk of pastoral care would be delegated to the nonordained who had received the appropriate gifts and training.

From the nonstipendiary clergy, nonstipendiary bishops would be drawn, ideally one per large parish or local geographical group of small parishes (no more than four) so that the bishop had real week-by-week experience of the people. From the administrative, stipendiary clergy, an administrator bishop would be drawn for a whole diocese. Also at a diocesan level would be two nonstipendiary discerner bishops elected from the parish-level bishops. The three diocesan bishops would make decisions together, and the administrator bishop would be the deacon-bishop, the servant of the discerners, to see that their decisions were effected, and would consult them as necessary. Such a limited structure would require both smaller dioceses and dedication on the part of nonstipendieries, but not independent wealth; there would be enough people to share the work.

The philosophy of organization would be: act only when absolutely necessary and be sure that every organizational group with potential to wield power has its own checks so that it does not become a self-perpetuating hierarchy. This would mean that much would be left up to local discernment.

At all levels, as far as possible, the discerning-liturgical ministry would be kept separate from administrative ministry to keep very clear in everyone's minds the kenotic priority of I WILL BE. Even with an emphasis on kenotic commitment at baptism, it is all too easy for those baptized or ordained to slip into the wrong power model if the models of power are not kept separate and if there are not checks on spheres of responsibility. The administrators would administer and would not be able to make decisions about people or exercise pastoral ministry.

The discerner-liturgist presbyters would have responsibility for discerning and providing spiritual support for the nonordained specialist ministers, for matching adults and children with spiritual discerners and nannies, for overseeing care of the catechumens, and in general discerning the emotional and spiritual needs of a parish. To emphasize that the celebration of the Eucharist is not the sole prerogative of the discerner-presbyters or bishops, but rather the offering of each life for the sake of the community, from time to time (at the annual meeting, for example) the community should name one of their number who is not ordained to preside at the Eucharist.

The above is only a sketch of what might be possible, practical ways for the institutional churches to return to their being in the humility of Christ, and any structural model would certainly have to be adapted to different cultural and denominational situations. What is important to realize is that we are not bound by our conventions, and that what we most need to do is to listen for the kenotic mind of Christ in this and every matter, developing theology and organization that grows from eucharistic engagement. We need to recognize the two different models of power, to separate them, and to put checks on the worldly, self-aggrandizing power that always seeks to fill a leadership vacuum in any group. We need to find ways to reverence and embody Christ's humility and make it the focus of the gathered community.

If it were possible for a community of ungrasping engagement to come into being, baptism would be *the* commitment to the Christian priesthood I have outlined above. No further "special" consecrations would be necessary; all who were baptized, no matter what their state of life, would make the same vows.

While there will probably always be some form of traditional communal monasticism, further commitment would be to the community only; the commitment to God would have already been made once for all. The false elevation of religious life as "higher" or "special" would be eliminated, at least in terms of the signals the rites give to those not living in community. The dangers of mystique are always with us. There is already a movement toward reorienting religious consecration ceremonies, which call for the renewal of baptismal vows of all present.

The baptized not living in monastic community would already be committed to the nakedness of the wilderness encounter with God as solitaries—the commitment to meeting God in the stillness of interior solitude, no matter what their living conditions or marital status. Baptism is the commitment not only to be utterly, inviolably vulnerable before God, but to receive God's utter, inviolable vulnerability. The Holy Spirit both inspires and effects this commitment, and baptism is a covenant that puts us wholly at the disposal of the Spirit, expressed in our willingness for whatever, willingness especially for the unpredictability that is the Holy Ghost.

To use a more concrete image, the commitment is not only to be naked before God, but to be willing to bear God's terrible nakedness before us. From union in this painful revelation, salvation is born: new possibility, new life. Throughout Christian history, writers have used sexual imagery to describe engagement with God. This kind of imagery is entirely appropriate, just as eucharistic imagery is appropriate for chaste love-making. If these symbols seem repellent, it is simply further evidence of how deeply ingrained dualism, hatred of the notion of God's glory choosing to indwell creation, has become in our religious consciousness.

Present Realities

It is obvious that even if the churches could find within and among themselves the vision and generosity to effect the profound changes that mean the difference between death and life for institutional Christianity, there would still be enormous problems. Who would choose the initial discerners? How would this choice be made to ensure that the power-brokers who wished consciously or unconsciously to pass themselves off as discerners would be recognized and prevented? What would be the process by which the discerners were discerned? How would the sharing of different kinds of power among bishops in each diocese (or region or whatever division is appropriate) be put into practice? What would be the overall liaison between dioceses and between churches? It is not only far beyond the scope of this book to explore these practical questions, but to dictate solutions would be the very kind of presumption that is exposed in this book. New patterns and methods must come into being organically, discerned by the eucharistic community from within.

Until the churches reorient themselves to the humility of Christ, the gravest concern is for those already committed to kenotic living who feel isolated and unsupported. The churches need to find ways to establish networks for these people and, if appropriate, to offer them some kind of consecration that is *not* derived from any particular stereotype of monasticism or religious life of the past. Religious life has its place and originally derived from a noble vision, but these are people for whom it is inappropriate. Let us look at a typical couple for whom such a new way of consecration might be appropriate (consecration for single people is already becoming possible in some churches).

They might be of any age but seem to be most often of middle age (late thirties), stably married, with or without children. They have complementary personalities and share a deep and quiet commitment. They are intelligent, articulate, and have subtle and penetrating senses of humor. Both ·may be employed. If they are, they do their jobs responsibly. They are ordinary in the best sense.

There is a thread running through their life stories—which may be very different—of ever-deepening engagement with their Lord to plumb the deepest levels of human pain, and there finding, in this self-emptying immolation of becoming prayer, resurrection and new life, God's life. You can see it in the strength of their quiet but resonant presence. There is something about this couple that brings hope and a sense of well-being to those around them, without their doing or saying anything in particular. When they are present, the world seems to make sense. They embody *ihidayutha*.

Their prayer is simple and solitary except for the Daily Office which they say with each other or perhaps even over the telephone with another *ihidaya*. They respect each other's solitude and separate relationships, as well as delighting in those they share. Their understanding of each other's need for solitude is perhaps one reason their relationship seems so solid. Theirs is not a life of active devotions or shared prayer sessions; rather, we can glimpse in these two very different and unself-conscious people that prayer lives in them, that Christ indwells and prays them.

As were the *ihdaye* of the past, this couple is faithful to their parish and well integrated into it, although they are not particularly active in its special interest groups. Yet they are, in some inarticulate way, key members. But for all they give, there is little the parish does to affirm them. Although they rarely criticize it, the cozy parish liturgy, which they faithfully attend, does little in its liturgical action to enable their sense of renewing the kenotic commitment to be, the costliness of their sacrificial death and resurrection that mirrors and coinheres with Christ's in the re-creative Silence of God.

Ordination and religious life are not only not desired by this couple; such steps are out of the question. It would be entirely inappropriate to overlay their deeply focused spirituality with any other traditional form, no matter how admirable; to do so would be a kind of desecration. Their fidelity to God and God in each other is true chastity. Celibacy, essential for a few people to establish this focus, is for them irrelevant.

This couple lives simply but not ostentatiously so; they have ideas about the consecration of their lives, but they are willing to learn, to be fluid, to give up long-held stereotypes and whatever else is inappropriate for the sake of the integrity of their vision. This is true poverty: they are willing to give up their old ideas for an expanding vision and to wait in naked hope. To disturb this interior stripping with any added-on, outward practice beyond what already springs from their deep listening would be artificial, distracting, and destructive. Their wounded, open hearts express the attitude that the nondirective obedience of the desert monks prized above all other virtues. They are *ihidaye.*

They are haunted by a call to realize Christ's priesthood in personal dedication to finding resurrection for the world in the midst of its despair; to ungrasping engagement with the world in its despair, primarily in prayer, but also in careful, mostly hidden, action. They have been faithful for years to this vocation, but because there is virtually no one in their parish who shares or supports their vision or even wishes to try to understand it, they want and need the strength of consecration, perhaps of vowed commitment. And they want to make this commitment where they are in the midst of their ordinary lives and their parish. They realize that to "leave home" in a dramatic gesture would be self-defeating and purposeless; in a disintegrating society they are a focus of stability for all around them.

This couple, and people like them, married or single, are unable any longer to play political games that distract and prevent them from being at the heart of the world's suffering, their living-out of Christ's priesthood that indwells them. They want to live and to make hard decisions—and have the churches make hard decisions through discernment, discernment born of silence, humility, and prayer, not with an eye to career advancement or expediency. They want to be consecrated yet free to live out their vocations at risk.

Among these people are solitaries: some are solitaries within their marriages, their "enclosure" being their spouses and children; some are urban solitaries; some need the silence of wilderness. The discernment of these vocations has been the subject of study by Simon Holden, C.R., and his wise counsel is printed in Appendix B.

Also hidden among the hugger-mugger of today's Christianity are other people who are also its heart's blood. They often comprise a subgroup, dropouts or lookers-on. They are among the most creatively responsive to God, and their creativity, like creativity everywhere, frequently may be linked to an energy that is both inspired and irrupting from the effort of overcoming some enormous yet undefinable handicap, physical or mental. Their gifts of music or writing or discernment are wrested by grace and effort from suffering through unimaginable solitary darkness and despair. They are often tossed to and fro as their small ships plunge and pitch their way through stormy seas to a hard-won, often fragile serenity, clarity, and insight that cannot be bought at any other price. In addition to their creative gifts, some of them are solitaries as well.

People who have such gifts and energies have a sensitivity that is often too easily triggered in the ups and downs of ordinary life. They have discovered the hard way that their sensitivity cannot be modified without destroying the creative gift and the person with it. Thus, their lives are often so preoccupied with staying afloat that they have not learned or are not able to employ the politics of ordinary life, and because they are often receiving inaudible and invisible signals from outside themselves that rack them in their vulnerability, marginality is vital to them. These creative people are often rejected by society at large and by church communities.

It is these people whom the churches must sensitively and gently seek, draw out, listen to, allow to remain as they are, cherish, protect and, if they desire, eventually consecrate in some way. The churches must recognize these people on their own terms if fundamental institutional changes are to come into being that are not simply repeating the same old patterns of controlling power and co-dependence. The most important tool in attempting to bring the institution to mirror the humility of Christ is the practice of that humility by those who hold administrative power.

Models of Power and Spiritual Maturity

Spiritual maturity is not an option: it is our coming to be, our confluence with God, self, and community in ungrasping, eucharistic engagement. We cannot come into being if a controlling model of power is constantly set before us by the churches. Maturity is often confused with standardization, that is, standardized ideas of "normal" that (rightly or wrongly) may be considered appropriate for the factory assembly-line or office but have little to do with true maturity. The kind of maturity required for work in business is irrelevant in terms of spiritual maturity; the norms simply do not apply, and spiritual maturity must not be evaluated in terms of ability to cope in the marketplace. Sometimes the two kinds of maturity will coincide in the same person, but this is not a common occurrence. More often, the two kinds of maturity will be in conflict. What, then, do we mean by spiritual maturity?

Here is a cluster of ideas.

In spiritual maturity we move from dependence to independence to interdependence. We know that "normal" means true to each person's uniqueness in the Love of God and does not therefore mean shaping people up according to a universal standard. We know that in the love of God's creating, everything and everyone are intimately, inextricably interrelated, and that, as a result, our prayer and choices and acts must be considered and responsible and arise from the profound listening of interior stillness. God's *kenosis* is received and confluent with our kenotic response, which is co-creation. Here are the words of a woman struggling to free herself from the controlling model of power in order to move into spiritual maturity:

I suppose the problem of power has been in my mind this week. . . . I'm beginning to see why women often don't cope with it well, because perhaps they know only too well its underside, its ability to hurt and maim from their fear of male power and domination. . . . I found the comment about cooperating in becoming a victim very true, as I've seen it in myself on several occasions in the past, always catching it too late, it seems, after some damage has been done. I wonder about it, and where the driving force for such situations comes from. . . . Is it our need to please and be accepted; more deeply, our need to be loved; and why do I always long to grant another authority over me, initially . . . and then with time kick against that? The initial wanting of a spiritual *father*, but the growing realization that what is more demanding/satisfying/human is the need for a soul *friend* or companion, mutual relationship which precludes power, is common sense, and has love as its central source. I wonder if I dare push the analogy with my relationship with God. . . ."

In spiritual maturity we no longer mistake individuality for authenticity. We have learned the key distinctions between self-image and self-respect, self-reflection and self-forgetfulness; we have enough self-knowledge so that we can forget our desire for status and power in ungrasping, eucharistic engagement with others; we can act responsibly without being affected by "what people think," but with exquisite attention to the effects our acts might have on others; we listen, poised at the heart of silence in inviolable vulnerability. Our morality is ontological: what we do or do not do is not affected by any influence outside the focus of our chastity, our striving to become *ihidaye*.

In spiritual maturity we are able to live in ambiguity without leaning on props or propositions. We have deepening love for Scripture and symbol and liturgy, but realize that they are feeding us only so that we may go into the desert and wait, watching in the dark. Still-prayer becomes the core from which all other prayer flows and the silence to which it returns.

We are quick to realize and acknowledge when we do not know, when we cannot know, and when we presume. We are quick to admit errors, and we are willing to live in the ambiguity of not knowing without trying to manufacture a surrogate, a graspable substitute. We know that by remaining in unknowing, a truer, deeper engagement and insight will be given us: we will more deeply come to be.

In spiritual maturity we are willing to live in the tension of sustained paradox, in engagement with I WILL BE without trying to posit and determine and therefore control and make an idol of God. We refuse the temptation to come to artificial resolutions to impose on our selves and therefore on the outside world in order to make life easy and secure. We are willing to let go linear theology, the security of false polarity, to abandon the idea of God as the other "pole" from these dead ends. We engage God everywhere in everything and everyone, yet without confusing I WILL BE and creatures, without falling into pantheism or monism.

We recognize that there is suffering that will come to us that must not be avoided but embraced and lived through, that there is suffering that we must hand our selves over to in order to continue to mature. We are committed to long-term aspiration and are willing to suffer to have God's life grow within us, to expand us, to bring us to greater single-heart-edness and transfiguration.

In spiritual maturity we realize the necessity of healthy solitude for the sake of good community, that no relationship can be healthy, that is, we cannot have ungrasping engagement, unless we are comfortable in our own solitude. This does not mean we have to fix our selves up or be fixed up by others. In our solitude we come to accept the yoke of our gifts and griefs through self-care, learning what our real needs are and accepting them in humility; self-confrontation, distinguishing our needs from our wants disguised as needs; and from the tension of this engagement we receive, by grace, the gift of self-forgetfulness.

All of this involves risk. We risk, but we are not destroyed. Even if we seem to be, we know by faith that we fall through despair into the hand of God to be re-created, that we come more deeply to be in Christ's humility. Despair is destructive only if we insist on remaining in the hell of a closed system; the despair that breaks us out of the security of such a system to free-fall in the love of I WILL BE is the humility of Christ at work in our lives.

While we seek healing and to heal, we also see that only the devil is perfect, that only the beast has a mortal wound that is healed, that evil maintains appearances at any price and is unwilling for its image to be marred. We know that in the true vision of the resurrected Christ, Love is wounded, and that we are hidden in those wounds, transfigured and focused by them in their density of glory.

These are but a few elements of spiritual maturity. Much of what we would like to express about maturity is inarticulate, and always we need to be aware that within us there are different levels and seasons of maturity. We must ensure that in the future the minimal structures we create to keep the churches alive have one purpose and one alone: to set us free in the priestly humility of the kenotic Christ so that our lives *become* that priestly, sacrificial, and transfiguring offering for Love's sake; that we come to be; that we become spiritually mature.

We live in a desperate, dissonant age when our technological exploitation of the earth's material, psychological, and spiritual resources have made us fall from being into fragmentation and heedlessness that threaten to overwhelm us. We face tyranny and annihilation. The horror of the modern age is our refusal to accept the glory of our creatureliness, our refusal to enter our woundedness through which we may find the solitude and openness and salvation that lies in the Silence of God, from which is spoken the Word that is both First and Last who re-creates us and gives us our being.

To continue to insist upon a model of God that intensifies this noise, this fragmentation and tyranny, only adds to our sense of hopelessness. Ours is an age for which the only hope is the kenotic wisdom of engagement—in the deepest sense of biblical knowing—with God, whose single movement of self-emptying and transfiguring Love enables us to live in creation through the wholeness of paradox. Without in any way denying the appropriateness of ancient questions concerning Incarnation and Trinity for their time, we must understand that philosophical constructions of another age that depict an interventionist god for whom creation is a gratuitous afterthought and appendage are of limited value to a world that now perceives itself as inherently engaged with the universe of creation, within which it must discover its listening equipoise of response.

What we most need to discover in the tyranny and terror of our age is the meaning and creative potential that reside only in powerlessness, in the cry of dereliction that is the humility of Jesus the Christ. It is by entering our solitude in this humility that we find the ground of beseeching, that our being is gathered in all its creaturely glory, and from which the resonances of forgivenness and re-creation resound. It is from the resonances of this stillness of receptive and responsive being that we generate more change than by any action we may decide to take.

Jesus' age was also one of horror. His country was occupied

by a hostile force; thousands were crucified as a matter of routine. His response was not to attempt theodicy, or take refuge in elegant philosophical constructions, or to establish divine deterrence based on mutually assured destruction. His response was rather to penetrate condemnation, pain, suffering, and evil to their very core. By his humility they were broken open and transfigured; by his sacrificial, priestly incarnate being, which, in the resurrection, we share.

Run . . . and tell . . . that Jerusalem shall be a city without walls. . . . I will be a wall of fire round her, says the Lord, and a glory in the midst of her. . . . I am coming, I will make my dwelling among you, says the Lord. . . . Silence, all humanity, in the presence of the Lord! (Zech 2:4–5, 13)

Appendix A
Power Games: Methods and Models

Part 1: Models of Power: Theological Method and Doctrinal Evolution

1. In each of the pairs, what is the process by which an item moves from the right-hand column to the left-hand column?
2. What is the process by which the item may be returned to the right side and then pass through it?
3. Where am I (my minister, my parish, my parish council or vestry) within this continuum of seeming polarity? Or have I (we) begun to enter or pass through the narrow way to freedom?
4. On the left side, what are the seeming polarities brought to artificial resolution, and on the right, what are the seeming polarities held in the tension of paradox?
5. How many different kinds of notions (reading vertically) should perhaps be separated into what kind of categories? How many different ways of sorting are there?

Questions: "What do we mean by salvation?" (Answer: being sprung from a trap)

"What might it feel like to live without polarity on the other side of the narrow way?"

Explain the statement: "The devil is perfect." (Hint: look at resurrected Christ)

"Zeus" DEAD End		*I WILL BE [for you]* *THE WAY = Humility of* *Christ*	
linear thinking	≠	spatial thinking	
can be posited	≠	can't be posited (elusiveness of God; can't be named)	**WE**
can be defined (as object)	≠	can be engaged but not defined (subject, not object)	
Trinity as philosophical/political construct	≠	Trinity as lived prayer relationship	
dialectic	≠	dialogue	
definition that restricts meaning	≠	definition that enlarges meaning	
belief = self-comfort (easy falsehood, idolatry)	≠	belief = self-forgetfulness, gaze at God	
points toward self	≠	points away from self	
needs to decorate self	≠	naked	
impassible (impassibility is entailed in narcissism of pointing toward self; defended tower)	≠	impassibility not a question because can't be posited, points away from self; rather *apatheia* as described by R. Williams, (crudely put) readiness and appropriateness of response	**ARE**
closed system	≠	open system	
either/or	≠	both/and	
static	≠	dynamic	
immutable	≠	constancy in engaged and responsive love	
randomness a threat (negates, closed system)	≠	randomness a joy (possibility, hope, salvation)	**MEANT**
power: fission, diffuse	≠	power: fusion, dense, *kavod*	
maintenance exhausts energy	≠	energy generated even as used	

function	≠	being
noun	≠	verb
dualism (inherently hierarchical)	≠	paradox-continuum
asceticism = self-mastery, i.e. folly of the Greeks and debaters 1 Cor 1:18ff. because self-mastery is lust, *control* (cf., pain in Genesis)	≠	asceticism = acknowledgment of one's limits, willing powerlessness that invites grace; the Cross is giving up illusion of self-mastery and accompanying pride
spiritual rejects non-spiritual, e.g., matter	≠	spiritual and material are parts of the good creation, coinhering and interchangeable
Beauty rejects ugly	≠	Beauty becomes marred for Love's sake
disembodied spirit	≠	incarnate kenotic God
triumphalist mighty god	≠	humble King transforming death
lust (i.e., control and exploitation)	≠	kenotic sexuality
repression	≠	integration
exploitive pleasure in relationships (i.e., "fulfillment")	≠	communion (self-forgetfulness)
ecstatic vhs w/ instant replay; physical isolation; individualism	≠	solitude *for sake of* community
narrow-mindedness	≠	narrow place
genital intactness	≠	virginity (wildness as in unexploited; inviolate vulnerability, integrity; focus)
making a person into an idea (Mt 5:27–28 = lust)	≠	freeing a person to grow into God (unpredetermined possibility)
pornography	≠	eroticism
ritualism (to avoid face to Face encounter)	≠	sacrifice (ritual as *expression* of face to Face encounter)

TO

LIVE

hierarchical mediator	≠	indwelling Christ (which eucharistic leader expresses for gathered community)

HERE

personal devaluation to control group	≠	value of persons in interdependence within group
rule by fear	≠	rule by love
obedience to constraint	≠	obedience to aspiration
judgment/ condemnation	≠	grieving, tears, compassion
humility as submission, nonperson	≠	humility as lived truth, clear-eyed Godly creature
worry over appearances	≠	lived gospel in face of ridicule, criticism

IN

Magic Cookie	≠	we mirror God's going to heart of pain and generating new life (human kenotic life confluent with God's kenotic life in gathered community in all of life and in the Breaking of Bread)
addiction	≠	detachment
mystique	≠	mystery
fundamentalism (desire for security)	≠	faith (willingness to live in insecurity—mingled human and divine *kenosis*; primordial possibility; co-creation)
literal interpretation	≠	analogical and contextual interpretation

FREE-

passions (emotional clinging)	≠	passion (*apatheia*—balance of ready response, to God & community; conversion to single-heartedness)
defended tower	≠	readiness
ol' Forky Tail	≠	resonances of choice
uniformity	≠	unity in diversity

distortion of reality for control	≠	freedom to explore fluid reality for maturation

DOM

perfection (Latin: static, finished)	≠	perfection (Greek: dynamic, maturation)
ecstasy (watching self have pleasure)	≠	ecstasy (self-forgetfulness, other-oriented)
artificial complexity	≠	complex simplicity
much talk, noise	≠	much silence
gee whiz	≠	awestruck wonder
grandiosity	≠	grandeur
destruction of personality from without by tyranny	≠	transformation of personality from within by Paraclete
estrangement from self, nature, "truth" by dependant submission to dualistic, self-certifying authority	≠	estrangement into freedom by falling, i.e., self-knowledge and responsibility

AND

"muscular" Christianity (own bootstraps)	≠	grace at moment of despair; (willing powerlessness)
individualism	≠	authenticity
monastic romanticism (Manichean)	≠	"monasticism" as glory of creature found in humble Christ
sin leads to exclusion	≠	sin is necessary
no wounds	≠	wounds enable God to enter
limited perspective (all options known)	≠	limitless perspective (all options unknown)
knowable, graspable God	≠	unknowable, "elusive" God
self-indulgent expediency	≠	self-limited action-by-invitation, self-restraint, listening

LOVE

nuclear bombs	≠	weeping
AIDS as punishment (*de haut en bas* condemnation, creates abyss)	≠	*has* AIDS (suffers with) "neither will I condemn," bridges abyss, intimacy

fear of intimacy—mask	≠	intimacy, nothing to hide
status	≠	service
exploits for personal gain	≠	enables (self-forgetful)
rule of Christ = potentate	≠	rule of Christ, the humble
"On this rock. . . . " monarchical hierarchy	≠	"On this rock. . . . " on Peter, who is wholly emptied out by self-knowledge of depths of his capacity for betrayal in light of God's forgivenness
Prayer as saying prayers (quantity); creature as "I"	≠	being prayed (by Christ indwelling); creature as "thou"
legalism in the name of beauty (monasticism as a static, stunting art form)	≠	flexibility in the name of the Good ("monasti-cism" as a way to spiritual maturity); revaluing of baptismal covenant
emphasis on exterior observance	≠	emphasis on growth of interior virginity
competitiveness	≠	looking at and for God alone in solitude and community
normal = stereotype, fixed standard	≠	normal = true to one's nature as only-begotten
worldly wisdom	≠	wise foolishness
linear time	≠	relativity
technology	≠	wisdom
stasis	≠	stillness

IN

CHRIST

This is a chart of clusters of many different kinds of notions, that is, tensions within a continuum that tend to cluster when we refuse to wait through them. It is a chart of characteristics of two subliminal models of power most of us have that affect prayer, exegesis—every aspect of religion (and other areas of life) and a person's evolution toward spiritual maturity or devolution into immaturity. It is also a chart of spiritual characteristics and their counterfeits.

The left side is not merely a negative representation of the right side; it is simplistic, reductionistic, distorted. It is a dead end. The right side is not merely a positive statement but dynamic and ever-expanding. We move *through* the right side and keep going, in an expanding equipoise of conversion. Within the tension of paradox the "system" is kept open to possibility and transformation. Most of us seem to feel we must exist somewhere in the middle, caught in a false polarity, tending toward one side or the other in our responses, not realizing, or fearing to move through the right side into freedom.

It cannot be said that the left side is "evil" and the right side is "good." One reason is that there are many different kinds of things listed together; it is part of the game to sort them out. In addition, to know where we are in our thinking at a particular moment, to proceed in coherent fashion from one thought to another, we often have to come, temporarily, to some kind of artificial resolution. The danger arises when we regard this artificial, temporary resolution as natural and immutable, and, worse, when we impose it on the exterior world or other people. The left side tends toward the illusory security of a closed system, and yet there are times when we need a respite, when we need a safe haven, when we need security. The peril of this temporary shelter is the temptation to make it permanent.

It would also be inaccurate to say that this is a Jungian clustering, that the left side is "masculine" and the right "feminine." Every man or woman is equally capable of living toward one side or another. While I am cautiously feminist, I do not think it correct to say, as the militant often seem to today, that it is now possible only for women to save the world. This would make us hostages to fortune and to one another; one has only to look at Margaret Thatcher or Indira Gandhi to know that we women are as capable of the tactics of coercive power as men. Nor do I accept that there was once some idyllic prepatriarchal period; one has only to make an ethological extrapolation from the rape and infanticide common to the great apes to question whether such a concept is not mere fantasy. Women in every generation will always have to fight for their very physical lives, much less their mental and spiritual lives. Simply to say "no" means a woman has to look death in the face.

On the left side of the chart we can also see how the myth of objectivity contributes to hubris. Our "scientific" age insists on "objectivity." While we need to be as objective as we can, recent discoveries in both hard science and humanities question the presumption of an absolute objectivity. We cannot detach ourselves from creation—indeed, that we attempt to do so is at the heart of our problem. In addition there are too many variables (of which we are one) for our creatureliness to encompass. The myth of objectivity assumes a static universe, an illusory point of view from which, totally detached, we can regard the rest of creation. It denies interrelatedness and the tendency of the universe to appear as we wish to see it.

There are immense philosophical problems here, but when we are told, as we so often are these days, of technological perfection, of "absolutely safe" forms of nuclear energy, or a genetic breakthrough that will enable us to be "masters of our own destiny," we should realize the narrowness of the vision that is being communicated. God forbid that we should be masters of our own destiny: we have neither the perspective nor the wisdom to know what that destiny "ought" to be, to know what "perfection" is, to know what effects our actions will have in all possible worlds. We may already unwittingly have mastered our destinies down an evolutionary dead end.

The movement from the right side of the chart toward the left is often a response of fear: it is an effort to control, to support the illusion of control, and to maintain illegitimate authority over over ideas and illusions of our selves and other people. To effect relationships in terms of the left side is leading the "little ones" into sin (Mt 18:10ff); it does violence to the other, to the mystery of the human person and the integrity of the unique relationship with God each individual has. And the violation of the individual creates a reactive defensive situation that replaces the openness that grows out of true self-knowledge and thus violates also the true community that is formed by the interrelatedness of self-knowledge.

The response to violence is almost invariably violence. One person's patronage of another assumes a lack of potential and artificially locks the other in an inferior I-it relationship. It is a form of violence. Such a nonrelationship reinforces the patronizer's false sense of superiority and leaves the other feeling trapped and seething.

Abused children are in danger of abusing their own children, and the abuse of children creates an inheritance of violence that reaches far beyond the family; defeated and humiliated nations wait for an opportunity to get their own back; groups of people confined to ghettos and concentration camps become ruthless hunters of their persecutors and tend to pursue survival at all costs, even if it means using the very techniques that were used on them; individuals struggling toward the light become distracted from their task because their sense of reality is distorted, and in order to maintain and pursue their vision they lash out at those who would not allow different views of reality, who belittle and devalue what are often too penetrating, illuminating, and therefore threatening insights.

To be willing to expose to our selves to ourselves, to expose our secret desire to retreat permanently to the position represented by the left side of the diagram; to be willing, no matter how painful, to seek to receive God's unconditional love and forgivenness by allowing our selves to be moved within the continuum into the expansion (salvation) beyond the right side not only breaks us out of the cycle of sin, thereby creating possibility and bringing a small part of the Kingdom into being, but also is the expression of the commitment of our baptismal vows to grow into our fullness (maturity) in Christ.

The density of holiness on the right side creates its own energy (aspiration) that carries us into freedom. The energy of the left side, its counterfeit, tends to diffuse; there is no foundation or center, only the illusion created by constraint. An analogy to the density of holiness might be found in a theory of contemporary physics that tells us that if we could create a particle accelerator big enough (about the size of our solar system) that would bring a particle to unimaginable density, a new universe would emerge from that density.

The crisis of doctrine/authority/narcissism/lack of vision in the churches is as much a crisis of maturity as anything else, a desire by some to take permanent refuge in the "Zeus" cluster who are at odds with those who know that the survival of Christianity means constant maturation in I WILL BE. The left side is obviously a caricature of a popular cartoon idea of Zeus (*pace*, classicists); the right side shows some of the implications of understanding I AM as transactional and God as subject. There are very obvious philosophical objections to the creation of such a chart, for example, that to create such a diagram is in itself reductionistic, but this game is for heuristic purposes only, although there is a serious intent behind it, concern for the future not only of the churches but the planet also.

One of the biggest theological difficulties people seem to have in thinking about God is understanding that a kenotic God is *more* powerful than a self-indulgent puppet-master (for example rape is lust for control that is out of control and finds a temporary outlet in sexual expression but has nothing to do with sexuality. Sexuality is not control, and control is not focus; our sexuality needs focus because it is a pervasive energy in the goodness of our creation). The potentiality of "Zeus" is in the kenotic God, but the God of Sinai and the prophets and the New Testament reveal God's promise not to act that way. Thus, the kenotic God creates *ex nihilo*, some say, out of God's own being, acts in history not as an intervener but as one who is committed to suffer-with, one who indwells. What we perceive as God's triumphant power in the New Testament comes *only* through utter ungraspingness, through the solitude of the humility of Christ, that is, the Cross, and is in sharp contrast to the expanding hegenomy of the Zeus-god. The question is not God's power (whether God is omnipotent) but God's *use* of power. Thus we need to start theology with the mystery of God's in-historicization (this word signifying the entire salvific event, the Word who is First and Last), not of creator-God only: that is, we need to understand that it is a God who is committed to incarnation and its implications who creates.

Part 2: Implications for Spiritual Growth (combined under clustering above)

Three questions for discernment:
1. Where do [I, you, he, she, we, they] hurt? (self-care, asceticism)
2. What do [I, you, he, she, we, they] *really* want? (self confrontation)
3. What price am [I, you, he, she, we, they] willing to pay? (self-forgetfulness)

The clustering of ideas on the two sides of the chart is not dualistic because while the left side (closed system) cannot encompass the right side (indeed is threatened by it, tries to reject it), the right side (open system) can encompass the left side and transform it.

A fundamental temptation in life, thought, spiritual growth, and religion, is to expediency at the expense of discernment. Expediency can be expressed as control and presumption (original sin), reductionism, safety, dualism, fundamentalism. We constantly need to uncover how we (or they or an institution or whatever) are closing our systems and thus jeopardizing our salvation and how to reopen them by becoming willing to do what we must to move within the continuum and tension of paradox.

Related to this, we need to distinguish between the necessary tension of our limited perception and the paradoxical unity of the revealed God. For example, the tension between wrath and mercy is *our* perception and important for us to maintain, but we need to understand that it is not God who is wrathful but we who are vengeful, and that our perception of wrath is perception of what rebellion feels like in face of self-emptying Love. We need to be willing to live in the unresolved tension of these paradoxes because beyond them lies true freedom.

Bottom line: nothing is wasted, everything is loved (but you have to say "nothing is wasted" first because there is a lot we would like to reject).

Appendix B
Discernment of Vocation to the Solitary Life

SIMON HOLDEN, C.R.

The Reverend Simon Holden is Novice Master of the Community of the Resurrection, Mirfield West Yorkshire WF14 OBN, England, and Warden of the Society of the Precious Blood, Burnham Abbey, Maidenhead SL6 OPW, England

What I am writing comes from my personal experience over the last forty years. It echoes much of the Christian tradition, though at the same time it bears the marks of the times in which we are living, times in which there is a desperate search for the meaning of human nature.

I have known a number of men and women whose "listening" to life has led them to leave behind the conventional structures and securities of society and with the whole of themselves—body, mind, and spirit—penetrate what lies "beyond." All of them, in whatever way they live it out, hear the call to "go out" or "go beyond," and to "go alone." In every case the indications from the beginning are that this is in no way a self-indulgence but rather a self-transcendence.

The solitaries I have known share both this initial being called "out" from the conventions and norms they have observed in the past, as well as those that surround them as their lives unfold. But the manner in which this "going out" is expressed is as varied as the characters who follow it. Every solitary knows that if it is genuine, this vocation is no mere personal adventure, but in some way impossible to define, solitaries are "going out" on behalf of all of us.

Nevertheless there lies at the heart of the vocation a striking paradox. It is at once representative human nature that is making the dangerous exploration through the solitary way, and at the same time the exploration is made through the unique personal identity of each particular solitary.

If we reflect on this paradox we shall see that the vocation can make sense—and indeed, survive—only if both sides of this paradox are held in balance. This means attention to and appreciation for both aspects and at the same time protection during the time when one may overwhelm the other. To be oneself and at the same time to represent all the rest of us means being in touch with the pains, joys, fears, and hopes of all human beings through being in deeper touch with one's own pains, joys, fears, and hopes.

The universal nature of the vocation is mediated, indeed can only be experienced through the particular. For every solitary this means a terrifying confrontation with oneself. It is through the individual wounds, scars, and hang-ups of the solitary that some of the world's suffering is redeemed: it is through the particular love, faith, and hope of the solitary that some of the inarticulate aspirations of the world can be expressed. Underneath all of this, in the daily life of the solitary, no matter what the external life-style may be, there must be a further paradox of entering the self in order to be free of the self, losing one's life to find it. These factors, both those that are common to all solitaries and those that are the individual make-up of the particular solitary, bear directly on the matter of discernment as well as on the equally important factor of the care of solitaries.

The solitary will be by nature a highly sensitive person whose "pick-up" mechanism causes him or her to be wide open to others and to the world around with all that is potentially good or evil. This means that solitaries can often be judged by others as gregarious and extroverted, whereas the truth is that this very network of vibrations from the world around them requires solitude rather than community if it is going to lead to any kind of sane and discerning response.

The basic factors of the solitary vocation also indicate the great risk involved to the person mentally, emotionally, spiritually, and even physically. The risk of going out beyond the boundaries is only possible if there is a friend or friends who can act as a kind of bridge between the person going out alone and the rest of us whom they represent. These companions also provide a source of dialogue for the solitary about the experience of solitude.

It is not an exaggeration to say that the solitary needs a friend to prove not only by argument, but also by love and human converse, that he or she is sane and still a real live individual human being. My own experience with one solitary over the last seventeen years has been that from time to time I help to hold back the overwhelming force of the universal dimensions of what is going on or the force of the individual's own nature, both of which at times threaten to swamp the fine balance that has to be maintained. At these times I feel that I represent both the rest of us and the One Who is doing the calling.

I have known one solitary who lived for fifty years in one place as a recluse, with all the traditional disciplines, yet without any official attachment to a community. Her supports through half a century were the bishop and her spiritual director. On the other hand, the solitary I have traveled with for seventeen years lives on the grounds of her community and sees her vocation as part of the community's.

In both cases, however, these solitaries have been "free" of community domination. Discernment has come through the human, common-sense companionship of another Christian, who exercised the kind of relationship mentioned above.

I would suggest that the discernment of the solitary vocation necessarily must have this personal "friendship" dimension and cannot be exercised by large groups of people or an institution. Communities can often damage the freedom required by the solitary through unconscious projections and unlived expectations. Some solitaries may need the association of a community; others may not. But all of them need the strength that comes through contact with "the tradition."

This contact with the past and present stream of the faithful is mediated through the symbols of the bishop and vows. If the bishop can act as a kind of tap-root to this underground stream, yet at the same time leave the solitary free to explore the manner in which the call is lived out, the church fulfills a valuable and prophetic ministry.

Before commitment is made, however, there is need for a discerning friend or friends who will accompany the solitary, alongside as it were, encouraging and assuring, as well as warning and guiding. Thus common sense, mental stability (much threatened), a sense of humor, vows, a bishop, and a friend seem a basic recipe for any solitary.

Notes

Author's Note

1. Quoted in Brad Leithauser, "The Space of One Breath," *The New Yorker*, 9 March 1987, p. 69.
2. Mark C. Taylor, "Descartes, Nietzsche and the Search for the Unsayable," *The New York Times Book Review*, 1 February 1987, p. 34.
3. Unpublished doctoral thesis by Shafiq AbouZayd; at this writing still in process for submission to the University of Fribourg, Switzerland. For an introduction to Syrian Christianity, see Sebastion Brock, *The Syriac Fathers on Prayer and the Spiritual Life*, (Kalamazoo: Cistercian, 1987).

Introduction

1. Richard Preston, "Dark Time," *The New Yorker*, 26 October 1987, p. 72.
2. J. R. Lucas, "The Open Future," in *The Nature of Time*, Raymond Flood and Michael Lockwood, eds. (Oxford: Basil Blackwell, 1986), pp. 125–134.
3. Barry Lopez, *Arctic Dreams* (London: Picador, 1987).
4. Jeremy Bernstein, "The Life It Brings," *The New Yorker*, 2 February 1987, pp. 41–42.
5. Robert J. White, "Bioethical Shock," *America*, 28 February 1987, pp. 174–176.
6. Ursula K. Le Guin, *The Farthest Shore* (London: Bantam, 1969), p. 136.
7. Johann Wolfgang von Goethe, *Truth and Fantasy*, ed. Humphrey Trevelyan (London: Weidenfeld and Nicolson, Ltd., 1949).
8. Le Guin, *The Farthest Shore*, p. 66.
9. Ibid., p. 121.
10. Ibid., p. 67.
11. Ursula K. Le Guin, *A Wizard of Earthsea* (London: Bantam, 1969), p. 71.
12. Frank Rossi, "The Man Who Won the Class War," *Sunday Times Magazine* (London), 24 October 1987, p. 53.

Chapter 1

1. There are excellent critical studies available of the New Testament basis for this statement; see particularly books by Raymond E. Brown, S.S., *Priest and Bishop: Biblical Reflections* (Ramsey: Paulist Press, 1970) and *The Churches the Apostles Left Behind* (Ramsey: Paulist Press, 1984).
2. My thanks to the Rev. Reginald Rodman of Christ Church, Kealakekua, Hawaii, for this image.
3. Choan-Seng Song. *The Compassionate God* (Maryknoll: Orbis, 1982), pp. 123–124.
4. Andrew Reding, "Books on Latin America," *America*, 28 March 1987, pp. 262–263.

Chapter 2

1. Paul Bradshaw, *Liturgical Presidency in the Early Church* (Bramcote, Nottingham: Grove Books, 1983), p. 10.
2. Le Guin, *A Wizard of Earthsea,* p. 66.
3. Quoted in Peter Forbes, "Brodsky: Language Worship" in *The Independent* (London), 29 October 1987, p. 13.
4. R. Joly, *Le dossier d'Ignace d'Antioche* (Bruxelles, 1979).
5. Aloysius Grillmeier, S. J., trans. John Bowden, *Christ in Christian Tradition,* vol. 1 (London and Oxford: Mowbrays, 1975), p. 35.

Chapter 4

1. Isaac the Syrian, trans. A. J. Wensinck, *Mystic Treatises by Isaac of Nineveh* (Wiesbaden, 1969), pp. 211–212, adapted by S. P. Brock; Bedjan 316–317.
2. Isaac the Syrian, trans. Sebastian Brock in my *The Fountain and the Furnace,* (Mahwah: Paulist Press, 1987), p. 199; Bedjan 492.
3. I have borrowed Monica Furlong's image from *Wise Child* (New York: Alfred A. Knopf, 1987).
4. Isaac the Syrian, trans. S. P. Brock for this volume; Bedjan 463.
5. Kallistos Ware, *The Orthodox Way* (Crestwood: St. Vladimir's Seminary Press, 1980), p. 58.
6. St. Peter Damian, trans. P. McNulty, *Selected Writings on the Spiritual Life* (London: Faber, 1959), p. 57.
7. Alex Shoumatoff, *The Mountain of Names* (New York: Simon and Schuster, 1986).
8. Don Coville Skinner, "A Visit from Rosa Parks: Power of the Ordinary," *The Christian Century,* 1 April 1987, p. 30.
9. Isaac the Syrian, trans. Sebastian Brock, in *The Fountain and the Furnace,* p. 293.
10. Umberto Eco, trans. William Weaver, *Travels in Hyperreality* (London: Picador, 1987).
11. Robert J. McAllister, M.D., *Living the Vows* (San Francisco: Harper & Row, 1986), p. 225.
12. Ibid., pp. 253–254.
13. Cf., Robert Bellah, *Habits of the Heart* (New York: Harper & Row, 1986).
14. Arthur Hertzberg, "The Best Man," a review of Brian Urquhart, *Life in Peace and War* (New York: Harper & Row, 1987), in *New York Review of Books,* 5 November 1987, p. 27.
15. Quoted in Hertzberg, "The Best Man," p. 29.

Chapter 5

1. Isaac the Syrian, trans. Sebastian Brock in *The Fountain and the Furnace,* p. 165; Bedjan 506–508.
2. Isaac the Syrian, trans. Dana Miller, *The Ascetical Homilies of Saint Isaac the Syrian* (Boston: Holy Transfiguration Monastery, 1984), p. 247; Bedjan 350. It should be noted that Dana Miller's excellent translation is from the *Greek* version with reference to the Syriac version. There are significant differences between the two versions, and it is important to remember that while Isaac was familiar with the Evagrian tradition, he was theologically most emphatically in the Semitic tradition of Ephrem. The only translation

currently available from the Syriac is by A. J. Wensinck, a Dutchman whose English is somewhat stilted. Happily, Dr. Brock is working on a new translation from the Syriac of a selection of homilies in Bedjan's edition, along with the newly rediscovered and hitherto untranslated and unpublished Book II of Isaac's works.

3. Isaac the Syrian, trans. S. P. Brock, from Book II, in *The Fountain and the Furnace*, p. 316.

4. Lady Julian of Norwich, the fourteenth-century mystic, makes this observation in Chapter 13 of the short text and Chapter 27 of the long text of her *Showings*. While there are many editions available, to my mind none is satisfactory. First, no truly satisfactory Middle English text has been established. Second, the renderings into modern English rarely have an ear for the nuances of Julian's "sight" or the reflections of someone who has for long years lived in silence and solitude. Third, current work on the texts often refuses to relate the short and long texts with an eye to the way a writer writes. Translators past and present seem without exception to bring a personal or academic agenda to the text instead of letting the text work on them and actually entering Julian's experience in an interior way. A satisfactory text and modern rendering probably will not be available until a woman solitary with appropriate textual and linguistic skills—and no agenda but Julian's—undertakes the task.

5. Isaac the Syrian, trans. S. P. Brock, in *The Fountain and the Furnace*, p. 189; Bedjan 245.

6. Isaac the Syrian, trans. Dana Miller, p. 211.

7. Isaac the Syrian, trans. S. P. Brock for this volume; Bedjan 245–246.

8. Isaac the Syrian, trans. S. P. Brock and Dana Miller, from Book II, p. 196.

9. Isaac the Syrian, trans. S. P. Brock, pp. 185–186; Bedjan 125–126.

10. Ibid., p. 165; Bedjan 507.

11. Quoted in Carolyn Coman, "A Conversation with Helen Caldicott," *North Shore Life*, October-November 1986, p. 80.

12. Lopez, *Arctic Dreams*, pp. 109–110.

13. Quoted in Janet Watts and "Stewart," "Facing up to the Fight," *The Observer Magazine* (London), 12 April 1987, p. 63.

14. Isaac the Syrian, trans. S. P. Brock for this volume; Bedjan 259.

15. Etty Hillesum, *Etty, a Diary: 1941–1943* (London: Jonathan Cape, 1983), pp. 157 and 180.

16. Isaac the Syrian, trans. S. P. Brock in *The Fountain and the Furnace*, p. 253; Bedjan 163, 168, 166.

17. Ibid., p. 165; Bedjan 577.

18. *The Sayings of the Desert Fathers*, trans. Benedicta Ward (London: A. R. Mowbray, 1975), p. 176.

19. St. Ephrem, Hymns on the Epiphany, trans. S. P. Brock in *The Luminous Eye* (Rome: CIIS, 1985), p. 114.

20. S. P. Brock, *Syriac Perspectives on Late Antiquity* (London: Variorum, 1984), p. V 27–28.

21. *The Luminous Eye*, p. 117.

22. Ibid., p. 115.

23. See Chapter 1, note 3.

24. St. Ephrem, Hymns on the Church in *The Luminous Eye*, p. 19.

Epigraph

"Im all ways lissening thats how I know about every thing. . . . You know when I begun to lissen like that?"

I said, "When?"

He said, "When the Other Voyce Owl of the Worl begun saying the sylents."

I said, "Wil you tel me about that? . . .

This is what he tol:

The Lissener and the Other Voyce Owl of the Worl

There wer the Other Voyce Owl of the Worl. He sat in the worl tree larfing in his front voyce only his other voyce wernt larfing his other voyce wer saying the sylents. He had a way of saying them. He said them wide and far where he begun tnem he said them tyny when they come close. He kep saying the sylents like that in his other voyce and when he done it the sylents wer swallering up the souns of the worl then the owl wer swallering the sylents.

No 1 knowit he wer doing it. He wer trying to swaller all the souns of the worl then there wunt be no mor worl becaws every thing wud foller the soun of its self in to the sylents then it wud be gone. What the owl had in mynd wer to get it all swallert then fly a way. He only done it at nite he thot hewd get some of it swallert every nite and til he gone the woal worl a way.

No 1 knowit what the owl wer doing only a kid. He dint have no eyes he lissent all the time. When he heard the owl saying the sylents in his other voyce he heard the sylents swallering up the souns of the worl littl and big from the wind sying in the trees to the ants crying in ther hoals. The kid knowit the owl wer trying to say the woal worl a way and he knowit wer on him to stop the owl so he begun to lissen every thing back. He lissent them far and wide where he begun them he lissent them tyny when they come close. The eye of the goat and the dants in the stoan and the beatl digging a grave for the sparrer. He lissent them in to his ear hoals he kep them all safe there. The foot steps of the mof and the sea foam hissing on the stran he lissent every thing back.

The kid dint keap the souns of the worl in his ear hoals only at nite he kep them safe til morning. When the cock crowt in the middl nite it never foolt him nor when it crowt agen befor 1st lite. He kep them souns safe in his ear hoals til the day stood up and the cock of the morning crowt every thing a wake. Then the kid unheard the souns and they gone back where they livet. The kid wer larfing at the owl but the owl dint know it he thot he done a good nites work. He sat in the worl tree grooling and smarling all day thinking he wud get the woal worl gone only he never done it.

> The rivvers run
> My storys done

I said, "That owl tho he keaps trying dont he."

The Ardship said, "O yes he keaps trying and hewl do it 1 day too. All it takes is for no 1 to be lissening every thing back. Hewl go the worl a way and his self with it and thatwl be the end of it. But may be not for a wyl yet. Lissener is my calling name you can call me that."

Russell Hoban, Riddley Walker